The Second Vatican Council

STUDIES BY EIGHT ANGLICAN OBSERVERS

The Second
Vatican Council

Studies by Eight Anglican Observers

Edited by
BERNARD C. PAWLEY

Canon of Ely, first Representative of the Archbishops
of Canterbury and York in Rome 1960–65

LONDON
Oxford University Press
NEW YORK · TORONTO
1967

Oxford University Press, Ely House, London W.1

GLASGOW NEW YORK TORONTO MELBOURNE WELLINGTON
CAPE TOWN SALISBURY IBADAN NAIROBI LUSAKA ADDIS ABABA
BOMBAY CALCUTTA MADRAS KARACHI LAHORE DACCA
KUALA LUMPUR HONG KONG TOKYO

Printed in Great Britain by
Western Printing Services Ltd., Bristol

Contents

Acknowledgement

The portions of the *Directorium on Ecumenical Matters* on pages 241–5 are included by permission of the Secretariat for Promoting Christian Unity.

1 Introduction

BERNARD C. PAWLEY

*Canon of Ely, first Representative of
the Archbishops of Canterbury
and York in Rome 1960–65*

The essays in this collection are an unofficial report of the
Anglican observers at the Second Vatican Council to their fellow Anglicans and to any other Christians who are following
the evolution of the Ecumenical Movement. They are not dogmatic pronouncements or even agreed findings, but unco-
ordinated reactions and observations; for it is the latter which
the present situation seems to require. Such reactions, like the
opinions and impressions of the other great Christian confessions, are now always of importance. For it is one of the first
principles of the practice of 'ecumenism' that whatever any
one of the members of the Body is doing and thinking is of concern to all the rest. So far at least the Holy Spirit has led us
all.

The Church of England and her sister churches of the
Anglican Communion have a proud record in the history of the
Ecumenical Movement. In it from the first, these churches
have been instrumental in 'sparking off' most of the reunion
schemes which now proliferate throughout the world. And at
the present moment they are involved in so many attempts of
this kind that it is difficult for the ordinary member to keep
pace with their development. Perhaps by their very nature the
Anglican churches have had this duty thrust upon them.
Having a doctrinal and liturgical patrimony deriving deliberately from undivided Christendom and yet cherishing a liberty
of interpretation which has allowed them to embrace the insights of the Protestant Reformation as well, the Anglican
churches are clearly called to make a special contribution to
the work of restoring the unity of Christendom. This special
part the Roman Catholic Church has recognized both in the

Decree on Ecumenism itself[1] and in her courteous treatment of Anglican observers and commentators in interconfessional gatherings.

One of the particular emphases of the Anglican churches in the past half century has been on the importance of recognizing the central part which the Church of Rome must essentially play in the reunion of Christendom, and in reminding the rest of the Christian world that this dimension of the matter must always be kept in mind. It is true that the Anglican churches have not been alone in this, and that from the first the World Council of Churches has scrupulously kept contact with the Roman Catholic Church and encouraged her to join the movement at every stage, and that any official unwillingness has hitherto come entirely from the Roman side. But there has certainly been a hesitancy on the part of some of the major Protestant communions as to whether development on these lines would ever be seriously possible, and even whether, if it were, it would be right to encourage such development. The Anglican churches, however, have now for many years been pursuing deliberate and systematic contacts with their Roman Catholic brethren, especially in the countries of Northern Europe. During the years when dialogue was discouraged by the Roman Catholic hierarchies of the British Isles (which includes all the time up to the opening of the Second Vatican Council) Anglicans enjoyed in North America, in France, Belgium and Holland, and even in some cases in Italy itself, precious acquaintances which gave hope for the future. So Anglican observers had been reporting for some time the dawning of a new day in the Roman Catholic Church; for in biblical studies and theology, in liturgical and pastoral methods, and most of all in new ways of confronting the modern world, it was clear that Rome was on the move.

The eventual phenomenon of Pope John's Vatican Council was therefore not such a surprise in Anglican circles as it was in some, and it found a ready response in prayer, in thought, and in action. Archbishop Fisher's spectacular visit to Pope John in November 1960 was as spontaneous an act as had

[1] Decree on Ecumenism, section 13.

been that of Pope John himself in calling the Council. It was in tune with the aspirations of faithful people on both sides of the divide, and proved to be the first swallow of a splendid ecumenical summer. From that moment onwards the Archbishops of Canterbury, in the name of the primates of the Anglican Communion, have continued to keep a representative in Rome as a permanent liaison between the two churches. This office has now, since the Council, taken on a permanent character, and relationships have been further consolidated by the establishment in Rome of an Anglican Centre.[2]

The re-establishment of relationships broken for four centuries was rightly conceived as involving in the first place an exchange of accurate information, and consequently the deliberate abjuring of false propaganda and prejudice. The whole unhappy episode of the original separation, and even more the history of its perpetuation, had left a complex legacy of social, cultural, political and psychological undertones which it would be hard to eradicate. From the very first moment of the resumption of relationships this has been the aim of the enterprise. The method of its procedure has of course been based on mutual prayer and intercession, asking the Lord of the Church to help all concerned to remove those obstacles which lie so deep below consciousness as to be unperceived; and then asking for those rich blessings which are sure to come upon those who wait upon His will with simplicity.

The incidence of the Vatican Council has given immense impetus to what would otherwise have been a long, slow and difficult process. The reform of the Roman Church itself would have been impossible without a general Council, for one of the principal obstacles to progress within herself was the autocratic and reactionary control exercised by the Vatican departments in the name of the papacy. This only a worldwide gathering of the bishops could override. And the Council did itself present the necessary challenge to the rest of the world. As long as the Roman Church kept aloof from the other councils of Christendom it was not possible for her

[2] Via del Corso 303.

friends in other communions to make effective approaches to her, for the reactionaries in the Protestant world (and there were even some within the Anglican Communion itself) could demonstrate that such overtures were unwelcome. Any idea of union which involved the Church of Rome was ruled out as day-dreaming. But when Pope John declared for ecumenism, and for an attitude of realistic confrontation of other Christians, an entirely new situation had arisen. The rest of Christendom then had to show its hand, as to whether it was really concerned with total union including Rome or was to be content with limited confessional amalgamations. It is now a happy fact of history that most of the great confessions (with the exception, alas, of the Baptists) showed themselves ready to respond to this new opportunity, and with greater or less degrees of hesitation decided to accept invitations to send observers to the Second Vatican Council in 1962.

It must be remembered that the Council was not called primarily for the furthering of ecumenical relations. The objects of it had been stated by Pope John as follows:

The Council is to be celebrated for these special purposes, that the Catholic faith may increase, that the people may be brought to a new and higher standard of Christian morality and that Church law and discipline may be brought up to date according to the needs and conditions of our times. That will certainly afford a wonderful vision of truth, unity and charity—and we hope it will be a vision which those who are separated from this apostolic see may regard as a gentle invitation to seek and to follow that unity which Jesus Christ implored from His Heavenly Father with such fervent prayers.[3]

This quotation serves the double purpose of demonstrating how progress in unity was regarded in those days (1960) as a hoped-for by-product of a general renewal of the Church, and how limited was Pope John's own conception of unity, in comparison with the wider attitudes of his successor. For here, as often, he betrayed his deep-seated belief that unity was a 'gift' which the Church of Rome already possessed and which it was

[3] Encyclical *Ad Petri Cathedram*, 1960.

the duty of the 'separated brethren' to follow by any means they could.

The Second Vatican Council was therefore primarily a domestic affair of the Roman Church, and observers from outside had no expectations as of right from its proceedings, except perhaps that, as the subject of Christian unity had been mentioned, they might see an abrogation of prevailing Roman Catholic attitudes to other Christians. Chapters 3 and 5 demonstrate in detail how this change has been brought about, and how it operates. This particular pudding can be subjected to almost every proof in the eating. English Christians can compare the files of the *Catholic Herald* and the *Universe* for 1967 with those for 1957, and mark the difference. Missionaries in the 'new' countries can compare Roman Catholic missionary strategy of 1967 with that of 1957, and can be assured. Protestants of Colombia and other South American states, for whom something near persecution was the order of the day only a few days ago, are receiving invitations to 'dialogue'. The extent and the intensity of these changes of heart cannot be exaggerated. There are of course not wanting those who will point to conflicts still unresolved and to tensions still uneased. But these areas of difference have been very much reduced in number; and the pattern of success in so many other fields gives great hope of further progress. It must also be remembered that this fulfilment of hopes has been achieved not only against intransigent opposition in certain quarters in the Church of Rome herself but against the cynical chorus of those (on both sides of the ecumenical fence) who prophesied that it could never happen at all.

This observed phenomenon is, for the ordinary Christian, the end product of the Council: and it is exceedingly welcome. The most significant aspect of this change is that it has been brought about by the recovery of a sense of pastoral urgency which has been made to prevail over all other considerations. At one time or another there are many pressures upon the life and work of a Church, of any church—and in a church so extensive and so energetic as the Church of Rome these pressures are numerous, variable, and liable to be strong. The

claims of the theologian, the mystic, the prophet, the administrator, the pastor and the missionary, to name only some, are
continually recurring in church life. They all need to be
weighed against each other and to be kept in balance and harmony. From one age to another there is a danger that any one
of these pressures may predominate, and so distort the balance
of the Church's life. The task of the reformer is then to restore
other energies which have been lost sight of, until

the whole body fitly joined together and compacted by that which
every joint supplieth, according to the effectual working in the
measure of every part, maketh increase of the body unto the edifying of itself in love.[4]

In the case of the Church of Rome in the last century at least
the predominant pressure has been a formidable alliance between the theologian and the administrator, demanding rigid
orthodoxy in doctrine, and procuring it by an inflexible discipline. This imbalance has done much disservice to the Church,
as has been so often said. It can be argued that in the centuries
which followed on the Reformation, and because of its excesses,
this pattern of life was forced upon the Church in self-defence.
And in so far as it was good, it perhaps represented the Holy
Spirit's way of preserving for future generations those particular excellencies which had been entrusted to the Church of
Rome for her keeping—insights and inspirations to which
that part of the Catholic Church which had accepted the Reformation were becoming blind. In the nineteenth century,
especially under the impetus of the first Vatican Council, this
regimen had served the Church very well. It had not only
helped her to survive the first onslaughts of modernism, but
had carried her zealous missionaries to the far corners of the
earth. But the alliance of the dogmatic theologian and the
autocratic prelate was a method of church government which
did not stand up to the tests of the twentieth century. It had
given rise to an obscurantism in theology and philosophy
which was a hindrance to the Church's real progress: it had
achieved a totalitarian form of government which was widely
regarded as a tyranny; it had evolved an attitude to the world

[4] Eph. 4.16.

which was arrogant and censorious, and it had developed a way of behaviour to other Christians which was an offence to good manners. Anglican observers had been reporting for more than a quarter of a century that severe discontent and desire for reform existed among Roman Catholics in many countries, so that the spirit which inspired the Council came as no surprise to them. It was a longing to recover a vision of the wholeness of the Church. The pastor and the teacher were to have their say beside the theologian and the church politician; the layman was to take his proper place in the Church beside the priest. Yet this new régime found its way into power, let it be said in fairness, by the efforts of a new generation of theologians, and by reforms which were themselves administrative. They would not have been effective without the proposed changes in the organization of the Curia at Rome and in the Canon Law. But nowhere has the operation of this principle been more evident than in the change of relationships to Christians outside the Roman Church. Here the pastoral necessities of the situation, the common sense of the busy priest and bishop in contact with the modern world, had been scandalized by the divisions of Christendom and had shown itself impatiently dissatisfied with the old conception of 'the Church' as identified with the Church of Rome only and of all the rest of Christendom as being 'outside the Church' and thereby possibly outside salvation as well. The theologians therefore were sent back by the bishops to their text books and told to work out the implications of baptism for the whole question of Christian membership. This in turn led on to a new situation of tolerance and mutual esteem which is now seen, after all, to have a firm foundation in theology and a fine pedigree in the traditions of the Fathers. So the brakes have been taken off and fraternization has not only become permissible, but has been seen under many conditions to be a duty. This new state of affairs, which is of course a *sine qua non* of further meaningful encounters, has now been codified in the Directorium governing ecumenical work, and is being permanently provided for in the revision of the Canon Law.

It has already been stated, and needs to be repeated, that

the establishing of better relationships with other churches was only a secondary aim of the Second Vatican Council. It is therefore all the more pleasurable to record that its achievement is not merely an isolated part of the Council's conclusions, but that it is very surely woven into the whole texture of its proceedings. Theology, Biblical Scholarship, Ethics, Liturgy, all show a new awareness (at the high, official, level) of what other Christians are thinking and doing and hoping for. The essays in this collection are therefore all appreciative and encouraging; not that all their expectations are fulfilled, for they all refer to unsolved problems and highlight errors still remaining, but because their authors are sure that a new era of open discussion has been inaugurated by the Council. And here it would be appropriate to say that perhaps the Anglican observers have been more appreciative than most, because of their unique inheritance in the Christian tradition. It is therefore with much sympathy that they have watched the Roman Catholic Church beginning to come to terms with the Reformation, while acknowledging with humility their own need to recover and enrich themselves with some of those other treasures of catholic Christendom which, though not lost, have been neglected. It has been observed more than once that if the agenda for the Vatican Council could have been drawn up at Lambeth, it could not have been much improved upon. Perhaps the resolution of the Mixed Marriage question would have been put a little higher on the agenda; yet even there it is realized that this question presents problems for the Church of Rome much wider than Anglican relationships and that it will need a long and laborious solution. But in general the subjects of the Constitutions, Decrees, and Declarations are, as to their subjects, what Anglicans would have chosen. To an outside observer who is not familiar with recent developments in the Roman Church there might seem to be large fields which have not been covered, some of which need urgent attention. But here again account needs to be taken of the nature of the Council. It did not aim at a total restating of the whole syllabus of Roman doctrine, or even of those parts of it which particularly needed clarifying for the sake of better ecumenical discussions; but the selection was bound to be determined primarily by the number of those which were ready to be discussed. In the first grade of urgency could be included those on which the Roman Church herself needed further elucidation (particularly the papacy, bishops, the place of the Scriptures, the nature of worship, the place of the laity, and Marian doctrines). The second grade included those questions which were being forced on her notice by the modern world (non-Christian religions, atheism, modern economic and political theories, religious freedom, etc.) The third category, that of the expectations of the Christian world outside Rome, would in fact have included almost all the foregoing if it had been drawn up on its own, so that the subject of Ecumenism itself was the only one which needed to be added. The whole syllabus was commendably comprehensive; and the outcome is a series of documents which could well occupy the attention of all Christendom for some time. There were, however, four notable gaps. The first was the absence of any serious consideration of eucharistic doctrine (except in so far as it is treated in the Decree on the Liturgy). This omission has been a cause for regret because it touches one of the most controversial issues under debate. But there were at least two reasons for this. The first was that there did not seem to be sufficient need for such discussion within the Roman Church, and secondly that the non-Roman world is itself so divided on eucharistic doctrine (except when it is united in condemning certain Roman errors), that discussion of it by Rome did not seem likely to be profitable from an ecumenical point of view. The subject was by no means mature enough to be an obvious field of closer understanding. But it is encouraging to notice that since the Council signs have already been seen that there is unrest in certain schools of theology (particularly in Holland and in the United States of America) about the future of the scholastic eucharistic doctrines. And although the papal encyclical *Mysterium Fidei* was made to appear to stifle discussion, the reverse was evident from a closer reading. For though it not unnaturally discouraged the publication of undigested academic criticism of current doctrine, yet it ended by saying that the formulation (as distinct from the essence) of any doctrine could be subject to disciplined reappraisal at any period. There is no doubt that opportunity will be taken of this instruction to pursue new and eirenical eucharistic speculations further in the future. The progress of current attempts to prepare an eventual restatement of, e.g., the doctrine of transubstantiation are worth careful study, as illustrating both the inevitability of eventual change (in spite of repeated disclaimers) and also the present immaturity of the alternatives being offered. Such study makes it quickly apparent that discussion of this and allied problems would have been unprofitable at the Second Vatican Council. It also illustrates the fact that there is a clear ecumenical function here for Anglican scholars. It is to be hoped that they will not be content to wait in the wings, as it were, with Article 28, according to which transubstantiation 'overthroweth the nature of a Sacrament'. But knowing that some Roman Catholic theologians would agree that their doctrine *as it is now stated* does indeed come under this criticism, it is to be hoped that ecumenically minded scholars from the non-Roman side will be helping to prepare a workable alternative statement, keeping in close touch with the appropriate Roman Catholic theologians. In that way they would be helping to fill up a lacuna in Vatican II and perhaps even starting to prepare for Vatican III.[5]

The second notable absentee from the list of subjects under discussion was of course the classical question of Grace, of justification and sanctification thereby. And as this was perhaps the most violent of the Reformation controversies it might at first sight seem surprising that it did not come up for treatment. But the reason for this was most likely the opposite to that in the previous case, that there is now so much agreement on the modern restatement of this ancient discussion that unilateral treatment of it might easily do more harm than good. For decades before the Council this matter has been sub-

[5] A learned statement of the rearguard fight for the traditional formulas and an argument of the case, can be seen in the published lecture of Fr. Francis Clark S. J. given in Rome on 1 December 1965. See the Review *Unitas*, vol. for Summer 1966.

mitted to close joint argument, especially in Germany, its
native soil, and it will no doubt continue in that vein until in
the thinkable future joint statements will be able to be
achieved. It is worth reflecting how many of the classical 'irri-
tants' between Roman Catholics and other Christians can be
traced to misunderstandings under this head. Everything to do
with shrines, pilgrimages, pardons, and penitence is a deriva-
tive from it, from Canon Tetzel's saleable pardons to the most
recent vagaries of the administration of indulgences. It seems
strange that while there is now such a measure of agreement
on the deep theological issues involved, the work of clearing
up the 'debris' is so difficult—for the maladministrations
committed under this heading have left a very deeply un-
favourable impression on the non-Roman mind.

The third notable absentee from the Council's agenda, in
the general view, has been any discussion of the question of
Anglican orders. But this is also a matter which can readily be
explained, and on closer examination it will be found to be of
a much lower priority than might be supposed at first sight.
In fact those officially engaged in Anglican–Roman Catholic
relationships, on both sides, have positively discouraged the
re-opening of its discussion at the present. There are clearly
so many prior questions which need elucidation before it would
be advisable to enter into any close examination of it. The
whole sphere of the theology of the sacraments and of the
ministry, for example, needs much further clarification before
such a reappraisal would be profitable. And indeed it might
be said that the prolegomena to such studies must include some
agreement about the historical facts of the Reformation scene.
There is further the fact that Anglican orders themselves are
undergoing a considerable 'redeployment' in the course of the
various union schemes in which the Anglican Communion
is currently involved. Although it has not to our knowledge
been publicly stated, the Church of Rome can be presumed to
be waiting to see what Anglican orders will look like after
they have emerged from these transformations. And for this
purpose, presumably, all will have to be able to see the proposed ordinals for the united churches. These considerations

make it premature to pursue these matters at present and would have made such discussion unprofitable, and in fact impossible, either at the Council or in conjunction with it. Here again it appears that though there is much natural impatience to be getting on with this task, the reasons for delay are genuine and acceptable. But Anglicans can rest content in the knowledge that the background against which this question will be tackled in the future will be much more favourable than it has been in the past. At the time of the bull *Apostolicae Curae* there was no effective liaison between the two churches, and the examination of the question was vitiated by misinformation (because some of the main sources were not available) and by adverse prejudice on the part of the then Roman Catholic hierarchy in Great Britain, for whom the whole matter seemed to be a question of survival. But in spite of its strong language *Apostolicae Curae* is not an infallible document, and its conclusions could be put into reverse. In fact there are many Roman Catholic scholars who hope to see it so disposed of.

And, fourthly, there was the question of mixed marriages, which some hoped to see satisfactorily settled at the Council. But here again there are reasons why these hopes have been disappointed. First, this is largely a matter of canonical legislation, which is too detailed for disposal at a Council; and it has always been understood that such matters would be dealt with by a Canon Law revision committee after the Council. Second, it is a question which presents such complex problems to the Church of Rome that it is not capable of easy solution anyhow. The variety of practice and of teaching with regard to matrimony which are to be met with in Christendom outside Rome is so great as to discourage legislation from the Roman side. But as is widely known, a start, albeit a very limited start, has been made on this question by the *monitum* of 1966, whereby the excommunication on any Roman Catholic contracting a mixed marriage is lifted. But the great irritant of the promises demanded of the non-Roman partner remains. It leaves non-Roman brides and bridegrooms no alternative but to try to persuade their affianced to defy their church's discipline, and this is, of course, very distasteful. Such a situation, which is most unsatisfactory at the time of writing, is not only contrary to the Council's own requirement that these matters should be regulated in the spirit of the decree on Ecumenism,[6] but is out of accord with the general tone of the Decree on Religious Liberty.[7] Although therefore this matter must naturally continue to be an irritant as long as it remains as it is, and seems to clash with the spirit and intentions of the Council, yet it must be admitted that it is so complex that it would not have been possible, or even desirable, to have dealt with it in the Council itself. Anglicans confine themselves to hoping that the whole question will be adequately dealt with, at the latest, in the revision of the Canon Law.

It cannot be said, therefore, that the absence of any of the four controversial topics mentioned above from the agenda of the Council constitutes any kind of disappointment from the point of view of Anglicans, as there appears to be an evident reason for the omission in each case, and there is hope that they will be adequately developed in the future.

When we turn to consider the positive deliberations of the Council itself it soon becomes clear that on balance the whole Christian world has much to be thankful for. The achievements of the Council can perhaps be considered under the following heads:

(1) *The correction of past mistakes*

The Church of Rome herself had in her own eyes allowed habits and customs, ways of behaving and methods of teaching, to creep into her life in the past which she has come to regret, and much of the business of the Council has been an internal reformation along these lines. This process has proved not at all easy, and sometimes even painful, as indeed it would do in any church. On the whole prophets do not perish outside Jerusalem, and even the degree of prophecy which is likely to find its way into an assembly of bishops has had to fight hard against opposition. Yet it must be said in fairness

---

[6] *Votum* on the Sacrament of Matrimony, section 5.
[7] *passim*, but especially section 2.

that much of the reforming zeal of the Council came eventually
from the bishops themselves; and observers had the satisfaction of watching what began as a reforming minority win over
the allegiance of the uncommitted, and eventually triumph
over the entrenched opposition. The bishops had to take
account of the cries of the *periti*, or council experts, within the
gates. And beyond the range of the *periti* has been heard the
cry of the clergy in remote provinces, and even of the laity in
the modern world. So the spring cleaning has gone on. In defence of the doctrinal inerrancy of the Church, as it is alleged
to be, it has often been insisted that these reforms have not involved fundamental change, least of all doctrinal change, but
the process has been compared by the present Pope to the
pruning of a tree, cutting out dead wood but leaving the main
trunk and branches intact. This, we may suppose, is exactly
the way Cranmer might have described the English Reformation.

The main single defect which the present reformers hoped
to remove from the life of their church was the concentration
in Rome of too much administrative power. The interpretation of the first Vatican Council which had since prevailed
had led to the draining away of rights and privilege from the
bishops in their dioceses to curial departments in Rome who
had been claiming to govern in the name of the Pope. This was
a matter which could be considered quite separately from the
question of Infallibility. It was in the first place an administrative defect. As such it is gradually being corrected by a
series of organizational reforms under the present Pope. These
consist mainly in the down-grading of curial departments in
favour of a senate of bishops and of national conferences of
hierarchies. But behind all these reforms was seen to lie the
theological problem of the nature of the papacy, and the interpretation of the divine authority committed to the Church.
Chapters 3 and 4 examine in detail the way in which this problem was handled. That there has been a fundamental change
in the pattern of administration of authority there can be no
doubt. What is still being debated is whether the new doctrinal
definitions of the nature of a bishop's office and of the apostolic

'college' of bishops really constitutes a change from the doctrines of Vatican I. Some of the highest authorities said openly in the Council that the new principles ran contrary to accepted catholic doctrine; others hoped that the new augmented and developed the old. One thing emerged clearly from the debates, which is that there are now many Roman Catholic biblical scholars who are uneasy about the usual exegesis of such texts as Matt. 16. 18 which have been used in the past to ascribe absolute powers in Christendom to the Papacy.

Another inherited 'defect' which came up for correction was that of hierarchical autocracy, the total, even totalitarian, control of the Church by the clergy and the consequent aggrandizement and 'triumphalism' of that order, the honours, pomps and power surrounding the office of a bishop—to say nothing of the tendency of the whole Church to accumulate wealth and secular power. The old plea of Dante was heard again in the Council debates:

> Ahi, Constantin, di quanto mal fu matre,
>   non la tua conversion, ma quella dote
>   che da te prese il primo ricco patre.[8]

It can be said that it has been effectively heard, and that appropriate reforms have been begun. There have been deliberate and significant outward gestures calculated to show that the point has been taken, e.g., the simplification of dress and ceremonial in St. Peter's itself, the reduction of the mode of address in the Council from 'Reverendissimi, Illustrissimi et Excellentissimi Domini' to the simple 'Fratres Conciliares', the symbolic sale of the Pope's tiara, the Pope's journey to India to demonstrate a concern for the poverty and suffering of the world. All these can be considered in connexion with more profound reforms in the structure of the Church, such as the suggested use of colleges of priests to advise the bishop in the government of his diocese,[9] and the assignment at last to

---

[8] Ah, Constantine, it was not your conversion which was mother of so much ill, but that fateful endowment which first made rich a father of the Church. (*Inferno* 19.115)

[9] *On the Pastoral Office of Bishops* section 27 and the Motu proprio *Ecclesiae Sanctae*, 1966.

the laity[10] of some status, if not yet of an effective role, in the life and government of the Church. Some of the reforms in the Liturgy, too, can be said to come under this head, as bringing to an end an era in which in effect the Liturgy was something which the clergy performed, and at which the laity were merely present.[11]

The next major achievement of the Council which could be described as the correction of past mistakes was of course the reinstatement in a more effective role of the Holy Scriptures. To all observers, Orthodox, Anglican, and Protestant, this has been most welcome. It is important to state precisely what this change consists in, for it must never be suggested that the Church of Rome paid no heed to the Scriptures hitherto, even if the outward appearance of many of her rites and customs had not unnaturally given this impression. But the change is apparent in at least these four ways. First, that a real attempt has been made to restore the right balance (as we should say, to recover the proportions) of truly catholic Christendom between the Sacred Scriptures and church tradition;[12] secondly, that both by a return to the vernacular and by proposed revisions, the Scriptures are going to be much more effectively heard in the Liturgy;[13] thirdly, that the place of Scripture in the interpretation of doctrine has been made more apparent (see the abundant scriptural references in, and the deliberately scriptural basis of, the council documents themselves, in comparison with those of previous councils); and fourthly, the comparative emancipation of biblical scholars from regimentation by the curial departments.

A second category in the achievements of the Council might be described as:

(2) *Domestic pastoral reforms*

These will be found over all the Constitutions, Decrees, and Declarations, and are perhaps too numerous to list in detail. Many of them will find their expression in the reform of the

---

[10] *On the Church* Chapter 2 and *On the Laity* passim.

[11] *On the Liturgy*, section 11 etc.

[12] see Chapter II, passim, below.   [13] *On the Liturgy*, section 24.

Canon Law. Reference will of course be made to them in the chapters which follow. But they are mainly to be seen in the documents on the pastoral office of the bishops, on the life and training of the priesthood, on the laity, on the schools and seminaries, on the missions and on the life of the religious orders. The Council in this, as in so many other ways, is intended to be the inauguration of a period of development. The flowering of the 'Counter-Reformation' has often been quoted as a precedent for what should be the after-effect of this Council, if its suggestions are heeded and followed up with energy. The main fields of proposed development could perhaps be listed as follows:

1. Redeployment of the clergy, as between town and country, and as between the countries of the 'old' world and the 'new'.
2. More definite training of the clergy for adaptation to the needs of the modern world. The development experimentally of new pastoral techniques.
3. Training and effective use of the laity.
4. Thinking out of a new strategy for what used to be known as the 'mission field'.
5. Redeployment of the monastic orders, with special attention to their relations with the secular clergy and dioceses.
6. General implementation of the 'liturgical revival'.

To these can be added, no doubt, a long list of smaller developments, but the six fields enumerated above are probably those in which most progress can be expected. Taken together they could constitute a very potent revival of church life. To say the least, the easements and release of energy which they represent could put considerable new forces at the Church's disposal.

Another heading under which some of the Council's enterprises could be grouped would be:

(3) *Reforms undertaken for the sake of other Christians*

These are of course the stuff and essence of Ecumenism, which is treated at length in Chapter 5 below. As in the case of the two previous categories, the items can be seen scattered over all the decrees. The exercise of ecumenism was quite rightly given a starting point in theology, and the whole of Christendom stands indebted for the result. This might have been classified under the heading of the 'correction of past mistakes' as well, for much of the value of the new ecumenical attitudes of the Vatican consists in the passing away of the old order of things in which the rest of Christendom seemed to have no status whatever. Now, not only is this intolerable misinterpretation of the theology of the Church rescinded, at least by implication, but positive directions are given for the prosecution of constructive relationships with other Christians. The general outlines of behaviour which should be observed are stated in the Decree on Ecumenism, and this itself is being systematically followed up, not only by implementing decisions of national conferences of bishops, but by the Directorium already mentioned.

But the matters which were deliberated upon for the sake of other Christians were not only those which deal directly with ecumenical relations. Under this head we may also include, for example, that part of the text of the dogmatic constitution on the Church which deals with the problem of the Papacy. Some of the sections of the Constitution are deliberate explanations of doctrine, conceived with the commendable object of dispelling misunderstanding among non-Roman Christians. The best known of these is perhaps §25 in Chapter 3, in which it is explained that infallibility does not inhere in the private person of the Pope, but in his official function, and then only under certain carefully defined conditions— an attempt to remove misunderstandings on that point. For the good intention of such passages the whole Christian world is grateful, but it is necessary to say that there remain a number of doctrines peculiar to the Church of Rome, of which this is one, which no amount of clarification can render acceptable to the rest of Christendom. But even in such cases it is satisfactory to be able to report progress in the understanding of this situation. Before the council there were many high-placed Roman Catholic dignitaries who supposed that the 'difficulties' in the way of the eventual union of Christendom could be removed by further clarification: there was little trace of a suspicion that such doctrines could really be fundamentally wrong and would need to be totally changed or abandoned before the unity of Christendom could be restored. Pope John seemed continually to be under an illusion of this kind. He would say, for example, that

. . . it is only natural that such a Council will bring with it promises of the clarification of our doctrines . . . such as will encourage the aspirations of our separated brethren to return to unity and will hasten their steps towards it.[14]

Such expressions recall the pre-Council attitude of many prelates. Pope Paul would use a different approach to the same question, more realistic, sometimes sounding more stern, but nevertheless reflecting a more mature understanding that there is still much dialogue to be undertaken even when maximum clarification has been achieved. Yet clarification is not without its value. In the case of the treatment of the papacy in the Constitution On the Church the point has emerged even more clearly that the difficulties attaching to this doctrine cannot be resolved without profound and laborious mutual re-examination of the Scriptures in the light of modern knowledge, and in the context of patristic understanding of them. The knowledge that there are many Roman Catholic scholars who are not only willing but anxious to begin such an objective re-examination of fundamental beliefs is progress indeed.

Under this same heading, of subjects considered for the sake of other Christians, we should of course include Chapter 8 of the Constitution On the Church, concerning the Blessed Virgin Mary. It is one of the unhappiest features of the divisions of Christendom that the figure of our Lord's mother should be at the centre of our misunderstandings, when it is so certain that she herself would so gladly lead all Christians to peace and agreement in the service of her Son. Here again there is progress, much progress, to report, as will be seen in Chapter 3. One can recall the case of one English bishop (R.C.) who in a pastoral letter on the Council had only two hopes to express,

[14] Speech at the promulgation of the Bull *Humanae salutis* for the opening of the Council, Christmas Day 1961.

which were the promulgation of further Marian doctrines, those of *Maria mediatrix gratiae* and *Maria coredemptrix*. He is a disappointed, but a wiser, man as a result of the Council. For not only was the escalation of Marian doctrines deliberately halted, but Christians outside Rome could note with satisfaction a real endeavour to bring Marian doctrines and devotions within a compass which would not distort the totally Christocentric nature of our faith. The present Pope has frequently appealed to Roman Catholics to make this adjustment where necessary. And the Council document states that

the blessed Virgin is invoked by the Church under the titles of Advocate, Helper, Mediatress. This, however, is to be so understood that it neither takes away from nor adds anything to the dignity and efficaciousness of Christ the one Mediator. For no creature could ever be counted as equal with the Incarnate Word and Redeemer.... The Church does not hesitate to profess *this subordinate role* of Mary.[15]

That statement should be a help to many who find the excesses of Roman Marian devotion hard to understand, even if it suggests at the same time that there is still much to talk over. The labour involved in further progress here will be not so much in investigation of the Scriptures and patristic documents (for in them Marian devotion of the modern Roman pattern is hard to seek) but in a really deep attempt to discover what is the spiritual and psychological urge which impels our Roman Catholic brethren to seek the consolations of 'Marian' piety. Here particularly the Anglican has a part to play because the Blessed Virgin Mary has an honourable place in his formulas and devotions and he believes that the Anglican emphasis preserves the real catholic proportions, from which modern Roman Catholic practice is an aberration.

Under this same heading we should include the Declaration on Religious Liberty. Christendom outside the Church of Rome should welcome this most warmly, as putting beyond doubt the official position of the Church on the matter. Several really tough problems are eased by this Declaration, and it is by a further implementation of its teaching that we hope for

[15] *On the Church*, VIII, section 62.

further progress in such matters as mixed marriages. It is important for the reader to note how in the first half of Chapter 7 Professor Wolf traces the steps by which this Declaration won its way through to acceptance against the most intransigent opposition. A new freedom won after such a struggle will not easily be lost sight of—and this constitutes a 'clarification' for which all will be grateful.

The last category of Council material could be

(4) *New attitudes towards the contemporary world*

Here again the discussions have defied neat classification. The Pastoral Constitution on the Church in the Modern World, of course, addresses itself entirely to this problem. But so do large tracts of the Declaration on Religious Liberty, of the Declaration on the Church's attitude to the non-Christian religions, with its important section on the Jews, and of the decree on Missions. In fact the determination to come abreast of contemporary needs and problems was a dimension of the whole council, and its results can be detected in almost all the documents. There are also in this type of material quite a number of passages which might come under our first category, that of the correction of past mistakes. The spectre of Galileo hung over the debaters, and the much more recent memory of Teilhard de Chardin. The Church is anxious not to make those mistakes again, not only because it has suffered the consequences of committing them, but because new attitudes to contemporary knowledge and discoveries are seen to be demanded by the application of the gospel to the problems of modern times. The Council has not so much formulated these new attitudes as brought them out from where they have been hiding. Roman Catholic scholars, philosophers and psychologists, anthropologists and economists have been waiting for some time for a degree of emancipation in order to take up 'the dialogue with the contemporary world'. This they seem to have achieved in the Council, and the new freedom which allows them to emerge into the open forum is a matter for much satisfaction. The establishment of Secretariats in the

Vatican for non-Christian religions and for non-believers seems to have brought us a long way from the Syllabus and the Index. And this progress, we hope, is only the beginning of a new era.

This brief analysis serves as an appetizing introduction to the detailed study of the various new attitudes and documents which are the wholesome fruit of the Second Vatican Council. If they were to be reduced to a yet more compendious form they might be stated as follows:

1. The admission of the general principle that there is something more in truth than dogmatic exactitude, i.e., that pastoral instincts and intuitions must have their place in revelation.
2. The recognition of value (undefined) in the experience of other Christians and a resolve to come to terms with it.
3. The recognition of a place for the laity in the polity of the Church.
4. A restoration of the right use of the Holy Scriptures in the interpretation of revelation.
5. The recognition that there is a certain amount of traditional belief and practice which needs restating or even abandoning—though this is not held to apply to 'fundamental' dogmas.
6. A realistic confrontation with the contemporary world on a new basis, with a recognition that modern scientific knowledge can actually contribute to the sum of revelation.

Various valuations have been put upon this achievement by the observers of the several parts of Christendom. Perhaps the Anglicans, being traditionally more concerned with what is workable than what is able to be precisely defined, have been the most sanguine. The hopefulness of their judgement rests not so much on an evaluation of the position now reached as on an appreciation of the nature of the struggle which achieved it. Many of the highest officials of the Roman Curia have done their utmost to frustrate the intentions of the majority of the bishops and have shown themselves unwilling to 'cancel half a line'. But the renovating majority have gone steadily on because they have felt securely able to say that 'it seemed good to us and to the Holy Ghost'. Reactionary forces are still, some of them, in power, and their rear-guard actions in the interests of defeating the intentions of the Council are to be read of frequently in the newspapers. But the present Pope is treating them gently, and is gradually and skilfully replacing them by successors who will be more willing to following up the aims of the Council. One of the most potent forces for renewal in the Roman Catholic Church has of course not yet had its say, viz. the lay people. It is not easy for the English or American reader to realize how different is the position of the Roman Catholic Church in countries which are its traditional home from its much stronger condition in those two countries, where the immense thrust of Irish vitality has given it a vigour which is the envy of all its neighbours. But throughout the Latin world the Church is either languishing in a state of neglect or facing the active hostility of people who have forsaken it, where the outlook of the majority is anti-clerical. There are also large tracts of what are normally thought of as 'catholic lands' where there is an attitude of patronizing but incredulous conformity. The visitor, for example, to Italy, who has the time to enter deeply into the minds of the intelligent laity is amazed to discover the mental reservations of the apparently conforming Catholic. A very common lay attitude to recent dogmas is revealed in the formula 'let those who made them believe in them', a pattern of revolt against a clerically dictated standard of faith in the formulation of which the laity have had no hand. And to bring the matter nearer home, it can be observed how certainly the Roman Catholic laity of Britain and the U.S.A. are getting restive about the clerical domination of the Church, and how they are beginning to demand that, especially in matters concerning their personal morals, they should be taken closely into consultation. All these circumstances are bound to have a 'liberalizing' influence in the future. In fact it is possible that by the time these words are in print we may have seen a remarkable change in the Church's attitude to family ethics which could be directly traced to these influences.

If the attitude of the Anglican observers is here described

as hopeful that does not mean to imply that they under-
estimate, still less are unaware of, the magnitude of the obstacles still remaining in the path of reunion. It means rather
that they are sensitive to the more powerful motions of Him
who is the Lord of the Church. Many attempts have been
made to analyse the fundamental questions still at issue to their
depths. Perhaps from our side we should trace them to a need to
agree about the way in which God reveals his truth. To us the
Roman way appears so 'fundamentalist', too much inclined to
treat as eternal and sacred what are in fact only human formulations. We therefore see ourselves more naturally attracted,
when we look backward through history, to the Orthodox conception of God's revelation as a deep mystery, ever to be gazed
at and meditated upon anew. And that also is why we have to
take our place beside the Reformers, who in the sixteenth
century saw that the Church of Rome had in certain matters
taken a wrong turn. It therefore remains sadly true for us
that:

as the Church of Jerusalem, Alexandria and Antioch have erred,
so also the Church of Rome hath erred, not only in their living and
manner of Ceremonies, but also in matters of Faith.[16]

To the traditional Roman Catholic theologian this, of course,
constitutes a failure of belief. It amounts to saying that
Christ's promise that 'He, the Holy Spirit, shall lead you into
all truth', has failed. And that charge must be squarely faced.
We must likewise acknowledge the dangers implicit in a more
rational interpretation of God's way of revealing Himself, for
the fragmentation and disunity of non-Roman Christendom
testify to the need of a firm focus of authority and of a degree
of clarity in definition. The only hope of progress therefore lies
not so much in an attempt to unwind the tangled skein of the
past as to weave afresh the tapestry of Christian belief and
practice in the future, using all the given colours and materials
which are serviceable for the common enterprise. It is encouraging to note that the Pope has already agreed with leaders of
other churches to set up an institute of ecumenical research

[16] Art. 19 of the Thirty-nine Articles.

which will be sited near Jerusalem and will in the first instance study 'the history of salvation'. That is, it will begin by studying the way in which the saving Word of God dwelt among us 'from the beginning', and will then, presumably, consider the way in which that revelation is to be apprehended in the future by a united Christian family. That is at least a reasonable programme to which all Christians can readily give their assent and for whose success they will surely pray.

The task of 'observing', in the technical sense of the term, has always been both an active and a passive exercise. Thanks to the new Vatican attitudes expressed in the Secretariat for Christian Unity, all observers have been not only permitted, but encouraged to send in their observations on the Council themes. And so a series of memoranda was gladly contributed to the store of material from which the Council drew its inspiration; and beside these written contributions can be numbered the judgements and opinions delivered at the weekly meetings of the observers with the Secretariat. Anglicans can therefore count this among the achievements of the Council already to hand that the results of their experience have already been handed in, at the highest level, for the consideration of the Council Fathers. The Church of Rome, from the Pope downwards (and especially the present Pope) has shown itself anxious to hear and to understand what we have to say. The fact that she has not always felt able to accept or to respond to our opinions is no qualification of this principle. And the Council has been a passive experience: it has profoundly moved those who have taken part in it. There has been an unmistakeable experience of being under the same pressure to hear 'what the Spirit saith to the churches'. On the one hand we have been encouraged to observe how in certain matters the Anglican churches have preserved intact some of the truths of catholic Christendom which Rome has neglected or distorted, but on the other we have been humbled to see how our own failings and misapprehensions in the past have been responsible for some of our own present weaknesses. It would do the Anglican churches good to make a list of those things which they can admire in the Church of Rome in which they are

themselves defective—the certainty and faithfulness of her proclamation of what she holds to be the faith, the solidarity and
loyalty of her congregations, her struggle for the religious up-
bringing of children, the evangelical devotion of her religious
and her missionaries by the thousand in all parts of the world,
the splendid discipline because of which she is able to act as
one man in Christ throughout the world. All these things we
must acknowledge, admire, and emulate if we are to criticize
her for her rigidity of teaching, her misbegotten zeal for prose-
lytizing at any price, her toleration of superstition, her alliances
with oppressive governments, her doctrinal exaggerations and
her pomps. At the end of the day therefore the Anglican
churches acknowledge that while they speak the truth in love
(which it is now possible to do) they themselves must put on the
garment of penitence. They see their own need for an up-to-
date statement of the Christian faith as they hold it, in a drastic
revision of the obsolete Thirty-nine Articles, or the production
of an entirely new document. They see the need to recover
some respectable 'lawful authority' in matters of religion to
which clergy and laity alike can look up—and in England at
least this means the revision of the 'Establishment' of our
Church. Those who have applauded the Decree on the Liturgy
must bear in mind the urgent need for liturgical reform in the
Anglican churches. The Decree on Divine Revelation, which
has opened up new fields of development in the study of the
Scriptures for our Roman brethren reminds us that the
Anglican's hold on those sacred writings is not what it was.

The dialogue with Rome will therefore be taken up with
vigour. The Anglican churches have been pursuing it unofficially in one quarter or another for years, and the psychological effect of being able to bring it out into the open is considerable. Readers in England should bear in mind that the
situation in which they see these matters is untypical of the
rest of Christendom. Relations here have been bedevilled by
centuries of misbehaviour between the English and their Irish
neighbours; and it is difficult to disassociate the pursuit of
objective discussion from the undertones of historical controversy. We are already enjoying improved relationships in

England itself, but it must be remembered that the main thrust of this encounter is felt on the chief axis between the international Anglican Communion and the Roman Catholic Church at the centre. The Anglican bishops of, e.g., Ondo-Benin, or Kuching, or Washington D.C., or Porto Alegre in Brazil, do not wish their dealings with the Roman Catholic Church to be coloured by British memories or prejudices.

The new spirit of mutual recognition which is the outcome of the Vatican Council has now been given shape on both sides by the creation of organizations charged with diffusing it. We have already recorded the existence in Rome of the Secretariat for Christian Unity on the one hand, and of the Anglican Ecumenical Institute on the other. Through the churches of the Anglican Communion, following the Archbishop of Canterbury's memorable visit to the Pope at the beginning of 1966, provision has been made by the creation of special commissions or by the widening of the terms of reference of organizations already existing. In the United States of America, for example, there now exists the Committee for Relations with the Roman Catholic Church of the Joint Commission on Ecumenical Relations; and for England and Wales the Archbishops' Commission on Roman Catholic Relations.

The team of observers who have contributed these essays feel themselves under heavy debts of obligation; first to two successive Archbishops of Canterbury, Geoffrey Fisher and Michael Ramsey, who first sent and then encouraged them; secondly of course to two memorable Popes, John XXIII and Paul VI, whose personalities blazed a trail into a new era of the Church: to the Secretariat for the Union of Christians, in the persons of Cardinal Bea and Mgr. Willebrands and their staff: to their fellow observers from other Christian communions whose company and erudition they enjoyed in great measure: now to Mr. Geoffrey Hunt and the Oxford University Press who have made this production possible; but most of all to those loyal and expectant Anglicans throughout the world who have already received this testimony with interest and thanksgiving.

2 Divine Revelation

FREDERICK C. GRANT

Professor Emeritus of Biblical Theology
in Union Theological Seminary,
New York

The first *schema* (draft decree) debated by the Council was on *The Sacred Liturgy*. To it were devoted fifteen working days between 22 October and 13 November 1962. Then followed the *schema* on *The Sources of Revelation*. This was debated for six working days between 14 and 21 November. This order of procedure, taking up the Liturgy first, was doubtless diplomatic: the *schema* on the Sacred Liturgy would surely command more general assent than any other designed to come before the first Session. And this was in fact the outcome. The published Constitution on the Liturgy, issued after its adoption on 4 December 1963, reflects the wide unanimity—or at least the overwhelming majority—of the bishops approving its principles and proposals. The fifteen working days had sufficed to complete the discussion and authorization of the decree. Far different was the week that followed: Whereas the *schema* on the Liturgy reflected modern expert thinking and real pastoral concern, the one on Revelation was criticized from the outset as antiquated in outlook and presuppositions, and anything but pastoral in spirit and aim.

The *schema* was five chapters in length, including 29 articles, and filled thirteen pages in the beautifully printed, fully annotated Latin text, an example of the superb craftsmanship of the Vatican Press. It is the opening *schema* in *Series Prima* (*sub secreto*) of the *Schemata Constitutionum et Decretorum de quibus disceptabitur in Concilii sessionibus*: it was undoubtedly meant to come first in the council discussions, as arranged by those who drafted it. The subdivisions were as follows:

Ch. I. *The Double Source of Revelation.*
1. The Revelation of the Old and New Covenants.
2. The earliest propagation of the Revelation of the New Testament.
3. Its transmission.
4. The two sources of Revelation [sc. Scripture and Tradition: *non in sola scriptura, sed in scriptura et traditione*].
5. The relation between them.
6. The relation of both to the church's Magisterium [authority and teaching office].

Ch. II. *The Inspiration, Inerrancy, and Literary Genres of Scripture.*
7. The Inspiration and Canonicity of Holy Scripture.
8. The true nature and definition of Inspiration.
9. The many different human authors.
10. The personal inspiration of the sacred writers and the community.
11. The extent of Inspiration.
12. Inerrancy, a consequence of Inspiration.
13. How Inerrancy is to be judged.
14. The divine condescension.

Ch. III. *The Old Testament.*
15. The authority of the Old Testament in the Church.
16. The relation between the Old and New Testaments.
17. The true character of the Old Testament.
18. The human authors of the Old Testament.

Ch. IV. *The New Testament.*
19. The Gospels and their authors.
20. The historical value of the Gospels.
21. The truth of the works of Christ related in the Gospels.
22. The truth of the words of Christ in the Gospels.
23. The truth of the teaching of the Apostles in the canonical writings.

Ch. V. *Holy Scripture in the Church.*
24. The Church's care for the Holy Scripture.
25. The Latin translation of the Vulgate [free from all error in faith and morals].
26. The reading of the scriptures by priests, and
27. by the faithful.
28. Catholic exegetes.
29. The relation of theology to Holy Scripture.

The *schema* was presented to the Council by Cardinal Ottaviani, the President of the Theological Commission and for many years head of the Holy Office. It was seconded by Mgr. S. Garofalo, a member of the Theological Commission. The Cardinal stressed what he believed to be the genuinely pastoral tone of the document, since 'the foundation of all pastoral theology is provided by safe doctrine'. Since this doctrine is true, and traditional, it must ever remain the same, and hence cannot yield to the proposals of 'the so-called New Theology'. The *schema*, he insisted, was the work of honest and learned scholars, and must not be set aside for any of the three or more unauthorized private drafts which were then in circulation. None of the others could be adopted, even in part. Quite obviously, the aged Cardinal was aware that the document was already under fire, even before its formal presentation to the Council, and that it required apology and defence by those who would see it adopted. Mgr. Garofalo seconded the Cardinal's affirmations, adding that the Council's responsibility was to defend and promote Catholic doctrine in its exact form. It must condemn error and thus safeguard truth, and purge the world of error and evil. This echo of Pius IX's conception of the Church's function, viz. to sift out and condemn modern errors (see his famous *Syllabus of Errors*, 1864), was most ill-timed, and immediately aroused strong opposition.

Cardinal Liénart of Lille was the first to speak against the *schema*. 'There are not now, and never have been, *two* sources of divine revelation, but only *one*, the Word of God, the good news announced by the prophets and revealed by Christ.' The *schema* he viewed as cold, scholastic, and formal, not an account of the living Word of God to men. Moreover it would make no appeal to 'our separated brothers, who have such love and veneration for the Word of God'. He asked that the *schema* be entirely rewritten.

The second speaker was Cardinal Frings of Cologne, also a scholar learned in Holy Scripture. He objected especially to the non-pastoral tone of the document, its condemnatory attitude toward much of modern scholarship, and its erroneous assumption that Holy Scripture and Tradition are two different *sources* of Revelation. This use of the plural is very modern, and not in accord with the earlier usage of the Church, the Fathers and ancient theologians, or the Councils. There is but one *Source* of Revelation, namely God Himself. Finally, he insisted, the *schema* comes down on one side in the current debate among theologians and biblical scholars, and thus inhibits liberty of research.

Three conservatives followed the two 'liberal' Cardinals. These were Cardinal Ruffini of Palermo, Cardinal Siri of Genoa, who intimated that the errors to be condemned sprang from the 'Modernism' suppressed by Pope Pius X in 1908, and Cardinal Quiroga y Palacios of Compostela in Spain. After this interlude the speeches that followed were made by more modern-minded cardinals, first among them the immensely popular Cardinal Léger of Montreal, who insisted upon rejection of the *schema* as submitted, and pleaded for freedom of scholarship within the Roman Catholic Church. Both Cardinal König of Vienna and Cardinal Alfrink of Utrecht, who followed Léger, criticized the *schema* as inadequate and misrepresenting the aims of the Council as outlined by Pope John. Another 'liberal' Cardinal followed, Cardinal Suenens of Malines-Brussels in Belgium, who pointed out that the *schema* lacked relevance to the problems of today. Cardinal Ritter of St. Louis, in the United States, followed, and condemned the document as timid, pessimistic, dull, and unrealistic.

Cardinal Bea, the famous Rector of the Pontifical Biblical Institute in Rome and now head of the Secretariat for Promoting Christian Unity, spoke next. He pointed out that the *schema* was misdirected, and ignored the purpose of Pope John in calling the Council together. Instead of a patristic or scholastic approach to the Church's doctrine of Revelation, the *schema* should have been 'pastoral' in its attitude and should have demonstrated 'the love and good will that flow from our religion'. He also urged that the document be entirely re-done.

Following him, the Melchite Patriarch of Antioch, Maximos IV Saigh, rounded off the criticism by asking for immediate consideration of the *schema* On the Church, which would set this theological argument in its proper perspective. The *schema* on Revelation was 'still in the spirit of the Counter-Reformation'. The day's session closed with strong statements by two Archbishops from Indonesia, Abp. Manek and Abp. Soegijapranata, who opposed the *schema*, and by the Archbishop Gonzalez of Saragossa, who pleaded for its retention and revision.

Thus the debate on the very first day showed clearly the sharp division between those who accepted the *schema* and were prepared to defend it, and those who wished to reject it and demanded that it be rewritten. As early as the preceding Tuesday, 13 November, the African bishops had met and agreed to vote against it *en bloc*.

The background of all this debate was somewhat more involved than most of the observers realized. Efforts had been made to close the Jesuit Biblical Institute in Rome and the Dominican École Biblique in Jerusalem, and—it is said—to substitute for them a teachers' institute at St. John Lateran, the old mother church of Rome. These efforts were motivated by firm opposition to the freedom of research and teaching in both the Institute and the École Biblique. And the proposal to substitute the Lateran University for these great and world-famous institutions and make it the centre of biblical study for the whole Church, was what some speakers meant when they referred to the tension between 'theological schools', a tension which the Council had no right or duty to adjudicate. The attempt to prevent 'liberals' (they never used the term!) from being appointed to membership in the Theological Commission, or, once appointed, to counteract their influence and forestall their votes, was part of a strategy inspired by zealous but blind devotion to the past. As early as the preceding summer, Cardinal Léger, who visited Rome each month as a member of the Preparatory Commission, had protested against the attacks upon the Biblical Institute and the plan to curtail the freedom of Catholic scholars. And later in this opening week of debate over the present *schema* Cardinal Döpfner of

Munich·challenged the statement of Cardinal Ottaviani that the Theological Commission had worked in harmony and concord and had reached unanimous agreement upon the formula. Cardinal Döpfner cited the testimony of Cardinals Frings and Léger to support his denial of this statement. Naturally, Cardinal Ottaviani counter-charged the Cardinal from Munich with mis-information, and insisted that the minority had been heard in due course but their views had been submerged in the final unanimously adopted *schema*. He intimated that members of the Biblical Institute had been invited to share in drafting the *schema*. Finally, he insisted that the Council might adopt or amend its wording, but could not reject it *in toto*. At once the Cardinal's statement was opposed on the floor of the *aula*, and a reading of the Council Rules of Order was demanded. Obviously the Council was entitled to discuss, amend, or reject any *schema* submitted to it. (See Art. 33.1 of the Rules.) Someone—my notes on the debate do not include this incident—is reported to have observed that it scarcely need be said that His Eminence (Cardinal Ottaviani) was prevaricating: 'All the world knows it' (see Xavier Rynne, *Letters from Vatican City*, 1963, p. 157). This sharp rebuff led to further disclosures. One member of the Theological Commission testified that no representative of the Biblical Institute had been present at the deliberations of the Commission, and that opponents of the majority's views were shifted about, dismissed or threatened, and ignored when votes were taken—in their absence.

It is unnecessary to describe the debates that took place on the following days of that decisive week. The arguments advanced, *pro* and *con*, were much the same as those already presented. In fact, throughout the history of Vatican Council II, despite the continuous effort to save time by limiting speeches to ten minutes—a marked contrast to the endless oratory of Vatican I in 1869–70—the variety of possible points of view was limited and the resulting repetition was inevitable. After all, only a dozen or fifteen lines of attack or defence were open. One exception was the widely quoted speech of Bishop De Smedt of Bruges, a member of Cardinal

Bea's Secretariat (soon to become a Commission) for promoting Christian reunion, and in mind and attitude very close to Pope John. He stressed the ecumenical purpose of the Council, and argued that the *schema* should lead to friendly dialogue with non-Catholics. He even listed some rules that should be observed in preparing *schemata* for the Council (conveniently listed in Xavier Rynne, p. 162). Obviously the present *schema* reflected no interest in ecumenical dialogue. The Theological Commission had in fact spurned the offer of the Secretariat on Unity to co-operate, or even to form a mixed sub-commission for the drafting of the decree. The danger now was that Vatican II might destroy this last best hope for co-operation among Christians in interpreting their diverse allegiance to one common faith, one common Lord.

In view of the absence of a two-thirds majority either for adoption or rejection of the *schema*, it is not strange that on 21 November Pope John intervened and ordered the *schema* to be withdrawn and entrusted to a mixed Commission consisting of members of both the Theological Commission, headed by Cardinal Ottaviani, and the Secretariat for Promoting Christian Unity, headed by Cardinal Bea. This mixed commission was instructed to shorten and redraft the *schema* and place more emphasis on the general principles of Catholic doctrine already treated by the Council of Trent and by Vatican Council I. This last provision presumably meant the omission of detailed support for such obscurantist views of dates and authorship of biblical writings as appeared in the original draft, views which supported the Lateran University, for example, against the Biblical Institute in Rome and the École Biblique in Jerusalem. And clearly it meant that at last Cardinal Bea, one of the leading Biblical scholars in the Roman Catholic Church, was to have a share in drafting the *schema* on Divine Revelation.

Of course the majority were right. There are not two sources of divine revelation, but one, namely God, or the Word of God. 'Only God can reveal God.' It was a superficial, even an artificial, use of language to distinguish thus widely between scripture and tradition. The purpose of the distinction was evidently to place ecclesiastical tradition on a level with the Bible. Thus equipped, the Church could bring forth from its treasures things new and old, including explicit doctrines unheard of by the writers of the scriptures and not even faintly suggested in the sacred books, if historically interpreted. Scripture and Tradition imply each other. The oral sources of the Bible and the oral tradition of interpretation of scripture both precede and follow the written documents. This was recognized by the ancient Pharisees with their Oral Tradition of the Law. As Dr. Douglas Horton said, at a meeting of the observers with the Secretariat on Christian Unity in an afternoon conference during the first session of the Council, 'Scripture and Tradition *interpenetrate*'.

One excuse for the lamentable separation of scripture and tradition and the declaration of the latter's independence was the effort to offset the old Protestant slogan *sola scriptura*, which in its turn had been devised to undermine medieval doctrines, beliefs, and practices disapproved by the Reformers. But *sola scriptura* is now seen to be indefensible—save as a test for eliminating every development within Christianity after the second century. The full richness and power of later Christianity would be ruled out if *sola scriptura* were taken in full earnest. By the same token, *sola traditio* would be indefensible; and almost as bad is the dichotomy assumed when the source of revelation is described as *two* sources, separate and distinct though parallel. As Fr. Yves Congar, the eminent Dominican theologian, has pointed out, 'There is not a single dogma which the Church holds by Scripture *alone*, not a single dogma which it holds by tradition *alone*.' (See Rynne, p. 141.) 'The Bible and the Bible only' was once described as —or identified with—'the Religion of Protestants' (William Chillingworth, 1637). But the Bible is the Church's book, and it was both produced and preserved within the Beloved Community, and for that Community's purposes, not independently—like a book 'let down from heaven by a string', or as a private literary venture on the book market, or as a selected anthology of moving passages gathered from all the sacred literatures of mankind.

As Dr. Horton writes in his *Vatican Diary* (vol. i, p. 122f.), the liberals were not even understood by the conservatives. 'When the latter heard the phrase, "one source", they seemed to hear in it the old Reformation cry, *Sola scriptura*, scripture alone—whereas this was not the meaning of the progressives at all.' The opposing sides 'never really encountered each other'. And this is a situation repeated all over Christendom, not just at the Vatican Council, wherever Fundamentalists confront Liberals and completely misunderstand or misinterpret their views of holy scripture. The struggle in the Vatican Council is the battle we all are forced to wage, on one side or the other. Hence its interest and importance for all Christians everywhere. The progressives among the Roman Catholic Cardinals and Bishops have been engaged in a well-fought fight for religious and intellectual liberty, and the promise of 'still more light to break forth from God's Word'. Present-day Protestants and above all Anglicans, but also all other churches and schools of religious thought in the world today, should view with deep concern and warm gratitude the valiant defence of the Church's real interest in the preservation and true interpretation of the Holy Scriptures. Slowly the tide is turning. Once more, we believe, will dawn an age of renewed and vital faith, centred not in the memorization of lengthy theological formulae and confessions but in the fresh study of Holy Writ and in direct and unhesitating approach to the one and only Source of Divine Revelation. 'For whatever was written in former days was written for *our* instruction, that by steadfastness and by encouragement of the scriptures we might have hope' (Rom. 15. 4 R.S.V.).

At long last, the new draft of the *schema* was submitted to the Council at its fourth session, was adopted, and was promulgated by Pope Paul VI on 18 November 1965. Does the decree really go beyond Trent or Vatican I? Has it met the requirements of Pope John, who asked for a pastoral approach and less reference to theological controversy or the debates of the schools? Finally, from our own peculiar point of view, what will Anglicans make of it? Protestants have generally criticized Trent as vague on these points of Scripture and Tradition. In fact both Trent and Vatican I were brief and vague. The *Decretum de libris sacris et de traditionibus recipiendis*[1] issued on 8 April 1546 (text in Denzinger, *Enchiridion Symbolorum*, new ed. § 1501) described the Church's teaching as 'derived from the one source of both saving truth and moral discipline' and 'to be proclaimed to every creature (Mark 16. 15)'. This truth and discipline 'are contained in written books and in unwritten traditions which the Apostles received from the lips of Christ himself and were received from the Apostles themselves by the dictation of the Holy Spirit and as it were delivered by hand and have thus come down to us. All these scriptures of Old and New Testament are to be preserved, and also the traditions.' The questions before Trent had chiefly to do with the *contents* of Holy Scripture. (Compare the relevant Article VI, in our *Thirty-nine Articles*.) By 'all these scriptures' the Council meant to include the still-disputed books: Tobit, Judith, Wisdom, Ecclesiasticus (Sirach), 1–2 Maccabees, and parts of Daniel, in the Old Testament (i.e. in the Apocrypha), and Hebrews, 2 Peter, James, 2–3 John, Jude, Apocalypse (Revelation), in the New Testament. These words of Trent are repeated in the Constitution of Vatican I, 24 April 1870, entitled *Dei Filius*, 'On the Catholic Faith,' Ch. 2 (text in Denzinger, § 3006): *Haec porro supernaturalis revelatio, secundum universalis Ecclesiae fidem a sancta Tridentina Synodo declaratam continetur 'in libris scriptis et sine scripto traditionibus, quae ipsius Christi ore ab Apostolis acceptae, aut (ab) ipsis Apostolis Spiritu Sancto dictante quasi per manus traditae, ad nos usque pervenerunt'*.

The usual Protestant criticism of this language is its vagueness and its implication that Scripture alone is not adequate but must be supplemented by Tradition, which can thus become an independent source of doctrine, apart from the Bible. But the Protestant criticism is not very impressive, if the decree (either the original or its repetition at Vatican I) is read in the context of the deliberations and discussions at Trent. Certainly it does not favour the quite modern notion of 'two

[1] Decree on the holy books and on the traditions which are to be received.

sources' of Revelation. Another Protestant criticism is the inclusion of the Apocrypha as on a level with the Palestinian
(Hebrew) canon of the Old Testament, thus authorizing certain doctrines, such as prayers for the departed or the guidance
of angels, which are not found in the New Testament. This
argument likewise has lost much of its force. We no longer
look upon the Bible as a disguised treatise on systematic theology but as the record of a divine revelation, on one hand, and
of the human response to it, man's search for and discovery of
God, on the other hand.

The Anglican view of Holy Scripture and the growth of
Tradition is somewhat unusual in both Catholicism and Protestantism. As the *Book of Common Prayer*, in the sacramental
rites of Ordination, and also the *Articles of Religion* appended
to the Prayer Book (Article VI) presuppose, Scripture *contains*
'all things necessary to salvation'. It is *not* said that the Bible
is literally inspired, or infallible, or that it contains nothing that
is not inspired. The very text upon which such a claim might
be based can be variously translated and also interpreted: 'All
scripture is inspired,' or 'all inspired scripture' (2 Tim. 3. 16).
As in Judaism, the inspiration of the Pentateuch or Torah is
unquestioned: 'God spake these words and said . . .' (Exodus
20. 1; see the introduction to the Decalogue in the Communion Service). But no such claim is made for Joshua and
Judges, 1–2 Samuel, 1–2 Kings, the 'Former Prophets'. As in
Judaism, these were probably included as containing accounts
of the earlier prophets, i.e., those prior to the 'writing' prophets
beginning with Amos. But they similarly, like the writing prophets, spoke in the name of the Most High. Their messages
began, 'Thus saith the Lord'—a formula that continued long
after the writers began entitling their oracles, 'The word of the
Lord which came to (or by)' Amos, or Isaiah, or Jeremiah, or
Ezekiel, or whosoever book it was in which the formula was
used. The Wisdom books were also supposed to be inspired,
presumably because 'all Wisdom cometh from the Most High'.
The visions and dreams of the apocalyptists, Daniel for example, were supposedly 'sent' by God, and, as a literary genre,
took the place of the messages sent through the prophets.

Further elaboration of the Law, in the later codes of the Torah and in such Utopian codes as that of Ezekiel, was also thought to be inspired, like the ancient traditional codes derived from the primitive laws of Moses. Only the Megilloth [the Five Rolls], i.e., the Song of Solomon, Ruth, Lamentations, Ecclesiastes, and Esther, were questioned. But they were included in the sacred Canon because they were 'useful' or 'profitable', as the term is used in the New Testament (2 Tim. 3. 16; cf. the Collect for Advent II in the Prayer Book), and were in fact used by the Jews on various festivals. The other writings found in the Greek translation, i.e. in the so-called Alexandrian Canon (though it was scarcely a formal canon), were not admitted to the Hebrew Canon, i.e. the list of sacred books authorized in Palestine. Thus Ecclesiasticus (The Wisdom of Ben Sira or Sirach) was excluded even though it was an older book than Daniel, and though its original text was in Hebrew, a text which was still in circulation when the Hebrew Canon was drawn up at the Council of Jamnia in A.D. 90. To this Canon in its two-fold form, Hebrew and Greek, the Church added the New Testament, in the course of a long development ending in A.D. 364, though ninety per cent of the New Testament was formally complete by the year 180, and virtually so, long before that date, say by 125–150. By the middle of the second century the four Gospels and the Pauline Epistles (the *Euangelion* and the *Apostolos*) had long been familiar and in wide use. The Canon was no invention of Marcion,[2] or of the Anti-Marcionites, but grew out of the liturgical use of Holy Scripture in the early Church, the New Testament writings being gradually added to the Greek translation of the Old Testament. In fact, the Old Testament itself arose in this way.[3]

Thus the 'growth' of Holy Scripture was spread over a long

[2] Marcion (d. about A.D. 160) rejected the Old Testament, and as Scripture accepted only ten Pauline epistles and his own version of the Gospel of St. Luke, thus cutting the links (which he thought un-Christian) between Christianity and Old Testament religion.

[3] As I have tried to show in my book, *Translating the Bible* (New York and Edinburgh 1961). This volume was prepared at the request of the Episcopal Church for its observance of the 350th anniversary of the King James Version of the Bible.

period, and involved tradition from the outset, especially in the early, pre-literary period, and it took place on different levels. There were 'oral literatures' before there were written, as the Chadwicks of Cambridge demonstrated in three great volumes,[4] and as the more recent 'Form Critics' have assumed in their interpretation of the Gospel traditions. Moreover, there were different levels of inspiration, as much so in Holy Scripture as in any and all other literatures, the divine inspiration running parallel to the secular levels of poetic, dramatic, narrative inspiration, though on a higher level of subject and content and overruling impetus. The same is true of the interpretation of the Bible, which must be studied in the light of its own time, i.e. the many successive times represented in the authorship of the holy books. There is some 'timeless' writing in the Bible, and as a whole it speaks to the ages; but most of the writings were addressed primarily to their own generation: naturally, since the burden of the Bible's teaching had to do with living, not with metaphysical speculation. There are some sacred books in the world's literature which remind one of a plane cruising above the clouds, searching for a safe three-point landing in time and space, a well-laid-out port where the teaching can be applied. But the Bible emerges, by divine evocation, out of human need and divine response.

It is characteristic of Anglicanism that the Bible is used primarily in public worship, i.e. liturgically, not as a source-book for systematic theology. This use is selective. Some passages in the Bible are never read in church. Anglicans make no effort to systematize the whole Bible in a complete scheme of theology or doctrine. Development, which Anglicans take for granted, means that some parts are left behind, e.g. the *lex talionis*, 'an eye for an eye and a tooth for a tooth', or the death penalty for the adulteress. Anglicanism emphasizes a few basic teachings, upon which the rest depend. According to the Prayer Book, these begin with the Creed (i.e. the Apostles' Creed), the Lord's Prayer, and the Ten Commandments. This is the basis of the Catechism, a remarkable contrast to some of

[4] H. M. Chadwick and N. K. Chadwick, *The Growth of Literatures* (Cambridge, 1932–40).

the sixteenth-century confessions with their long explanations of theological ideas derived from the Bible—chiefly from St. Paul. As someone has affirmed, according to Anglicans 'Christianity is sixty per cent. practical.' There is a very early precedent for this. The earliest church council, described in the Book of Acts, issued a 'decree' and introduced it with the words: 'It has seemed good to the Holy Spirit and to us to lay upon you no greater burden than these necessary things...' (Acts 15. 28 R.S.V.). The few things 'necessary to salvation', assumed by the *Book of Common Prayer*, are in marked contrast to the long theological definitions provided by the Schoolmen and the Reformers. On many points of belief certainty is both impossible and unnecessary, and upon them equally sincere and loyal Christians may disagree. And 'to require men to accept as authoritative teaching for which there is no real evidence is to strain and weaken faith. If men are asked to accept indiscriminately anything that individuals choose to teach, the inevitable result is that as soon as they learn the precariousness of part of the teaching, they reject not that part only but the whole.' This is quoted from a well-known standard textbook used in Anglican seminaries the world over, E. J. Bicknell's *A Theological Introduction to the Thirty-nine Articles of the Church of England* (p. 166). Another well-known textbook testifies: 'The Christian religion has more to do than to formulate a true system of thought. Dogma misses its end unless it is used to mould life'—this is quoted from Darwell Stone's *Outlines of Christian Dogma* (p. 5). Thus it is from a somewhat different point of view than either Roman Catholicism or the conservative Protestant standards that Anglicans will study the Constitution on Divine Revelation issued by the Vatican Council—a view-point of considerable agreement and sympathy, but also of dissent and even disagreement.

The final draft of the decree appeared at once in newspapers, as in *The New York Times*, 19 November 1965, pp. 16f. The translation had been prepared by the National Catholic Welfare Conference and was endorsed by the Bishops of the United States. It was as adequate a version as could be had, in marked contrast with some of the earlier press releases which were obviously done hastily and by translators (in Italy) who were not wholly familiar with English. The decree contains a Preface and six chapters, as follows: I. Revelation Itself. II. Handing On Divine Revelation. III. Sacred Scripture, Its Inspiration, and Divine Interpretation. IV. The Old Testament. V. The New Testament. VI. Sacred Scripture in the Life of the Church.

The Preface begins on a lofty note, comparable to the beautiful Preface to the Constitution on the Sacred Liturgy.

Hearing the word of God with reverence and proclaiming it with faith, the sacred Synod takes its direction from these words of St. John: 'We announce to you the eternal life which dwelt with the Father, and was made visible to us. What we have seen and heard we announce to you, so that you may have fellowship with us and our common fellowship be with the Father and His Son Jesus Christ' [cf. 1 John 1.1–3]. Therefore, following in the footsteps of the Council of Trent and of Vatican I, this present council wishes to set forth authentic doctrine on divine revelation and how it is handed on, so that by hearing the message of salvation the whole world may believe, by believing it may hope, and by hoping it may love.

Following explicitly the example both of Trent and Vatican I, the opening chapter speaks of revelation as the work of God, in His goodness and wisdom. That is, 'God chose to reveal Himself, and to make known to us the hidden purpose of His will by which through Christ, the Word made flesh, man might in the Holy Spirit have access to the Father and come to share in the divine nature.' This weighty statement of first principles is completely biblical, and echoes in every phrase the language of the Bible and of the ancient theologians, the church Fathers. It is 'God speaking' and declaring His 'plan of revelation' which is realized in the deeds and words of the 'history of salvation' and form an inner unity: the deeds wrought by God 'manifest and confirm the teaching and realities signified by the words; while the words proclaim the deeds and clarify the mystery contained in them. By this revelation . . . the deepest truth about God and the salvation of man shines out for our sake in Christ, who is both the Mediator and the fulness of all revelation.' This language also is traditional, and embraces the wide comprehensiveness of Catholic theology at its best. It is universal, beginning with 'our first parents'; it is biblical, stressing the enduring hope that spurred men on, even after the fall; it is soteriological, emphasizing the 'waiting for a Saviour' which the church has always seen in the Old Testament; it is rational, and it recognizes the general revelation made to all men. After emphasizing the completeness and finality of the Christian revelation—'to see Jesus is to see his Father'—the chapter concludes with a summary: It was God's will to 'show forth and communicate Himself and the eternal decisions . . . regarding the salvation of men' and to 'share those divine treasures which totally transcend the understanding of the human mind'.

Then follows, almost as an appendix, the widest possible statement:

As a sacred synod has affirmed, 'God, the beginning and end of all things, can be known with certainty from created reality by the light of human reason'; but [it] teaches that it is through His revelation that 'those religious truths which are by nature accessible to human reason can be known by all men with ease, with solid certitude and with no trace of error, even in this present state of the human race'.

This is quoted from Vatican I, *Constitutio de Fide*, 2 (see Denzinger, new edition, § 3004f). It also sounds like Trent, as well as Vatican I (without the anathemas!). But it is no appendix. It is a statement that crowns and binds together the whole chapter, and will strongly appeal to all who believe in measures of grace and illumination granted to all men everywhere, from the beginning of history and before. It is also a biblical note, and one that needs to be stressed in these days when Christianity is credited with a kind of narrowness and exclusiveness that comports poorly with the facts of the history of religions. It may also point the way toward further realization of the meaning of revelation to those Christians who share the narrower view. 'Religionless' Christianity is a contradiction in terms. Christianity cannot be understood except in its natural setting in the history of religions. There is a direct line of continuity from the 'general' revelation to all mankind, including the most primitive people, and the 'special' revelation reflected in the Old Testament, first upon its lowest historical levels, then upon ever higher ones as God's increasing revelation took place, and men found that a nobler conception of God required a nobler human ethics, a higher ethics a purer idea of God. Finally, the continuity of Judaism and early Christianity is undeniable and not to be ignored. If St. Augustine could say[5] that 'What is latent in the Old Testament is patent in the New,' and if a modern scholar can maintain that 'everything in the New Testament has its roots in the Old', then the continuity of the process from the beginning is clear. God has not left himself 'without witness' in any age, in any place, in any nation (cf. Acts 14. 15–17).

There are always people totally uninterested in history, and in consequence incapable of historical judgements. For some of them, logic is the only guide to decision, and systematic or theoretical constructions take the place of immediate insight, especially in religion. But this situation does not alter the facts. Christianity, like Judaism, is an out-and-out historical religion.

To Anglicans this will seem a very natural conclusion, for we are heirs to a wide outlook, older than the *Aufklärung* or the modern study of History of Religions—witness the Cambridge Platonists of the seventeenth century. Hence we may assume that this statement by the Council will be warmly welcomed among us. Moreover, we may also be sure that increasing numbers of other Christians will share in welcoming it. The closing statement balances two ideas: the totally transcendent conception of God and His purpose (the 'divine decrees') which may lie outside the range of human understanding, and the things that are known from reason and the phenomena of nature.

Chapter II deals with the subject 'Handing on [the] Divine Revelation'. It describes the way in which God has provided

[5] *Quaest. in Hept.* 2.73.

for the transmission of His revelation to all generations. Tradition is the key: the process is a 'handing down' or 'on' (*traditio*), and it may be either oral or written. Tradition is the work of God, not of men: Christ the Lord, 'in whom the full revelation of the Supreme God is brought to completion', commissioned the Apostles to preach the Gospel to all mankind—the Gospel which is 'the source of all saving truth and moral teaching'—and to impart to men 'heavenly gifts'. This statement is really a reaffirmation of what Trent and Vatican I have said. The Church's Tradition is derived from Christ, by way of the Apostles and the 'apostolic men' (Eusebius's term, used in his *Church History*), who under the inspiration of the Holy Spirit 'committed the message of salvation to writing'. Thus both Scripture and Tradition are derived from one and the same Source, and belong together in the long course of 'handing on' the tradition to the bishops and they to their successors, along with the authority to teach. Both Scripture and Tradition are like a mirror 'in which the pilgrim Church on earth looks at God ... until she is brought finally to see Him as He is, face to face'. The Apostolic preaching, based on direct communication from Christ, is 'expressed in a special way in the inspired books', and at the same time was to be 'preserved by an unending succession of preachers until the end of time'. Hence the Apostles warned their readers to 'hold fast the traditions' which they had learned 'either by word of mouth or by letter'. There is no *growth* in tradition: all things necessary to salvation and holiness were contained in the original deposit. But, under the guidance of the Holy Spirit, there is a growth in understanding. This takes place through study and contemplation, a widening experience of the religious life, and by the preaching of 'those who have received through episcopal succession the sure gift of truth. For as the centuries succeed one another, the Church constantly moves forward toward the fullness of divine truth until the words of God reach their complete fulfillment in her.'

So much for tradition. It is not a separate source or even channel of divine revelation, but part and parcel of the total process of transmitting divine truth, now orally by word of mouth, now in writing, now in formal transfer from one Apostle or bishop to other Christians, now by the special selection and authorization of the canonical scriptures, segregated from all other writings whether heretical or only well-meant but erroneous and inadequate. 'Sacred tradition and sacred scripture form one sacred deposit of the word of God.' 'Sacred tradition, sacred scripture, and the teaching authority of the Church . . . are so linked and joined together that one cannot stand without the others.'

Not only is this a highly desirable elucidation and amplification of the earlier statements of Trent and Vatican I, but in approach and in terminology the decree is modern. The whole emphasis upon tradition which now prevails in biblical studies—ever since 1900 and especially since 1918—has provided a more sympathetic approach to such a statement as the Council has produced. In the modern view, tradition preceded, accompanied, and followed the sacred writings, in both Old Testament and New. They were not literary *jeux d'esprit*, but arose within the holy community, the *Qahal ha-kodesh*, the *Ekklesia tou Theou*, and often only crystallized what had previously been the current teaching or belief or cultic utterances of the group. 'Form criticism' is not a very good name for the study of the tradition underlying the Gospels, but everyone knows what it is concerned with, viz. the oral tradition, partly stereotyped, then partly written, finally woven together into the finished books of the evangelists. Tradition was the cradle in which sacred writings grew. Whether or not, and to what degree, tradition itself grew as time went on, is a nice question for experts. It can hardly be maintained that there was *no* development—e.g. in Mariology, or in the theory of succession, or the unique office of the papacy, or in a dozen other beliefs and practices of historical Christianity. But as far as it goes—and the Council carefully limits its definition— the statement is true and sound, and in Chapter II as in Chapter I speaks in modern language.

Chapter III, on 'Sacred Scripture, its Inspiration, and [its] Divine Interpretation', affirms the inspiration of both the Old Testament and the New 'in their entirety' (as Trent affirmed).

They were 'written under the inspiration of the Holy Spirit', and 'have God as their Author, and have been handed on as such to the Church herself'. Hence 'everything asserted by the inspired authors or sacred writers must be held to be asserted by the Holy Spirit.' Accordingly, these writings are 'without error' in teaching 'that truth which God wanted put into the sacred writings for the sake of our salvation'. 'All scripture is divinely inspired' (see 2 Tim. 3. 16)—nevertheless 'God speaks ... through men in human fashion', and the interpreter of Scripture has the task of making clear the real intention of the words spoken, and must pay special attention to 'literary forms'. 'Truth is expressed differently in texts which are variously historical, prophetic, poetic, or [in] other forms of discourse'—a fine statement that echoes the great encyclical of Pius XII, *Divino afflante Spiritu*[6], in which, he himself echoing St. Augustine's *De doctrina Christiana*, the Pope insisted that biblical interpreters (expositors as well as translators, and especially teachers) must begin by studying 'tropes', figures of speech, the figurative and symbolic language current in the ancient Orient—and still common there. At the same time, the Council insists that due regard must be paid to the unity of Scripture, its total meaning, its unity in diversity as well as its diversity in unity. Moreover, 'the living tradition of the whole Church must be taken into account, along with the harmony which exists between elements of the faith'. And the exegete must be subject to the judgement of the Church, which is the final authority for Christian doctrine, since the Church 'carries out the divine Commission and ministry of guarding and interpreting the word of God'.

Quite clearly this broad statement of principles is no theoretical or speculative composition, spun like a silky skein of theorems with their proofs: it is meant for guidance in the actual life, work, and worship of the Church—especially its teaching and preaching. It deserves careful study, not a mere once-over reading, by all Christians—by Catholics, Orthodox, Anglicans, and Protestants of all persuasions from the most rigid fundamentalists to the broadest of liberals. For we all use

[6] 30 September 1943; see Denzinger§ 3825ff.

the Bible, read it, interpret (or misinterpret!) it, preach from it, and translate it incessantly—a new version every year!

Whether the actual administration of the decree will make adequate provision for freedom of scholarship, enabling qualified researchers to investigate and propose new and promising channels of study, and identify the ever-fresh Word which is to spring forth from the written words—this is not guaranteed by Chapter III. And one hesitates to assume that it will be forthcoming in every area of Catholic influence. Pope Paul VI has issued more than one warning against the pursuit of 'novelty'[7]—what some Anglicans, for example the late Francis J. Hall, used to call 'neology' or 'neologism'. The 'Instruction', approved by Pope Paul, 'Concerning the Historical Truth of the Gospels', appended to Cardinal Bea's recent book, *The Study of the Synoptic Gospels* (Harper, 1965), contains an admonition to 'ordinaries' (bishops and superiors) to 'keep watch with great care over popular writings', such as 'books and articles in magazines and newspapers, on biblical subjects'. This is clearly censorship, and may quite possibly fall into the hands of ecclesiastical authorities who have not the slightest interest in biblical or historical research or in scientific exegesis or in the whole modern way of approaching the Bible, interpreting it, and using it both publicly and privately.

From the Anglican point of view, one must regretfully acknowledge that incredibly bad history and exegesis are frequently expounded from our own pulpits and even in formal and official church documents; at the same time we must continue to insist that freedom of research be guaranteed despite its risks. A Church which has produced an outstanding succession of biblical scholars through the centuries (observe the Anglican participation in the record, e.g. in the new *Cambridge History of the Bible* edited by S. L. Greenslade)—such a Church surely cannot consent to see scholarship muzzled in the interest of uniformity, or even of reunion, or in an effort to preserve the unruffled calm of the uneducated laity (or clergy!), however 'faithful'. As a matter of fact that 'unruffled calm' is swiftly disappearing, as the laity are becoming better educated

---

[7] See my *Rome and Reunion*, O.U.P., New York, 1965, p. 186.

and are asking embarrassing questions, everywhere, not only in the Roman Catholic Church. It is no sign of submission to popular modern 'liberalism' that the Anglican Communion demands freedom for its scholars: it is in our blood, and antedates the whole period of the Reformation, the Counter Reformation, the *Aufklärung*, the age of Rationalism, and the rise of modern science. It dates from a far earlier period. Robert Grosseteste, the famous Franciscan Bishop of Lincoln in the thirteenth century, was a biblical scholar long before the Reformation. He was no radical, but he opened the door to biblical and scientific research. It is a pity the Decree says nothing about the responsibility of teachers and interpreters of the Bible to seek and follow truth above all things, since it 'endures and is strong for ever, and lives and prevails for ever and ever. . . . Blessed be the God of truth!' (1 Esdras 4. 38–40 R.S.V.). And the corollary of that search for truth is the freedom of the scholar, which the Church must guarantee.

Chapter IV on the Old Testament and Chapter V on the New Testament set forth the traditional view of Holy Scripture. The books of the Old Testament, for example, 'give expression to a lively sense of God, contain a store of sublime teachings about God, sound wisdom about human life, and a wonderful treasury of prayers; and in them the mystery of our salvation is present in a hidden way. Christians should receive them with reverence.' 'The New Testament is hidden in the Old, and the Old is made manifest in the New'—this view (as we have seen) is as old as St. Augustine. But what of the modern *historical* view of the Old Testament, and its interpretation as religious *history*, and the 'preparation for the Gospel' in ancient Judaism, and also in the religious thought of the Gentile world, contemporary with the Old Testament and shedding a flood of light upon the religious development of Israel and its literature? This chapter reads as if its authors had 'grown weary in well-doing', perhaps in endless revising of the *schema* in order to satisfy the demands of extremists on one side or another, and had given up hope of saying anything new and constructive.

The same criticism may be made of Chapter V, which

hews to the traditional line. Christ 'established' the Kingdom of God on earth, manifested God and Himself by deeds and words. The record of his life and teaching is contained in the four Gospels, which are of apostolic authorship: 'the foundation of faith, namely, the four-fold gospel according to Matthew, Mark, Luke, and John'. 'Holy Mother Church has firmly and with absolute constancy held, and continues to hold, that the four gospels just named, whose historical character the Church unhesitatingly asserts, faithfully hand on what Jesus Christ, while living among men, really did and taught for their eternal salvation until the day He was taken up into heaven.'

Yes; but how much more can be said of the Gospels—and also of the Epistles—than this warm encomium and assertion of authenticity! No doubt the limitations of space and time had something to do with this truncated statement. No doubt the world should be grateful for the general drift of the affirmation, even though some phrases need (and will receive) criticism. But Protestants and Anglicans, as well as Liberals, probably will find the Decree more or less unsatisfactory. The 'how much more' that is left unsaid deserves full recognition and statement: the literary charm and fascination of these marvellous books; the *mysterium tremendum* of the divine utterances that lie behind them; the long process of advancing revelation, step by step, ethical insights and new motives marching forward *pari passu* with religious inspiration; the flashing brilliance of certain sayings and passages that shine like new stars in the sky, illuminating whole wide areas of human problems, frustrations, defeats, and despairs; the calm assurance of God's love and care, even in the most desperate situations; the reward of loyalty and fidelity and self-sacrifice in God's cause; the assurance of a deep and everlasting *meaning* in human life, under the guidance and tutelage of the Holy Spirit; the compelling example of Christ and his inspired teaching set forth in unforgettable words, simple to grasp, profound to comprehend, uplifting and challenging to observe in one's daily life; the call of the Christian, and of all men, to believe in God and submit to His law, rely upon His grace and forgiveness, and share in extending His reign throughout all the earth; the transforming power of the new life, the 'new being', in Christ Jesus, by which human nature is actually metamorphosed and remade more like the divine pattern; growth in grace, in holiness, and the promise of a better world not only hereafter but also here in this present one. Alas, these meanings of scripture which Protestants, Anglicans, and Liberals cherish, though perhaps taken for granted, are not stated. The dull hand of ecclesiastical authority clamps down firmly and decrees that the Bible must be taught, but the teachers must conform rigidly to the requirements set forth by the dogmatic and canonical regulations of Holy Mother Church. That Church, alas, in our experience, has too often been a step-mother!—cold, legal, unsympathetic, dictatorial, and merciless. All the accumulation of dogmatism that ruled the Byzantine period, all the legalism of imperial Rome in its latter days, is still dominant in ecclesiastical Rome. That is why we suspect that omissions in the present decrees are ominous. We shall study them, and learn from them, and thank God for the progress being made by Roman Catholicism, especially in biblical studies; but we shall not rush into any plan for reunion that overlooks elements in the Christian faith which are not only precious to us and to most Christians, but absolutely essential to any statement of what we believe and affirm as true, and what we aim to convince others that they also shall find in our religion.

Chapter VI 'Sacred Scripture in the Life of the Church', stresses the changeless continuity of the Church, its worship, its faithful dispensation of the Word and Sacraments, especially the Holy Eucharist. This must prevail in the future as in the past. 'Easy access to Sacred Scripture should be provided for all the Christian faithful.' Adequate translations, like the Greek Septuagint and the Latin Vulgate, have been accredited by the Church in the past; other translations, into modern languages, must be undertaken now. 'And should the opportunity arise and the Church authorities approve, if these translations are produced in cooperation with the separated brethren as well, all Christians will be able to use them.' This last sentence is almost funny, in view of the recent adoption of the American *Revised Standard Version*, produced by Protestants, with the approval of the hierarchy in Great Britain, and also its widespread use among Roman Catholics in other countries. The emphasis upon patristic studies is sound, and will be welcomed by Anglicans and many others—certainly by our Orthodox brethren. But the teaching office of the Church did not expire with the ancient church fathers or the medieval schoolmen; biblical scholarship is even more alive today, and more active, and uses better tools, than ever before in the long history of the Christian Church. Why not mention this ongoing function of the *Ecclesia docens*? Instead, the decree insists that 'all the clergy must hold fast to the sacred Scriptures through diligent sacred reading and careful study'— especially the sacred text found in the liturgy, in instructions approved by the bishops, and ... accompanied by constant prayer. Biblical scholars are encouraged 'to continue energetically, following the mind of the Church, with the work they have so well begun, with a constant renewal of vigor'.

This all sounds very good, as also does the admonition to distribute the Holy Scriptures, including annotated editions, especially those adapted to use by non-Christians. But where is there any word about the hard, relentless task of mastering the languages, the idiom, the structure, the interrelations of holy scripture, or its setting in the ancient world, or the long historical evolution of the religious life that lay behind and led up to the divine revelation, or the inescapable duty of following the truth in interpretation and exegesis, whatever the traditional interpretations have been, and especially the duty of rejecting the inflated allegorism of days gone by which made selected texts mean anything the writers chose and thus transformed the Bible into a book of riddles and their answers, and expounded it past all recognition? Not that the Roman Catholic clergy are the only ones that need such admonition. Everyone knows clergy in all churches who lightly excuse their incompetence ('My professors would not approve this exegesis, but ... !'), and then proceed with outrageous misinterpretation and mangling of sacred texts.

The decree can only be temporary—let us hope that it will be! There is much more to be said of the Bible and its use, and we trust that in the present Roman Catholic revival of biblical studies there will be a long and fruitful harvest of modern understanding and application of divine wisdom to human need and inquiry.

3 The Church

EUGENE FAIRWEATHER

Keble Professor of Divinity,
at Trinity College, Toronto

I

... The council is to be a new spring, a reawakening of the mighty spiritual and moral energies which at present lie dormant. The council is evidence of a determination to bring about a rejuvenation both of the interior forces of the Church and of the regulations by which her canonical structure and liturgical forms are governed. The council is striving, that is, to enhance in the Church that beauty of perfection and holiness which imitation of Christ and mystical union with Him in the Holy Spirit can alone confer.[1]

These words of Paul VI in his first papal address to the Second Vatican Council express succinctly the paramount concern which inspired the Council's activities from 11 October 1962 to 8 December 1965. The Council's primary purpose was the renewal of the Roman Catholic Church in its doctrine, worship and common life, with a view to the more faithful and effective fulfilment of its mission in the world of today. Of course, it would be misleading to suggest that all who shared in the work of the Council saw either the Church's need of renewal or its resources for renewal in the same light. But it would be idle to question the commitment of the Council as a whole to the ideal of a reinvigorated Church.

Any truly responsible effort to bring about the renewal of the Church must be based on a reasonably clear idea of what the Church is and what it is called to do. This requirement was clearly stated by Pope Paul VI in the address already quoted.

The time has now come [he said] ... when the truth regarding the Church of Christ should be examined, coordinated and expressed. The expression should not, perhaps, take the form of a solemn

[1] Pope Paul VI, allocution of 29 September 1963, quoted from Floyd Anderson (ed.), *Council Daybook: Vatican II, Sessions 1 and 2* (Washington: National Catholic Welfare Conference, 1965), p. 147.

dogmatic definition, but of declarations making known by means of the Church's magisterium, in a more explicit and authoritative form, what the Church considers herself to be. . . . The principal concern of this session of the council will be to examine the intimate nature of the Church and to express in human language, so far as that is possible, a definition which will best reveal the Church's real, fundamental constitution and manifest its manifold mission of salvation.[2]

It is hardly too much to say that, if Vatican II had failed to respond to this summons to serious and prolonged reflection on the nature of the Church, it might just as well not have happened at all. Without the guidance of a definite ecclesiology, it could have done little more than tinker at ecclesiastical machinery. Happily, however, well before the close of the first session the Council Fathers were showing themselves aware of the theological requirements of their task,[3] and as the months and years passed their projects of reform were ever more clearly illuminated by a fresh apprehension of the Church's nature and mission.

Among the sixteen constitutions, decrees, and declarations—all of them bearing on the Church's doctrine, worship, structure, inner life or role in the world—which survived the test of conciliar debate, pride of place unquestionably belongs to *Lumen Gentium*, the first, in order of promulgation, and by far the longer of the Council's two dogmatic constitutions.[4] In this text, as nowhere else, we find a systematic exposition of the doctrine of the Church's being and calling which came more

[2] ibid., p. 146.

[3] At the 'general congregation' (plenary session) on 28 November 1962, Cardinal Ottaviani proposed that discussion of the draft constitution on the Church, which was ready for presentation to the Council, should be deferred in favour of the *schema* on the Blessed Virgin Mary, which (he said) might well be dealt with before 8 December, the closing date of the first session. The Council presidents considered this proposal and rejected it. Ottaviani introduced the draft *De Ecclesia* on 1 December, and discussion continued to 7 December. Cf. Anderson, *Council Daybook*, pp. 102–12.

[4] For brevity's sake the dogmatic constitution on the Church will be cited throughout this essay as *Lumen Gentium* and other documents will be referred to by their Latin titles, derived in each case from their opening words. (For a list of titles and opening words, see Appendix 1.)

and more fully to inform the work of Vatican II. As we shall see, some points of ecclesiology, including more than one major doctrinal consideration, were handled more effectively in other conciliar documents, but no other document gives us such a comprehensive account of the mystery of the Church and its place in the saving purpose of God.

The history of the dogmatic constitution on the Church, from the introduction of the first draft (*schema*) on 1 December 1962 to the promulgation of the final text on 21 November 1964, formed one of the most dramatic episodes in the story of the Second Vatican Council. The long and complex debate in and around St. Peter's, which itself epitomized a lengthy and crucial development in modern Roman Catholic thought, cannot be adequately reported here.[5] I can only speak of the final product and say that, in my judgement, the eventual promulgation of *Lumen Gentium* was the worthy *dénouement* of a dramatic tale.

In effect, *Lumen Gentium* has 'canonized' a strikingly fresh self-definition of the Roman Catholic Church—a self-definition heavy with consequences both for the domestic economy of Roman Catholicism and for its stance in the world. Of course, it must be acknowledged that the essential elements of the 'new look' are not alien to the traditional heritage of the Roman Church. If they had been sheer novelties, the recent transformation would have been inconceivable, because it would have demanded an unacceptable breach of continuity. It must also be recognized, however, that in recent centuries these elements were obscured both in official statements and in conventional teaching and practice. If they had been widely expounded in the theological schools and embodied in ecclesiastical practice, no transformation would have been necessary.

But the significant transformation of Roman Catholic ecclesiology is an indisputable fact. This transformation may be summarily described as a shift from the juridical and institu-

---

[5] An informative account of the debates which eventuated in *Lumen Gentium* (and of many other matters) will be found in Xavier Rynne, *Letters from Vatican City* (New York: Farrar, Strauss, 1963); *The Second Session* (New York: Farrar, Strauss, 1964); *The Third Session* (New York: Farrar, Strauss, 1965).

tional emphasis of the past four centuries or more to a primarily theological and missionary vision of the Church.[6]

The typical ecclesiology of Counter-Reformation Roman
Catholicism—that is to say, of the Roman Church from Trent
to the eve of Vatican II—viewed the Church first and foremost as an institution to be reverenced, supported and (if need
be) defended.[7] The one point about the Church which apparently interested the authors of theological manuals was its
authority as doctrinal instructor and moral mentor.[8] Being a
member of the Church meant being a subject of the institution.[9] To attend public worship was to assist at the institution's
official approach to God.[10] The aim of the missionary enterprise was to make the institutional means of salvation available
to human beings.[11] Of course, it must immediately be added
that the living faith and devotion of Counter-Reformation
churchmanship transcended this juridical framework. The
loyalty, piety and missionary zeal of countless Roman Catholics in the centuries since Trent are indeed beyond criticism.
Nonetheless, it must be confessed that the vital religion of
millions of post-Tridentine Catholics has been individualistic
rather than corporate; for them the Church has pertained (so
to speak) to the skeletal structure rather than to the flesh and
blood of religious life. We are told that Jesuit government has
been somewhat extravagantly described as 'an absolute mon-
archy tempered by the insubordination of the subjects'.[12] Per-

[6] Cf. J. Hamer, O. P., *The Church is a Communion* (London: Geoffrey Chapman,
1964), pp. 13-34; Y. Congar, O. P., 'Konzil als Versammlung und grundsätz-
liche Konziliarität der Kirche,' in J. B. Metz (ed.), *Gott in Welt: Festgabe
für Karl Rahner* (Freiburg: Herder, 1964), Vol. II, pp. 135-65.

[7] It would be unfair to suggest that this distortion was confined to Roman
Catholicism. Parallels can certainly be found— e.g. in Anglican presentations
of episcopal order and in Reformed accounts of church courts and church
discipline.

[8] See Note A at end of this chapter.

[9] Cf. Hamer, *op. cit.*, pp. 83f. (on the ecclesiology of Cardinal Bellarmine).

[10] Cf. L. Bouyer, Cong. Orat., *Liturgical Piety* (Notre Dame, Indiana:
University of Notre Dame Press, 1955), pp. 1-9.

[11] Cf. H. de Lubac, S. J., *Le fondement théologique des missions* (Paris: Seuil,
1946), pp. 33-51.

[12] F. E. Crowe, S. J., 'The Exigent Mind', *Continuum*, 2 (1964-65), 317.

haps it would be less extravagant to describe Counter-Reformation Roman Catholicism as institutional churchmanship enlivened by individualistic piety. In the light of New Testament teaching the compound must surely be judged unsatisfactory. Ambrose and Augustine, Leo the Great and Gregory the Great would have thought it a sadly impoverished version of Christianity.

In *Lumen Gentium* and other documents, Vatican II has set its seal of approval on a very different ecclesiology, much closer in spirit to the Bible and the Fathers. This ecclesiology is theological, rather than juridical, in character. It continues to take historic Christian institutions seriously, but it penetrates beyond the institutional shell to a deeper, sacramental meaning. (In the end, of course, to think in these terms is to treat ecclesiastical institutions with truer seriousness.) Viewing the Church christologically and organically, as the Body of Christ, it can show, as a juridical institutionalism could not, how an authentically Christian life is essentially a churchly life. Furthermore, based as it is on a theology of salvation which has burst the bonds of individualism and 'spiritualism' and attained to a genuinely historical and cosmic vision of God's saving action, this ecclesiology is uniquely equipped to appreciate the Church's role in the drama of the divine purpose. In a doctrine of the Church shaped by such principles as these there is obviously no room either for an individualistic view of personal Christian existence or for an external and legalistic view of the Church's life and mission.

It would be unrealistic to claim that this radically renewed ecclesiology was explicitly and consistently taught in all of the sixteen documents promulgated by the Second Vatican Council. In fact, even *Lumen Gentium* itself retains more than a few significant traces of the older outlook. Nonetheless, only the most determined pessimist could assert that the overall movement of thought in Vatican II was other than consistent and promising. To any careful and open-minded student of the Council's work, one of its most impressive features was the way in which the conciliar majority laboriously, and not seldom painfully, reoriented itself under the impetus of new ideas and went on to express its new orientation in the next phases of its programme. Certainly, on the crucial questions of ecclesiology the direction of the Council's thought, once the decisive reorientation had begun, became more unmistakable month by month.

In attempting, in the following pages, to expound the basic ecclesiological teaching of Vatican II, I shall both follow the systematic order of *Lumen Gentium* and draw the bulk of my material from that primary text, but I shall of course feel free to refer to any other conciliar documents in which particular points are more clearly stated or fully developed. (As I have already said, I am quite persuaded that, as time went on, the Council's work was progressively informed by an increasingly clear ecclesiology.) I need only add that my task is to explore doctrinal principles rather than to discuss the application of those principles to the shaping or reshaping of organizational structures.

II

The opening chapter of *Lumen Gentium*, entitled 'The Mystery of the Church',[13] definitively sets the tone for the entire constitution. What is crucially important about it is the way in which it interprets Christ and the Church conjointly in the setting of an all-embracing vision of God's creative and redemptive purpose and action.

Christ [the document begins] is the light of all nations. . . . By her relationship with Christ, the Church is a kind of sacrament or sign of intimate union with God, and of the unity of all mankind. She is also an instrument for the achievement of such union and unity. For this reason, following in the path laid out by its predecessors, this Council wishes to set forth more precisely to the faithful and to the entire world the nature and encompassing mission of the Church.[14]

---

[13] Translation in Walter M. Abbott, S. J. (ed.), *The Documents of Vatican II* (New York: Herder & Herder—Association Press, 1966), pp. 14–24. (All parenthetical page references are to this edition.)

[14] *Lumen Gentium*, no. 1 (pp. 14f.).

A little later, the same point is made in more explicitly Christological terms.

In the human nature which He united to Himself, the Son of God redeemed man and transformed him into a new creation (cf. Gal. 6.15; 2 Cor. 5.17) by overcoming death through His own death and resurrection. By communicating His Spirit to His brothers, called together from all peoples, Christ made them mystically into His own body.[15]

As Christ's Body, the document goes on, the Church lives by Christ's life and is called to total conformity to its crucified and risen Head.

From Him [it adds], 'the whole body, supplied and built up by joints and ligaments, attains a growth that is of God' (Col. 2.19). He continually distributes in His body, that is, in the Church, gifts of ministries through which, by His own power, we serve each other unto salvation so that, carrying out the truth in love, we may through all things grow up into Him who is our head (cf. Eph. 4. 11–16, Greek text).[16]

The most obvious benefit of this Christological view of the Church is no doubt the fact that those who share it must necessarily view the Church as a mysterious and theological reality rather than a merely sociological and juridical entity. They are thus compelled at once to reverence the Church as the gift and sign of God's grace and to accept more than simply human and political standards for the conduct of its life and the accomplishment of its mission. To have assimilated that lesson is already to have learned more about the Church than a good many Christians seem to know.

It is possible, however, to state the great merit of the Council's Christological interpretation of the Church rather more precisely. To describe the Church, Christ's Body, as 'the universal sacrament of salvation'[17] is to affirm its unique role in the saving purpose of God the Creator. Provided only that God's saving purpose is adequately set forth, the outcome must be a comprehensive and compelling insight into the Church's mission under God.

Fortunately, the Fathers of Vatican II were well aware of

[15] ibid., no. 7 (p. 20).   [16] ibid., (p. 21).   [17] ibid., no. 48 (p. 79).

this prerequisite of a satisfactory ecclesiology, and in the course of their deliberations they worked out a full and balanced statement of the Christian doctrine of salvation. It will (I think) be best to let them speak to us directly on this fundamental issue.

We may begin by looking at what *Lumen Gentium* itself has to say about God's creative and redemptive purpose.

By an utterly free and mysterious decree of His own wisdom and goodness [the Council tells us], the eternal Father created the whole world. His plan was to dignify men with a participation in His own divine life. He did not abandon men after they had fallen in Adam, but ceaselessly offered them helps to salvation, in anticipation of Christ the Redeemer, 'who is the image of the invisible God, the firstborn of every creature' (Col. 1.15). All the elect, before time began, the Father 'foreknew and predestined to become conformed to the image of his Son, that he should be the firstborn among many brethren' (Rom. 8.29). . . . The Son, therefore, came on mission from His Father. It was in Him, before the foundation of the world, that the Father chose us and predestined us to become adopted sons, for in Him it has pleased the Father to re-establish all things (cf. Eph. 1.4–5 and 10). To carry out the will of the Father, Christ inaugurated the kingdom of heaven on earth and revealed to us the mystery of the Father. By his obedience he brought about redemption.[18]

In sum, God wills that the men whom he has made should know, love and serve him as his sons. To achieve his purpose, he has given his perfect Son and Image to disclose his mystery and initiate his kingdom.

So far, so good—perhaps. But what has this will of God to do with the men we know—the men we are? The constitution on 'The Church in the Modern World' offers at least a partial answer.

The truth is [it insists] that only in the mystery of the incarnate Word does the mystery of man take on light. For Adam, the first man, was a figure of Him who was to come, namely, Christ the Lord. Christ, the final Adam, by the revelation of the mystery of the Father and His love, fully reveals man to man himself and makes his supreme calling clear. . . . He who is 'the image of the invisible God' (Col. 1.15), is Himself the perfect man. To the sons

18 ibid., nos. 2–3 (pp.). 15f.

of Adam He restores the divine likeness which had been disfigured from the first sin onward. Since human nature as He assumed it was not annulled, by that very fact it has been raised up to a divine dignity in our respect too. For by His incarnation the Son of God has united Himself in some fashion with every man.... Born of the Virgin Mary, He has truly been made one of us, like us in all things except sin.... From bondage to the devil and sin, He delivered us, so that each one of us can say with the Apostle: The Son of God 'loved me and gave himself up for me' (Gal. 2.20). By suffering for us He not only provided us with an example for our imitation. He blazed a trail, and if we follow it, life and death are made holy and take on a new meaning.... Such is the mystery of man, and it is a great one, as seen by believers in the light of Christian revelation. Through Christ and in Christ, the riddles of sorrow and death grow meaningful. Apart from His gospel, they overwhelm us. Christ has risen, destroying death by His death. He has lavished life upon us so that, as sons in the Son, we can cry out in the Spirit: Abba, Father![19]

To state the point more succinctly: man was created for life with God; the deepest mysteries of human life are intelligible only in the light of that supreme calling; Christ alone makes man's calling clear and effectual. In a word, the Christian gospel is the essential clue to human existence.

Again—so far, so good. But is man's supreme calling, realized in Christ, 'relevant'—blessed word!—to the activities of his daily life? In what sense is the 'secular' world the arena in which man wins 'the prize of the upward call of God in Christ Jesus' (Phil. 3. 14)? Is earthly life nothing more than a trial to be endured? Are earthly realities simply to be feared as a threat to man's ultimate salvation? Some versions of Christianity undoubtedly come very close to such a negative evaluation of man's earthly experience. But Vatican II—notably in its decree on 'The Apostolate of the Laity'—has something more positive to say:

Christ's redemptive work, while of itself directed toward the salvation of men, involves also the renewal of the whole temporal order. ... The spiritual and the temporal orders..., although distinct, are so connected in the one plan of God that He Himself intends

[19] *Gaudium et Spes*, no. 22 (pp. 220–22).

in Christ to appropriate the whole universe into a new creation, initially here on earth, fully on the last day. . . . It has pleased God to unite all things, both natural and supernatural, in Christ Jesus 'that in all things he may have the first place' (Col. 1.18). This destination, however, not only does not deprive the temporal order of its independence, its proper goals, laws, resources, and significance for human welfare but rather perfects the temporal order in its own intrinsic strength and excellence and raises it to the level of man's total vocation upon earth.[20]

In other words, earthly goods, intrinsically valuable because they are God's creatures, are integral to his full purpose for man. Indeed:

. . . After we have obeyed the Lord, and in His Spirit nurtured on earth the values of human dignity, brotherhood and freedom, and indeed all the good fruits of our nature and enterprise, we will find them again, but freed of stain, burnished and transfigured. This will be so when Christ hands over to the Father a kingdom eternal and universal: 'a kingdom of truth and life, of holiness and grace, of justice, love, and peace'.[21]

It is on this conception of the eschatological Kingdom of God, in which all that is truly human is destined to find fulfilment, that the Council's understanding of the Church's mission is based. The Kingdom of God was announced in Christ's preaching and inaugurated in his redemptive acts, and it will be perfected when he finally brings human history to completion. In the mean time, however, it is 'present in mystery'[22] in the Church, which consequently has an essential part to play in God's plan of salvation.

When Jesus rose up again after suffering death on the cross for mankind, He manifested that He had been appointed Lord, Messiah, and Priest forever (cf. Acts 2.36; Heb. 5.6; 7.17–21), and He poured out on His disciples the Spirit promised by the Father (cf. Acts 2.33). The Church, consequently, equipped with the gifts of her Founder and faithfully guarding His precepts of charity, humility, and self-sacrifice, receives the mission to proclaim and to establish among all peoples the kingdom of Christ

---

[20] *Apostolicam Actuositatem*, nos. 5, 7 (pp. 495, 497).
[21] *Gaudium et Spes*, no. 39 (p. 237).   [22] *Lumen Gentium*, no. 3 (p. 16).

and of God. She becomes on earth the initial budding forth of that kingdom. While she slowly grows, the Church strains toward the consummation of the kingdom and, with all her strength, hopes and desires to be united in glory with her King.[23]

Thus the earthly Church and its mission constitute a distinct stage in the realization of the Kingdom of God.

The Council's statement of the relation between the Church and the Kingdom is noteworthy for its balance. On the one hand, any tendency to identify the earthly Church with the Kingdom in its perfection is carefully excluded. For example, together with the last sentence of the passage just quoted, we may note the following contrast between the perfection of Christ and the imperfections of the Church:

While Christ, 'holy, innocent, undefiled' (Heb. 7.26) knew nothing of sin (2 Cor. 5.21), but came to expiate only the sins of the people (cf. Heb. 2.17), the Church, embracing sinners in her bosom, is at the same time holy and always in need of being purified, and incessantly pursues the path of penance and renewal.[24]

On the other hand, the Church's mysterious, ontological relation to Christ and his Kingdom remains unbroken. The Church 'is given strength . . . to show forth in the world the mystery of the Lord in a faithful though shadowed way.'[25] The Church is no mere witness to a reality external to itself—a past event or a future expectation. Rather, it witnesses to a reality which is present in its own life.

Once the Church's participation in the mystery of the Kingdom of God is rightly understood, two inferences seem inescapable. In the first place, in so far as the Church is really united to Christ, it necessarily shares in his mission to inaugurate the Kingdom of God; thus it is essentially a missionary body. Secondly, in so far as it already embodies the reality of the Kingdom, it is itself (so to speak) part of the very substance of its own mission; that is to say, it calls men into the Kingdom

[23] ibid., no. 5 (p. 18). K. E. Skydsgaard, 'The Church as Mystery and as People of God', in G. A. Lindbeck (ed.), *Dialogue on the Way* (Minneapolis: Augsburg, 1965), pp. 145–74, is for the most part very enlightening, but the author hardly gives due weight to this statement when he writes (pp. 168f.): 'In this document the church always takes precedence over the kingdom of God.'

[24] *Lumen Gentium*, no. 8 (p. 24).   [25] ibid.

by drawing them into its own life, in which they find fellowship with God through Jesus Christ. It is not the least of the Second Vatican Council's contributions to the better understanding of the Church and its mission that it draws both these inferences quite explicitly. For example, in its decree on 'The Missionary Activity of the Church' it puts them forward as first principles of the Christian mission to the world:

> The pilgrim Church is missionary by her very nature. For it is from the mission of the Son and the mission of the Holy Spirit that she takes her origin, in accordance with the decree of God the Father. This decree flows from 'that fountain of love' or charity within God the Father. From Him, who is 'the origin without origin', the Son is begotten and the Holy Spirit proceeds through the Son. Freely creating us out of His surpassing and merciful kindness, and graciously calling us moreover to communicate in life and glory with Himself, He has generously poured out His divine goodness and does not cease to do so. Thus He who made all things may at last be 'all in all' (1 Cor. 15.28), procuring at one and the same time His own glory and our happiness. But it has not pleased God to call men to share His life merely as individuals without any mutual bonds. Rather, He wills to mold them into a people in which His sons, once scattered abroad, can be gathered together (cf. John 11.52).[26]

In short, mission is integral to the Church and the Church is integral to mission.

What has been said so far in this essay has been based mainly on the opening chapter of *Lumen Gentium*. We must turn now to Chapter II, 'The People of God',[27] in which the theme of the Church's place in the unfolding purpose of God is more fully developed. To begin with, the text appeals to the biblical idea of the People of God to illuminate the unique significance of the Church in the history of salvation. Next, the role of all the Church's members in the priestly and prophetic activity of the People of God is expounded. Thirdly, the document considers all those who in varying degrees share in the life of the one People of God: the Roman Catholic faithful; the 'separated brethren' of other Christian churches; Jews; Muslims; other believers in God and all men of good

[26] *Ad Gentes*, no. 2 (pp. 585f.).   [27] Abbott, *Documents*, pp. 24–37.

will. Finally, the universal mission of the People of God is reaffirmed. Let us briefly consider each of these topics.

In the opening paragraphs of the chapter the principle of the corporate embodiment of God's saving purpose is elaborated, first with reference to Israel and then in relation to the 'new People of God'. The essential point is that God's saving action has always been directed towards the shaping of a people. On this question, it is hard to improve on the Council's own statement:

At all times and among every people, God has given welcome to whosoever fears Him and does what is right (cf. Acts 10.35). It has pleased God, however, to make men holy and save them not merely as individuals without any mutual bonds, but by making them into a single people, . . . which acknowledges Him in truth and serves Him in holiness. He therefore chose the race of Israel. . . . With it He set up a covenant. . . . These things, however, were done by way of preparation and as a figure of that new and perfect covenant which was to be ratified in Christ. . . . Christ instituted this new covenant . . . in His blood (cf. 1 Cor. 11.25), by calling together a people made up of Jew and Gentile, making them one, not according to the flesh but in the Spirit. . . . That messianic people has for its head Christ, 'who was delivered up for our sins, and rose again for our justification' (Rom. 4.25), and who now, having won a name which is above all names, reigns in glory in heaven. . . . Its goal is the kingdom of God, which has been begun by God Himself on earth, and which is to be further extended until it is brought to perfection by Him at the end of time. . . . So it is that this messianic people, although it does not actually include all men, and may more than once look like a small flock, is nonetheless a lasting and sure seed of unity, hope, and salvation for the whole human race.[28]

This statement, which it is almost criminal to abbreviate, because of its profundity and eloquence, lays the groundwork for the rest of the chapter—and indeed for much that the Council has to say elsewhere about the Church's mission.

The Constitution goes on to show how all the members of the People of God have a share in its mission of witness and service. Though the 'ministerial or hierarchical priesthood' and

[28] *Lumen Gentium*, no. 9 (pp. 24–26).

the 'common priesthood of the faithful' must never be confused, neither must they be separated, since each of them is a sharing in the true Christian priesthood, which is the 'one priesthood of Christ'. In the performance of his office, and above all in the celebration of the Eucharist, the ordained priest 'molds and rules the priestly people'. But the priestly people themselves exercise no less genuine a priesthood, when they join in offering the Eucharist, participate in the other sacraments, fulfil their responsibilities in the Christian family (the 'domestic Church', as the Council calls it), and offer the sacrifice of a holy, self-denying and charitable life.[29] Similarly, 'the holy People of God shares ... in Christ's prophetic office', not only by its witness in life and worship, but also in its common proclamation of the one faith, which is one manifestation, at any rate, of the Church's infallibility. The Constitution certainly does not overlook the distinctive teaching authority of the hierarchy. But at this point in its argument it lays greater emphasis on the 'charismatic gifts' which the Spirit freely distributes among 'the faithful of every rank'. These, it insists, are to be thankfully received as 'useful for the needs of the Church'.[30] It seems fair to cite the doctrine of these paragraphs as a particularly striking example of the shift in modern Roman Catholic ecclesiology from a narrowly institutional to a communal and missionary mode of thought.

In the next paragraphs the subject of the Church's universal significance in God's plan of salvation is taken up again and discussed in the light of the actual religious diversity of the human race. The basic statement of the 'catholic unity of the People of God',[31] in virtue of which the Church must always be open to men and women of all nations and cultures and receptive to their human gifts and resources in all their rich variety, invites attention—both as a positive recognition of the contribution of diverse human cultures to the life of the Church and as a warning against cultural imperialism disguised as concern for the unity of the Church. We must move on, however, to certain doctrinal issues raised by the assertion of

[29] ibid., nos. 10-11 (pp. 27-29).
[30] ibid., no. 12 (pp. 29f.).   [31] ibid., no. 13 (p. 32).

the Church's universal mission: the relationship between the one Catholic Church and the Roman Catholic communion; the relation of other Christian communions to Roman Catholicism; the relation of Jews and other non-Christians to the one People of God.

Vatican II, while it sought and found fresh and positive ways of stating the relation of both non-Roman Catholic Christians and non-Christians to the Church which is Christ's Body, by no means abrogated the claim that the Roman Catholic Church is a 'church' as other Christian bodies are not—in other words, that the Roman Catholic Church can, in some unique sense, be identified with '*the* Church' of Christian faith. On the contrary, on the explicit presupposition that 'the unique Church of Christ ... subsists in the Catholic Church, which is governed by the successor of Peter and by the bishops in union with that successor',[32] it affirms that 'whosoever, ... knowing that the Catholic Church was made necessary by God through Jesus Christ, would refuse to enter her or to remain in her could not be saved'.[33] While warning that ecclesiastical status is of itself no guarantee of salvation, it carefully distinguishes Roman Catholics from other Christians:

They are fully incorporated into the society of the Church who, possessing the Spirit of Christ, accept her entire system and all the means of salvation given to her, and through union with her visible structure are joined to Christ, who rules her through the Supreme Pontiff and the bishops. This joining is effected by the bonds of professed faith, of the sacraments, of ecclesiastical government, and of communion.[34]

It is reasonable to argue that the claim advanced in this statement is deliberately and very precisely limited, but it would be questionable (to say the least) to deny that a significantly distinctive claim was being made. To put that claim as mildly

[32] ibid., no. 8 (pp. 22f.). The word *subsistit* should not be construed as necessarily implying any modification of traditional Roman claims.

[33] ibid., no. 14 (pp. 32f.); cf. the Declaration on Religious Liberty (*Dignitatis Humanae*), no. 1 (p. 677).

[34] *Lumen Gentium*, no. 14 (p. 33).

as possible, being a 'Catholic Christian' involves being in communion with the Roman See.[35]

Nonetheless, as we read on in *Lumen Gentium* it quickly becomes apparent that the way has been opened for an unprecedentedly positive appraisal of non-Roman Catholic communions. The precondition of this appraisal is, of course, that replacement of a primarily institutional by a primarily sacramental ecclesiology which has already been emphasized. Once the Church is presented, first and foremost, as the People of God, the community of those who have been baptized into Christ, rather than the society composed of the subjects of a single government, it becomes difficult, if not impossible, to limit the People of God to one ecclesiastical communion. Recognizing—or better, perhaps, exploiting—this difficulty or impossibility, the Council carefully states the distinctive meaning of communion with the Roman See in the language of 'incorporation' into the society of the Church (which, it explicitly suggests, admits of degrees) rather than of 'membership' in the Church (which might easily be taken to demand an 'either/or' judgement). It is now in a position to recognize the 'many ways' in which the Church (the one Church, which 'subsists' in the Roman Catholic Church) is 'linked with those who, being baptized, are honored with the name of Christian', in spite of their less-than-Catholic faith and their separation from Rome. Indeed, it even finds it possible to speak of the separated communions as 'Churches or ecclesial communities'.[36] While the import of this development should not be exaggerated—after all, the Roman Catholic communion does remain the unique embodiment of the Christian Church, other churches being interpreted and evaluated in relation to it—its obvious theoretical and practical consequences must not be ignored. On the level of ecclesiological theory, it invites Roman Catholic theologians to consider the problem of schism (as theologians of other traditions have long been considering it) in other than crude 'in-or-out' terms. On the level of ecumenical

---

[35] These remarks should be read as a report, not a complaint. We cannot rightly invite other Christians to compromise their convictions.

[36] *Lumen Gentium*, no. 15 (pp. 33f.).

action, it enables Roman Catholics to meet other Christians on the ground of a common 'churchmanship'. These are no small benefits.

When Vatican II turns from the various Christian communions to the non-Christian world, it first looks, naturally enough, at the Jews and their religion.

In the first place [it remarks] there is the people to whom the covenants and the promises were given and from whom Christ was born according to the flesh (cf. Rom. 9.4–5). On account of their fathers, this people remains most dear to God, for God does not repent of the gifts He makes nor of the calls He issues (cf. Rom. 11.28–29).[37]

Later on, in the Council's Declaration on The Relationship of the Church to Non-Christian Religions, these points are elaborated; furthermore, the 'spiritual bond linking the people of the New Covenant with Abraham's stock' is strongly affirmed as an essential principle of ecclesiology. The Church, we are told, 'acknowledges that, according to the mystery of God's saving design, the beginnings of her faith and her election are already found among the patriarchs, Moses, and the prophets.'[38] In view of the common spiritual heritage of Jews and Christians, the Council goes on to recommend common study and fraternal dialogue—in the hope, presumably, of clarifying the Church's own self-consciousness, as well as of promoting mutual understanding.[39]

Moving on to others who acknowledge the Creator and are included in his plan of salvation, *Lumen Gentium* looks next at the Muslims. Like Christians and Jews, they see in Abraham the father of the faithful.[40] The Declaration on the Church and Non-Christian Religions (*Nostra Aetate*) develops the theme

---

[37] ibid., no. 16 (p. 34).   [38] *Nostra Aetate*, no. 4 (pp. 663f.).

[39] Cf. ibid. (p. 665). The Council's handling of this question provoked criticism from two very different standpoints. On the one hand, although its interest in the Jewish people was plainly theological and ethical, not political, the Council was violently attacked by the enemies of the Israeli state, who feared that clarification of the religious issue would deprive them of a political weapon or, worse still, provide the other side with a new one. On the other hand, precisely because it viewed Judaism in the perspective of Christian faith, the Council could not and did not speak altogether acceptably to Jews.

[40] Cf. *Lumen Gentium*, no. 16 (p. 35).

further. Islam, it observes, worships one God, submits to his decrees, venerates Jesus as a prophet, honours Mary as his virgin mother, awaits the judgement day, prizes morality, prays, gives alms, fasts. With all this in mind, the Council appeals once again for sincere effort towards mutual understanding and co-operation.[41]

Finally, *Lumen Gentium* speaks of those who have no tangible connexion with the biblical revelation. There are men and women who 'in shadows and images seek the unknown God', men and women who, though ignorant of the gospel and the Church, sincerely seek God and, under the impulse of grace, seek to follow conscience, and men and women who, without knowing God explicitly, respond to his grace and try to live well.[42] All these are embraced by God's saving purpose; all may share in the destiny of God's People.

By this time it must be obvious that the ecclesiology of Vatican II entails no narrowly ecclesiastical view of God's plan of salvation. On the contrary, it explicitly recognizes both the universal scope of his saving purpose and the universal presence of his saving grace. At the same time, the Council clearly has no intention of obscuring the Church's unique place in the history of salvation. In its view, as we have already seen, the Church is the unique and universal sacrament of God's saving love. The Church alone bears witness to God's self-giving and self-disclosure in Jesus Christ; the Church alone is the 'budding forth' of God's eschatological Kingdom. By the Church's teaching, as by no other doctrine, men are freed from crippling error; in the Church's communion, as in no other fellowship, men fully and visibly share in the life of God's People. Consequently, the Church's mission has no limits.

The Church has received from the apostles as a task to be discharged even to the ends of the earth [the] solemn mandate of

---

[41] *Nostra Aetate*, no. 3 (p. 663). It is surely to be hoped that Christians will undertake serious theological study of Islam as well as of Judaism. A recent Roman Catholic work, Michel Hayek, *Le mystère d'Ismaël* (Paris: Mame, 1964), offers at least a suggestive sketch of what might be attempted.

[42] *Lumen Gentium*, no. 16 (p. 35); cf. *Nostra Aetate*, nos. 1–2 (pp. 660–63).

Christ to proclaim the saving truth (cf. Acts 1.8). . . . The Church is compelled by the Holy Spirit to do her part towards the full realization of the will of God, who has established Christ as the source of salvation for the whole world. By the proclamation of the gospel, she prepares her hearers to receive and profess the faith, disposes them for baptism, snatches them from the slavery of error, and incorporates them into Christ so that through charity they may grow up into full maturity in Christ.[43]

To round out this exposition of the Church's task in the world, as seen by Vatican II, I need only add that the Council's view of the Christian mission is as broad as its vision of Christ's own work. Thus there is nothing individualistic or narrowly 'spiritual' in its definition of missionary aims.

Missionary activity [it tells us] is nothing else and nothing less than a manifestation or epiphany of God's will, and the fulfilment of that will in the world and in world history. In the course of this history God plainly works out the history of salvation by means of mission. By the preaching of the word and the celebration of the sacraments, . . . missionary activity brings about the presence of Christ, the Author of salvation. But whatever truth and grace are to be found among the nations, as a sort of secret presence of God, this activity frees from all taint of evil and restores to Christ its maker. . . . And so, whatever good is found to be sown in the hearts and minds of men, or in the rites and cultures peculiar to various peoples, is not lost. More than that, it is healed, ennobled, and perfected for the glory of God, the shame of the demon, and the bliss of men.[44]

III

Apart from the vision of the Church which I have been trying to communicate, the Second Vatican Council could have done little more than play aimlessly at rearranging the ecclesiastical furniture. It was this new vision that made Vatican II a truly momentous event in Christian history. All the same, the furniture really did need to be rearranged—and the new insight into the Church's nature and vocation only made the need more disturbingly obvious.

As it happened, the Council Fathers did devote a good deal

[43] *Lumen Gentium*, no. 17 (p. 36).   [44] *Ad Gentes*, no. 9 (pp. 595f.).

of attention to the reform of ecclesiastical institutions. The practical proposals which emerged directly from their discussions can be studied in several conciliar decrees—notably in the decree on 'The Pastoral Office of Bishops in the Church' (*Christus Dominus*).[45] The Council's fundamental pronouncement on ecclesiastical institutions is, however, to be found in *Lumen Gentium* itself. It is Chapter III of that document, entitled 'The Hierarchical Structure of the Church, with Special Reference to the Episcopate',[46] that provides the essential link between the Council's theological and missionary ecclesiology and its initial programme of ecclesiastical reform.

There is, indeed, some reason to question the internal consistency of this crucial chapter, which was hammered out in prolonged and (at least occasionally) acrimonious debate. At times, the spirit of Vatican I and the spirit of Vatican II seem to be striving together for the mastery. We may grant that the Council's claim to be 'following in the footsteps of the First Vatican Council'[47] is not wholly unfounded. To cite the most obvious point of contact, Vatican I, in the midst of its emphatic assertion of the primatial jurisdiction of the Roman Pontiff, affirmed the 'ordinary and immediate power of episcopal jurisdiction' of the bishops, as successors of the apostles,[48] and it would very likely have gone on to elaborate the latter statement, if external circumstances had not interfered;[49] in the end, the task was left to Vatican II, which performed it competently. Nonetheless, a great chasm gapes between the two councils. Vatican I showed no serious interest in the nature of the Church.

---

[45] Abbott, *Documents*, pp. 396–429. [46] ibid., pp. 37–56.
[47] *Lumen Gentium*, no. 18 (p. 37).
[48] First Vatican Council, dogmatic constitution *Pastor Aeternus*, c. 3; cf. Denzinger-Schönmetzer, *Enchiridion Symbolorum*, 33rd ed. (Barcelona: Herder, 1965), no. 3061.
[49] That Vatican I, however long it had sat, would ever have promulgated anything like the doctrine of 'collegiality' is nonetheless very doubtful. Even the *Declaratio collectiva episcoporum Germaniae* (1875), which was approved by Pius IX in the apostolic letter *Mirabilis illa constantia* (4 March 1875), confined itself strictly to an assertion of the divine right of the bishops as pastors of particular dioceses; cf. Denzinger-Schönmetzer, *Enchiridion Symbolorum*, nos. 3112–17.

... Contrary to what is commonly said, Vatican II does not put itself forward as a simple complement of Vatican I, as if the council of 1870 had written the first chapter of an ecclesiology whose second chapter was written by Vatican II. In fact, there was no conspicuous preoccupation with ecclesiology at Vatican I. Certainly there was a *schema* on the Church. But *Pastor Aeternus*, the constitution on the papacy, was not put forward as a first chapter of this *schema*. On the contrary, it supplanted it and pushed it aside. The desire to define the prerogatives of the pope did not in fact proceed from any demand for an investigation of the nature of the Church. The predominant concern was altogether different.[50]

Vatican II, on the contrary, was deeply preoccupied (as we have seen) with the question of the Church's nature and mission. Much of the drama of Vatican II lies in the tension between the Council's answer to that question and its inheritance from Vatican I.

It would be futile to pretend that this tension did not palpably hamper the effort of the Second Vatican Council to lay the groundwork for the reform of ecclesiastical institutions. At the same time, it would be most unfair to suggest that the fundamental ecclesiological principles of Vatican II had no serious effect on the Council's proposals for institutional reform. In point of fact, the pertinent chapters of *Lumen Gentium* clearly reflect those principles, both in their approach to the institutional aspect of the Church and in their treatment of particular institutions. Admittedly, there are some awkward juxtapositions of the new and the old, but that is hardly surprising, in view of the massiveness and complexity of the institutional tradition with which Vatican II had to reckon. What is really surprising is the extent of the Council's reversal of agelong trends in Roman Catholic theory and practice.

Probably the most celebrated feature of *Lumen Gentium* is its statement on episcopal 'collegiality'. At any rate, that statement has overshadowed everything else that the Council had to say about the Church's hierarchical priesthood. The consti-

---

[50] René Laurentin, *L'enjeu du concile: III. Bilan de la deuxième session* (Paris: Seuil, 1964), p. 44.

tution does touch, however, on all three of the major orders—
episcopate, presbyterate, diaconate—and makes an appreci-
able contribution to the renewal of each. Furthermore, Chapter III, which concentrates on the ordained ministry, is com-
plemented by Chapter IV, 'The Laity',[51] which emphasizes the
ministry of laymen in the Church and seeks to free them for
more effective witness and service. In these two chapters,
which manifest the Council's firm resolve to make its fine theological words count towards the reshaping of ecclesiastical institutions, we find an encouraging picture of a church seeking
to order itself according to God's will, with a view to the more
adequate performance of its task in the world.

On each level of the Church's ordered life, it is apparent
that the sharpest stimulus to reform is a renewed appreciation
of each distinct form of ministry in the Church as a participation in the Church's apostolic mission to mankind. It would be
instructive to explore the resultant plan of reform, point by
point, in this perspective. For brevity's sake, however, we must
focus our attention on the Council's proposals for the renewal
of the primary order of the hierarchy, the episcopate.

The conciliar teaching on episcopacy is plainly dominated
by the idea of the apostolic mission. *Lumen Gentium*, for instance, after discussing Christ's commission to his apostles,
goes on to state, as the basis of its exposition of the episcopal
office:

That divine mission, entrusted by Christ to the apostles, will last
until the end of the world (Matt. 28.20), since the gospel which
was to be handed down by them is for all time the source of all
life for the Church. For this reason the apostles took care to
appoint successors in this hierarchically structured society. . . .
Among those various ministries which, as tradition witnesses, were
exercised in the Church from the earliest times, the chief place
belongs to those who, appointed to the episcopate in a sequence
running back to the beginning, are the ones who pass on the
apostolic seed.[52]

---

[51] Abbott, *Documents*, pp. 56–65. On the Ministry as treated by the Council,
see also Chapter IV of this book.
[52] *Lumen Gentium*, no. 20 (p. 39).

Despite the echoes of Vatican I,[53] the accent is unmistakably different, just because in the text of Vatican II Christ's mission and gospel are set in the forefront.

But there is more to come. In describing the apostolate, as constituted by Christ, *Lumen Gentium* says explicitly that the apostles formed a 'college' or 'fixed group'.[54] It follows that apostolic succession must be corporately rather than individualistically conceived; in other words, the 'nature and meaning of the episcopal order' are 'collegial'.[55]

Just as, by the Lord's will, St. Peter and the other apostles constituted one apostolic college, so in a similar way the Roman Pontiff as the successor of Peter, and the bishops as the successors of the apostles, are joined together.

The episcopal mission, then, no less truly than the papal mission, is universal in scope.

The order of bishops is the successor to the college of the apostles in teaching authority and pastoral rule; or, rather, in the episcopal order the apostolic body continues without a break. Together with its head, the Roman Pontiff, and never without this head, the episcopal order is the subject of supreme and full power over the universal Church.[56]

In sum, the argument moves without interruption from apostolic mission to episcopal collegiality. To say the least, something is thereby added to the teaching of Vatican I. *Pastor Aeternus*, while it certainly acknowledged the inherent authority of the bishops as pastors of their several churches,[57] seemed to vest the government of the universal Church in the Roman Pontiff as sole sovereign. *Lumen Gentium*, on the other hand, while it emphatically reaffirms the supreme jurisdiction of the Bishop of Rome, also stresses the universal mission and authority of the episcopal college, acting in union with its primate. From the standpoint of old-fashioned Ultramontanism such an addition must appear revolutionary.

[53] Cf. Vatican I, *Pastor Aeternus*, prol. (Denzinger-Schönmetzer, *Enchiridion Symbolorum*, no. 3050).   [54] *Lumen Gentium*, no. 19 (p. 38).
[55] ibid., no. 22 (p. 42).   [56] ibid. (p. 43).
[57] Cf. Vatican I, *Pastor Aeternus*, c. 3 (Denzinger-Schönmetzer, *Enchiridion Symbolorum*, no. 3061): 'tamquam veri pastores assignatos sibi greges singuli singulos pascunt et regunt.'

Just how fully Vatican II appreciated the revolutionary implications of its own action is another question. It is certainly not clear that the Council achieved an adequate synthesis of episcopate and papacy. While *Lumen Gentium* carefully integrates the episcopate with the Roman primacy, it fails to integrate the primacy completely with the episcopate. The episcopal college may not act apart from its head, yet the head is left free to act apart from the college.[58] Peter thus seems to be something more than the head of the college of apostles and the pope something more than the head of the college of bishops.[59] We may well ask whether the essential idea of the Roman primacy really demands such an elevation of the pope above the rest of the episcopate. If that question is answered affirmatively, we can hardly help asking whether, in that case, a robust and consistent doctrine of collegiality can ever be digested by Roman Catholic ecclesiology.[60] Unquestionably, it would be much easier to read the future of Roman Catholic institutions if the Council had only grasped this nettle more boldly.

Yet even as things now stand there is some ground for optimism. (This essay is, of course, written by an Anglican who is, as such, a partisan of collegiality.) The signs of the times point to a rethinking of the Roman primacy in the light of the principle of collegiality, rather than to the reverse. As time goes on, the evolving theology and practice of collegial episcopacy may well alter the context of the papal primacy so effectively and drastically that the primatial authority itself can no longer be conceived or exercised as it has been in recent centuries. At any rate, the way to such a development has not been blocked by Vatican II, whatever imperfections we may

[58] Cf. *Lumen Gentium*, no. 22 (p. 43).

[59] I do not mean to suggest, by this sentence, that I accept the parallelism: Peter–apostles, pope–bishops. My criticism is formulated in the Constitution's own terms. I do not, in fact, believe that the continuity between the Petrine office and the Roman primacy has been effectively demonstrated.

[60] There is no 'conciliarist' dogma lurking behind these questions. I am merely asking whether a full 'coinherence' of papacy and episcopate is conceivable. If it is, members of episcopal churches separated from Rome may well find the notion of a Roman primacy less uncongenial.

have detected in the Council's synthesis of papacy and episcopate. On the contrary, new paths have been opened up which could scarcely have been imagined a decade ago.[61]

Before we leave the subject of episcopacy, we must note a further important contribution of the Council to the reform of the ordained ministry. By stressing the apostolic mission as the basis of the episcopal office—and thus as the criterion of authentic episcopacy—Vatican II has renewed the image of the Church's ministerial priesthood in at least three respects.

In order to understand the Council's achievement, we must glance quickly at what can fairly be called the dominant trend in Roman Catholic thinking about the priestly ministry. From the Middle Ages onwards, Latin theology has tended to define the Christian priesthood too narrowly as a 'cultic' office, defined essentially by the power to offer the eucharistic sacrifice. To put it very simply, the priest has been seen as a man ordained to say Mass. One inevitable consequence of this view is a questionable exaltation of the presbyterate. Since the presbyter possesses the power to say Mass by virtue of his ordination—in fact, the traditional ceremony symbolizing that power has been widely regarded as the sacramental 'matter' of ordination to the presbyterate[62]—ministerial priesthood and the presbyteral order are easily taken to be virtually synonymous. This exaltation of the presbyterate leads in turn to a depreciation of the episcopate. The most that can now be said of the bishop, as distinct from the presbyter, is that he enjoys the fullness of priestly power. No doubt, as long as this proposition is taken to mean that the bishop alone possesses the power to ordain others to the priesthood, the episcopate retains at least some theological significance. But even that limited significance has been called into question by the hypothesis that the Holy See might empower presbyters to ordain to the diaconate

[61] Cf. E. R. Fairweather and E. R. Hardy, *The Voice of the Church: The Ecumenical Council* (Greenwich, Connecticut: Seabury Press, 1962), pp. 65–72. These pages were written some time before Vatican II opened. I am now more hopeful that what I was asking for may be achieved by peaceful evolution without a spectacular volte-face.

[62] Cf. art. 'Instruments, Tradition of the', in F. L. Cross (ed.), *Oxford Dictionary of the Christian Church* (London: Oxford University Press, 1957), p. 696.

and presbyterate. It is true that this hypothesis has rarely, if ever, been acted upon,[63] but the very fact that the question could be raised is indicative of the bent of much Roman Catholic theology. To say the least, the juridical has heavily outweighed the theological in the common Roman Catholic attitude towards the episcopal office.

By setting forth a properly theological view of episcopacy, Vatican II has contributed significantly to the recovery of a more balanced view of ministerial priesthood as a whole. It has restored the true picture of the bishop as missionary and pastor, as chief priest and chief teacher in his own church—thereby relegating his administrative and juridical functions, so long overemphasized, to a properly subordinate position. As a result, it has been able to portray the bishop and presbyters of a diocese in their true mutual relationship as partners, each in his own order, in the ministry and mission of the local church. Moreover, in the light of the apostolic mission of the episcopate it has presented the priesthood which the bishop shares with his presbyters in broadly evangelical, sacramental and pastoral terms, in contrast to the narrowly 'cultic' interpretation which long distorted conventional Roman Catholic views of the ministerial office. The consequences, both internal and ecumenical, of this thoroughgoing reorientation can hardly be exaggerated.[64]

IV

It would be rewarding to make a careful study of Chapters V–VII of *Lumen Gentium*—'The Call of the Whole Church to Holiness'.[65] 'Religious',[66] and 'The Eschatological Nature of the Pilgrim Church and Her Union with the Heavenly Church'[67]—since these chapters contain many interesting developments and applications of the document's fundamental

---

[63] Cf. Tanquerey, *Synopsis Theologiae Dogmaticae Specialis*, Vol. II, pp. 603f.; T. G. Jalland, 'The Parity of Ministers', in K. E. Kirk (ed.), *The Apostolic Ministry* (London: Hodder & Stoughton, 1946), pp. 342f.

[64] See Note B at end of chapter.   [65] Abbott, *Documents*, pp. 65–72.
[66] ibid., pp. 73–78.   [67] ibid., pp. 79–85.

principles. We must turn immediately, however, to what is unquestionably the most important of the Constitution's later chapters—namely, Chapter VIII, 'The Blessed Virgin Mary, Mother of God, in the Mystery of Christ and the Church'.[68]

The first important fact to be noted about Chapter VIII is its presence in the Constitution on The Church. This chapter does, indeed, form a superb ending to *Lumen Gentium*, inasmuch as it portrays Mary both as archetype of the Church's role in the history of salvation and as pre-eminent member of the heavenly Church—in effect, as a personified synthesis of ecclesiology. Nonetheless, it was added to *Lumen Gentium* only after prolonged deliberation and acrimonious dispute. In fact, the decision to include it in the Constitution may well be described as one of the great turning-points in the story of Vatican II.[69]

The issue at stake must be briefly considered. At the risk of oversimplification, it may be said that two major tendencies can be traced in Roman Catholic Mariology. One tendency, which for centuries has been very influential in Roman Catholicism, accentuates Mary's distinctive role in the history of salvation, to the point of seeing its obvious analogue in the work of Christ himself rather than in the mission of the Church. (Thus this line of thought is often called 'Christotypical'.) Spokesmen for this tendency undoubtedly helped to promote the definitions of Mary's Immaculate Conception (1854) and Assumption (1950) and their successors continue to press for further definitions—e.g. for the definition of Mary's role as 'Co-Redemptrix'. The other tendency, while it acknowledges our Lady's unique place in the history of salvation, sees her essentially as an archetypal member of the Church, foreshadowing (albeit in a unique manner) its calling, nature and destiny. (Thus this trend is often referred to as 'ecclesiotypical'.) As a rule, spokesmen for this tendency deprecate any suggestion of further Marian definitions—and indeed can

[68] ibid., pp. 85–96.

[69] For a clear and succinct narrative of events, cf. John Moorman, *Vatican Observed: An Anglican Impression of Vatican II* (London: Darton, Longman & Todd, 1967), pp. 70–77.

sometimes be heard expressing the wish that the earlier definitions had never been promulgated.[70]

While the Council is careful to state that it does not intend
to settle all the outstanding issues and formulate a comprehensive Mariology,[71] it is hard to resist the conclusion that in fact
Vatican II has come down hard on the ecclesiotypical side.
It is not just that the problems of Marian doctrine and devotion have been dealt with in an ecclesiological setting—though
that fact is of some importance. What is still more significant is
the obvious orientation of the conciliar teaching about our
Lady.

In the first place, while Mary's distinctive contribution to
the fulfilment of God's saving purpose is not only recognized
but presented in detail,[72] all this is done in the light of her acknowledged relation to the Church. 'She stands out', the Council tells us, 'among the poor and humble of the Lord, who confidently await and receive salvation from Him.'[73] If it is said
that, because of her calling to receive 'the Word of God in
her heart and in her body', Mary 'far surpasses all other creatures', it is promptly added that 'she is one with all human
beings in their need for salvation' and is to be 'hailed as a pre-
eminent and altogether singular member of the Church, and
as the Church's model and excellent exemplar in faith and
charity'.[74] On balance, it seems fair to say that Mary's role in
the history of salvation is presented as analogous to (though of
course not simply identical with) the role of the Church as re-
cipient and instrument of redeeming grace.

This impression is confirmed when we turn to the other
main point of Chapter VIII—Mary's relation to the earthly

[70] The issues are fully discussed in René Laurentin, *La Vierge au concile* (Paris:
Lethielleux, 1965). Instructive comments will also be found in *Lexikon für
Theologie und Kirche*, 2d ed., supplement, *Das zweite Vatikanische Konzil*, I
(Freiburg: Herder, 1966), 326–47 (commentary by Otto Semmelroth, S. J.),
and in E. del Sgdo. Corazón, O.C.D., 'El Capitulo "De Beata Maria Virgine"
en la Constitución "Lumen Gentium",' *Salmanticensis*, 12 (1965), 685–734.

[71] Cf. *Lumen Gentium*, no. 54 (pp. 86f.).

[72] Cf. ibid., nos. 55–59 (pp. 87–90).

[73] ibid., no. 55 (p. 87).

[74] ibid., no. 53 (p. 86).

Church now. While she is indeed presented as the supreme intercessor, after Christ himself, for the pilgrim Church, there is no suggestion that her intercessory role is different in kind from the intercessory task of the other saints in glory.[75] On the contrary, even when she is described by the question-begging term *mediatrix*, the text emphasizes that her mediation is akin, not to the unique mediation of Christ, but rather to the mediatorial acts of the ministerial priesthood and indeed of all the faithful.[76]

When it is added that *Lumen Gentium* warns against eccentric and unbalanced Marian devotions and commends that 'true devotion' which 'consists neither in fruitless and passing emotion, nor in a certain vain credulity', but in 'filial love' and 'imitation',[77] it should be clear that Vatican II has made a genuine contribution to the renewal of Marian doctrine and piety in the Church at large. Far from promoting dubious trends in Roman Catholicism or widening the gulf between Roman Catholics and other Christians, the Council has taken a decisive step towards a biblical and patristic Mariology—and therefore towards what most Christians can be expected to recognize as common ground. Indeed, it might even be suggested that, by pointing to our Lady's role in the divine economy as archetype of the Church's mission, *Lumen Gentium* has furthered our understanding, not only of Mary, but also of the place of the Church in the purpose of God.

NOTES TO CHAPTER 3

Note A (page 57). *Theological manuals*

Since it is sometimes alleged that the 'manuals' are unfairly criticized on this and other scores, it may be useful to cite chapter and verse. I happen to possess A. Tanquerey's *Synopsis Theologiae*

[75] Cf. ibid., nos. 50, 60 (pp. 81–83, 90f.).
[76] Cf. ibid., no. 62 (pp. 91f.).
[77] ibid., no. 67 (p. 95).

Dogmaticae Fundamentalis, 14th ed. (Rome-Tournai-Paris:
Desclée, 1911), and his *Synopsis Theologiae Dogmaticae Specialis*,
2 vols., 13th ed. (Rome-Tournai-Paris: Desclée, 1911). The only
serious treatment of the Church is contained in the former work,
where a treatise 'De Ecclesia Christi' appears between 'De Vera
Religione' and 'De Fontibus Revelationis'. This treatise is divided
into two parts: 'I. De Inventione Ecclesiae Christi,' and 'II. De
Ecclesiae Constitutione'. The latter does begin with a preliminary
note (pp. 538f.) on the relations of Christ with the Church, which
leads to the conclusion that Christ is the invisible Head and
perpetual Bridegroom of the Church, as well as its Founder, but
the author adds: 'Now that this has been said, let us go on immediately to the proper object of this part. In three chapters we shall
speak: 1. of the *power* of the Church; 2. of the *exercise* of that
power; 3. of the *relations* between *Church and State*' (p. 540). As
for the larger work, it contains no section, however brief, on the
Church, while its index turns up only one reference: '*Ecclesiae*
jura quoad matrimonium, II, 650'! Enough said!

Note B (page 79)

Of course, not everyone would agree that the promulgation of
a high doctrine of episcopacy was ecumenically constructive. Cf.
W. A. Quanbeck and G. A. Lindbeck, 'Paul VI Becomes Pope:
Second Session', in Lindbeck (ed.), *Dialogue on the Way*, p. 57:
'It is strange that practically none of the Catholic bishops and
theologians at the council showed awareness that this affirmation
of episcopal sacramentality can be considered unfortunate from
the ecumenical point of view. It is perhaps the only point at
which this council has increased the gap between Catholics and
Protestants. For the Protestant, the highest office in the church
"*de iure divino*" is that of pastor, that of preaching the Word and
administering the Sacraments. He cannot but regret this exaltation
of the episcopal office at the expense of the pastoral one. He recognizes, to be sure, that from other points of view it does represent
an advance. It increases the emphasis on the pastoral, as distinguished from the purely administrative, functions of the bishop,
and, by providing a basis for collegiality, it helps balance the papal
office.' Quanbeck surely misses the point, however, when he speaks
of an 'exaltation of the episcopal office at the expense of the
pastoral'. In fact, Vatican II identifies the bishop as the pastor
(and priest and teacher) *par excellence*, and sees presbyters as
pastors (and priests and teachers) in so far as they share depend-
ently in his pastoral (and sacerdotal and magisterial) office. This

view of the ordained ministry is certainly very different from medieval quasi-presbyterian theories and Protestant doctrines of the parity of ministers. But we may well ask if it is not a truer view than either of those alternatives—and, ecumenically speaking, a more promising one, obviating as it does the antithesis between an administrative episcopate and a pastoral presbyterate, which has been such a troublesome factor in our Western discussions of the ministerial office.

4 The Ministry

JOHN MOORMAN
Bishop of Ripon

1. *Introduction*

Christianity was conceived and born in a community which
was essentially hierarchical. It is, therefore, natural that the
Church should itself have evolved some hierarchical structure.
This was something which took time. When Christ ascended
into the heavens and sent the Holy Spirit to guide and sanctify
the Church, the Christian community knew that their responsibility was to continue the work of Christ in so far as this was
possible. To guide them in their work they had the apostles,
the men whom Jesus had chosen and, to some extent, prepared for leadership in the Church. They themselves appointed
others to perform certain tasks in the life of the Church. Meanwhile other types of ministry sprang up as it were spontaneously.

Our records of the apostolic Church do not give us enough
material to form a very clear picture of what the ministry consisted of in those early days. The Church's main task was, in
obedience to its Lord's command, 'to preach the Gospel to
every creature', and this could only be done by following the
dictates of the Holy Spirit and adapting the ministry to the
conditions in which the evangelistic task had to be carried out.
This meant that there was need of two types of ministry, one
dynamic as the Christian evangelists set out for places where
the faith was yet unknown, and the other more static as communities of believers gathered together mostly in the larger
cities. We thus get a very wide range of ministries. The New
Testament writers speak of bishops, elders, a presbytery, over-
seers and deacons; but there are references also to prophets
evangelists, pastors and teachers (Eph. 4. 11), to miracle-
workers, healers and speakers with tongues (1 Cor. 12. 28), and

to a ministry which included prophecy, ministry, teaching, exhorting, giving, ruling, and shewing mercy (Rom. 12. 6–8).

Many of these terms belong, no doubt, more to functions of the Church than to specific officers, and no one would expect to find the Church so efficiently organized that it could produce a well-defined hierarchy such as developed in later years. But, within a generation or so of the death of the last of the apostles, it is clear that a form of ministry, with fairly clear-cut features, had emerged. St. Ignatius of Antioch refers over and over again to Bishops, Presbyters, and Deacons, as if such a ministry was the normal thing in the Church as he knew it.[1] So quickly and so firmly had this structure become established that it has survived to the present day in the greater part of the Christian Church.

The ministry of the Church is one, and all members have their part to play in it according to the *charismata* with which they are endowed. In a sense, all aspects of the Church's ministry are shared by all its members. The Church is the People of God, set in the world to proclaim the truth that is in Christ and to offer prayer and intercession for the needs of mankind. When St. Peter tells the Christian community to whom he is writing that they are a 'holy' or 'royal priesthood' (1 Pet. 2. 5 and 9), he means that all of them, clergy and laity alike, must share in the offering of sacrifices to God and all other priestly acts. When St. Paul talks to his converts about ministry, he means it to be something in which all have a part to play. The priests are ministers of Christ like everyone else. If they are to share in the ministry of Christ, then they must become the servants of the people. Nothing can be beneath the dignity of one who, like Christ, is prepared 'not to be ministered unto but to minister'.

The work of the Church, as the *laos* of God, is something which is shared by all its parts and all its members. But if we think of the Church as the 'Body of Christ' or as the 'Household of God', or adopt St. Clement's analogy of the Church as an 'army', we realize that there must be differentiation of

[1] J. B. Lightfoot, *The Apostolic Fathers* (London, 1891), pp. 137–8, 143, 144, 146, 147, 158.

duties and co-operation between the various parts. St. Paul explains this at some length in 1 Cor. 12. 12–27, or, in the words of St. Clement, 'the great without the small cannot exist, neither the small without the great'.[2] The Church is one, and its ministry is one; yet it must contain many different kinds of ministry 'according to the grace that is given us'.

The Vatican Council made no attempt to formulate any theory as to the origins of the ordained ministry within the Church. They would have agreed with the opening statement of the Anglican Ordinal that 'it is evident unto all men diligently reading Holy Scripture and ancient Authors, that from the Apostles' time there have been these Orders of Ministers in Christ's Church; Bishops, Priests and Deacons.' While other Christians are busy arguing as to whether episcopacy is of the *esse*, the *bene esse*, or the *plene esse* of the Church, and whether Methodists will feel happier if the word 'presbyter' is substituted for the word 'priest' in discussions on reunion, the Vatican Council was in no doubt as to the form of the ministry. It would never have occurred to the Fathers to doubt that episcopacy and the priesthood are, together with the papacy, the gift of God to his Church, to be used to the glory of God and the edification of his Church. The question that occupied them was how the various parts of the Household of God should act if they were to be faithful to their vocation.

Five decrees deal specifically with the ministry of the Church—one on The Pastoral Office of Bishops in the Church, one on Priestly Life and Ministry, followed by another on Priestly Training, one on The Adaptation and Renewal of the Religious Life and one on The Apostolate of the Laity. Each of these, however, was intended to draw its inspiration and to find its theological foundations in the Constitution on the Church (*De Ecclesia*) known (from its opening words) as *Lumen Gentium*. To understand these five decrees it is, therefore, necessary to read them against the background of *Lumen Gentium*, which is perhaps the greatest contribution which the Council has made to the Christian world of today—and which has been dealt with in the previous chapter of this book.

[2] op. cit., p. 73.

2. Bishops

One of the greatest achievements of Vatican II was to complete the work begun by Vatican I by clarifying what was to be the proper relationship between the Pope, as successor of St. Peter, and the Bishops, as successors of the other Apostles. By the declaration of Papal Infallibility in 1870 the whole status of the episcopate had been, to some extent, down-graded; and it took Vatican II to restore the balance and raise the Bishops to a proper place of responsibility in the hierarchy of the Church. This was done, in the Constitution De Ecclesia, by the theory of 'Collegiality' which put the ultimate responsibility for the Church in the hands of the 'College' of Bishops 'with' (or 'under') Peter as their visible head. An account of how this was achieved has been given in the previous chapter (pp. 54–84) but it is essential to realize the importance of the principle of Collegiality if one is to appreciate the conciliar decree on The Pastoral Office of Bishops.

The fundamental question as to the status of a bishop was put to the Fathers on 30 October 1963 when they were asked to say whether or not they believed that episcopal consecration constituted the highest degree of the sacramental order.[3] On the question of the status of a bishop there had long been two points of view. According to the first of these, a bishop is really a priest to whom additional authority has been given. It is based on the belief that the highest office which man can perform is to offer the sacrifice of the Mass and to bring down upon the elements the blessing of God so that they became, in truth, the Body and Blood of Christ. This would make the priesthood the highest degree of sacramental order. All that the bishop can do, in addition to this, is to ordain those men who shall exercise this ministry and to confirm those who shall receive the Body of Christ at their hands. If this is so, then episcopal consecration is a gift of grace together with jurisdiction and authority, but cannot be said to raise the priest to any higher sacramental order since he has already been raised to a

[3] Yves Congar, O.P., Report from Rome II: the second session of the Vatican Council (London, 1964), p. 91.

point of such dignity and importance that it is impossible to go any further.

The other point of view is that, although the priest does exercise the highest of all ministries, yet he depends upon the bishop for the grace and power to carry this out. The bishop can give him this power because he has himself been chosen by God for his high office, and has, by his consecration, been admitted into the apostolic fellowship and given a special responsibility for both the *magisterium* and the government of the Church. This means that a bishop is not just a priest who has been given, by the Church, authority to perform certain additional functions, but a kind of 'high-priest' chosen by God to perform the highest offices in the Church.

When the Fathers of the Council were asked whether or not they believed that episcopal consecration admitted them to 'the highest degree of the sacramental order', 2,123 said 'Yes' and only 34 said 'No'. This was a very significant vote, for on it rested the whole doctrine of episcopacy in the Church. 'Although it was the doctrine of collegiality that stole the headlines', wrote Abbot Butler, 'the crux of the Constitution's teaching on the episcopate is perhaps contained in the affirmation that a bishop receives in his consecration the "fullness" of the ministerial priesthood derived from Christ, and therefore, as is explicitly asserted, not only the "office" (*munus*) of "sanctifying" (by sacramental ministrations) but the offices of teaching and ruling. Thus episcopal authority is not something received from the pope, but something given directly by God in the sacrament of holy orders.'[4]

It was on the basis of this vote that the Council could discuss the draft decree on The Pastoral Office of Bishops. The title was important with its emphasis on the bishop as pastor. Having made sure that they were the holders of the 'highest degree of the sacramental order', and were united with the Supreme Pontiff in the Apostolic College, the bishops could now concentrate on what they wanted to be the image of the bishop in the world of today. Feudal conceptions of the mighty

---

[4] *De Ecclesia: the Constitution on the Church of Vatican Council II.* ed. Gregory Baum, with Foreword by the Abbot of Downside (London, 1965), p. 12.

prelate, the stern administrator of a rigid code of Canon Law, the man wielding immense power over the lives of every man, woman and child in his jurisdiction, was something which the Fathers were now prepared to dispense with. What they now wanted was to impress upon the faithful that their bishop was a pastor, a father-in-God, a man to whom they could turn for help and advice, the good shepherd who cared for his sheep and would do everything in his power to promote their welfare.

The decree, therefore, sets the bishop's pastoral ministry in a wide setting. As a representative of the Church and of Christ, his responsibility is not only to the pious faithful who may, in fact, represent no more than a small minority even in so-called 'Catholic' countries. He must, therefore, concern himself with the special needs of those who have lapsed, of priests who are failing in their duties, of the 'separated brethren' and of those who have no faith at all. In order to do this, he must acquaint himself with the way in which people live and think in present-day society. He must make some study of social, demographic, and economic problems, and of the outlook of what Cardinal Léger called 'homo technicus'. He must be able to give guidance on such subjects as Art, Science, and Economics, and must advise people what to think about such controversial matters as nuclear warfare. Whereas in earlier drafts of the decree phrases about the Good Shepherd had been regarded as sufficient, later drafts introduced St. Paul's words to Timothy about a man of God being 'sanctified and meet for his master's use, and prepared unto every good work' (2 Tim. 2. 21).

The picture here is of a man fully in touch with what is going on around him. He has studied the way in which people live in order that he may know how best to commend the Gospel to them. He knows that the old days of magisterial teaching and authoritative injunction are passing away, and that the Christian faith is more likely to be imparted by discussion and dialogue. He knows also that his own Church is not the only Christian body which is at work in the world, and that he must be prepared to meet his fellow-Christians and collaborate with them wherever possible.

Throughout the decree the *pastoral* duties of the bishop in his diocese are constantly emphasized. But the decree also recognizes the fact that, as a member of the College of Bishops, a man has responsibilities which extend far beyond the boundaries of his diocese. Meeting other bishops at the Council no doubt did much to make men realize how great were the needs of some parts of the world very different from their own, and the decree lays upon every bishop the duty of helping where the need is greatest. He must also accept some responsibility for the central government of the Church, especially since there is now to be a permanent Synod of Bishops, many of whom will be elected by their fellows.

The picture of the episcopate, and of the life and work of a bishop, as presented in this decree is encouraging from an ecumenical point of view. Churches which dispensed with episcopacy in the sixteenth century are apprehensive of taking into their systems something which seems to them unnecessary, unbiblical, and even un-Christian. Many of them are still frightened by the bogey of 'prelacy', of the feudal, monarchical conception of a bishop, living in luxury and lording it over both clergy and laity in his jurisdiction. It was in an attempt to remove this conception that the Anglicans who took part in the Anglican-Methodist Conversations set out a statement of what they regarded as the essential nature of the bishop's office. This declares:

(1) The episcopate symbolises and secures in an abiding form the apostolic mission and authority within the Church; historically the episcopate became the organ of this mission and authority.

(2) In early times the continuous successions of bishops in tenure of the various sees were valued because they secured the purity of apostolic teaching as against, for example, the danger of the introduction of novel and erroneous teaching by means of writings or secret traditions falsely ascribed to apostolic authors. No doubt the need for this safeguard became less urgent when authoritative formulations of doctrine were drawn up and the canon of Scripture finally fixed. But it has remained a function of the episcopate to guard the Church against erroneous teaching.

(3) The bishop in his official capacity represents the whole Church in and to his diocese, and his diocese in and to the councils

of the Church. He is thus a living representative of the unity and universality of the Church.

(4) The bishop in his diocese represents the Good Shepherd; the idea of pastoral care is inherent in his office. Both clergy and laity look to him as chief pastor, and he represents in a special degree the paternal quality of pastoral care.

(5) Inasmuch as the unity of the Church is in part secured by an orderly method of making new ministers, and the bishop is the proper organ of unity and universality, he is the appropriate agent for carrying on, through ordination, the authority of the apostolic mission of the Church.[5]

Everything in this statement would be endorsed by the decree on The Pastoral Office of Bishops in the Church.

After so much emphasis on the *pastoral* office of bishops it was, perhaps, a little disappointing that the Council did not give rather more consideration to the use of episcopal orders, not for any pastoral reason but as a 'status-symbol'. The Roman Catholic Church recognizes two kinds of episcopal consecration, one 'relative' and the other 'absolute'. Relative consecration is the term used when a man is made bishop of a particular diocese with both jurisdiction over, and pastoral responsibility for, the people living within his territory. All that is said in this decree about the pastoral office of a bishop, about his attitude towards his flock, and about the qualities needed for a man who is to perform the function of a 'good shepherd' falls to the ground when episcopal orders are conferred on curial officials, masters of ceremonies, secretaries of commissions and so on. This 'absolute consecration' carries with it no pastoral responsibilities, for the titular sees to which these bishops are appointed are usually more or less deserted villages in Asia Minor or North Africa, the inhabitants of which are Moslems. The traditional, and I think we may say 'Catholic', conception of what episcopacy means was abandoned by the Roman Catholic Church when this practice arose of appointing as bishops, and even as archbishops, men who, by the very nature of things, could exercise none of the functions of a bishop in caring for his flock.

[5] *Conversations between the Church of England and the Methodist Church: A Report* (London, 1963), pp. 24–25.

The situation has, however, been partially remedied by the declaration of the Council on collegiality. This has given to every bishop some slight share in the pastoral responsibility which the episcopate as a whole, including the Supreme Pontiff, bears for the people of God. As Karl Rahner says:

If the episcopal college is one, and as such has a function in the Church, and if consecration as such brings the person directly into the college, then constitutional *theology* cannot recognise any purely 'absolute' ordination in the straightforward sense of the word: in every ordination, in addition to the sacramental power of order, there will be granted membership of the episcopal college —which is the holder, not only of the power of order, but irrevocably of pastoral authority.[6]

This is one of the by-products of the conciliar statement on collegiality, but it is of great importance in defending the Church against the charge of having allowed a complete cleavage to arise between episcopacy and the cure of souls.

3. *Priests*

Having given themselves the highest degree of sacramental order, allied themselves with the Pope in an apostolic college, and defined their jurisdiction in the diocese and in the world, the bishops could now turn to the priesthood and consider in what ways the Council could help them in their work. Two decrees were concerned with the priesthood, one on Priestly Life and Ministry, the other on Priestly Formation or training.

To understand these decrees one must again go back to the Constitution on the Church where a short section (no. 28) deals with the priesthood. Here it is made clear that the main function of the priests is to assist the bishops in their work. They have their duties as preachers, shepherds, and celebrants of the holy mysteries; but they do all this in so far as they are ordained and appointed by the bishops. But if the priests were a little disappointed at the rather casual way in which they were mentioned in the Constitution on the Church, they felt even worse treated when they discovered that the first *schema*

[6] Karl Rahner, S. J., *Bishops: Their Status and Function*, trans. Edward Quinn (London, 1964), p. 31.

on the priesthood consisted of only ten propositions covering three pages of print. When this was presented to the Council it was quickly seen to be totally inadequate to the subject, and, indeed, almost an insult to a fine body of men. It was, therefore, rejected by the Council in 1964 and came back, in a longer and more adequate form, in 1965.

In its new form the *schema* was a considerable improvement on what had gone before. Instead of declaring that the priest was the bishop's assistant, it now spoke of the priest sharing in the ministry of Christ as Teacher, Priest, and King. The objective (*finis*) of priestly ministry is described as being *ad Dei gloriam augendam simul ac ad hominum vitam promovendam*, a phrase reminiscent of the first question put by the bishop in an Anglican ordination when the candidate is asked whether he believes himself to be inwardly moved by the Holy Spirit to take upon himself this office and ministration 'to serve God for the promoting of his glory and the edifying of his people'. Having set out the final objective of his ministry, the *schema* goes on to consider the three ways in which this aim will be achieved—by teaching (on which considerable emphasis is laid), by sanctification (with special reference to the Eucharist), and by ruling or edifying the Church. It later goes on to describe the co-operation which must exist between the bishop and his priests, and among the priests themselves if they are to help and encourage one another. It rightly sees that the ministry can be carried out, not only in the parochial sphere, but in many other ways where priests bear their peculiar witness as teachers, research workers, or even working with their hands—an apparent reference to 'Priest Workers'. Later on in the *schema* a good deal is said about a priest's spiritual life and the necessity for regular reading of the Bible, the making of a retreat, the importance of making a daily examination of conscience and of living simply and chastely.

All this was encouraging since it was clearly meant to be of help to priests of all kinds, both those who were satisfied with traditional types of ministry and those who were anxious to find new ways in which they could 'promote the glory of God' and 'edify the people'. There is no doubt that some priests were far too prone to separate themselves from the world, to feel that so long as they offered the daily sacrifice of the Mass, said their offices, and ministered to the faithful in the confessional they were doing all that could reasonably be expected of them. For such men this *schema* was intended to be something of a jolt, to show them that they were living in an age when people were drifting from the Church, and when it was the duty of the priest to go out and win souls for Christ.

That encouragement of this kind was needed was shown by Dr. Foley, the Bishop of Lancaster in England, who referred to an article which he had read in the *Osservatore Romano* describing a parish priest 'who had visited six hundred homes in his parish in a single year'.

This [he said] was written of as something unheard of and almost heroic; a book was written about it in which the priest was said to have brought back many to the Church, to have comforted many aged and sick, and so on. Surely [he went on] this is an extraordinary state of affairs. Is it not the strict duty of *every* priest working in parishes to be constantly, regularly and systematically visiting the homes of his people? How otherwise can he perform his apostolate? How can he be said to 'know mine and mine know me'? How can he bring comfort to the aged and help them in distress; how will he bring back the lapsed without going to them in their homes? If in some nations and regions there is still an intense religious practice, it is not because they have a more advanced liturgy, or great theological schools. It is because they have a truly pastoral clergy who faithfully perform their pastoral visitations, and who clearly know by name every least child in their parish or district.[7]

But if there are some priests who neglect their pastoral duties there are others who are depressed, frustrated, uncertain of their usefulness. As with clergy of all denominations, there is a proportion of Roman Catholic priests who are in danger of falling into dark despair, who are suffering from a kind of creeping paralysis, who are beginning to doubt the relevance of the Church's ministry altogether, and who, in the face of so much difficulty and indifference, are losing confidence in themselves

[7] *English Bishops at the Council: Third Session*, ed. D. Worlock (London, 1965), p. 96.

and perhaps even in God. As so often, it was Cardinal Suenens of Malines-Brussels who put his finger on this.

> In the world today, [he said] and particularly in the West, there has been a progressive loss of the sense of the sacred. Priests are becoming more and more strangers to the world. The difficulty of their work frightens them. They are looking for dialogue and searching for contact, and this makes them keenly aware of the paradox of their mission, that at the heart of the world they must keep apart from it in order to be at the service of the Gospel. Priests have come, because of the increased emphasis on the rôle of the laity, to question their own specific rôle in the Church.[8]

Properly meditated upon and implemented, this decree should do much to help the clergy, both those over-complacent and those over-anxious. It was certainly a great improvement on all that had gone before it. No one could describe it as 'an insult to the clergy'. The picture which it portrays is a good one, worthy of its subject and, as such, it should bring hope and encouragement where they are most needed.

Together with the decree on Priestly Life and Ministry goes the one which deals with Priestly Formation. How a priest *thinks* of his job, and how he *does* it, will depend largely on how he is trained, what is said to him during the long years in the seminary, what ideals are put before him, what standards of prayer, study, and discipline he knows that he will be expected to adopt.

Like the *schema* on Priestly Life and Ministry this draft was also first offered to the Council as a series of propositions, which were soon recognized as inadequate for a subject of such importance. In the debate on it the following points came up for discussion:

(1) That the method of training priests should vary from country to country. This was very popular among the bishops and was quickly accepted. For far too long the organization and planning of seminary training had been carried out by the Congregation of Seminaries, Universities and Studies in Rome. This was something which many of the bishops had

[8] Daily Bulletin for 15 October 1965.

long resented. It was all right in the days of the Council of Trent for a Roman congregation to control the work of the seminaries, but how could a group of men in Rome know what was best for the Church in Japan, the United States, or the Congo? The suggestion, therefore, that all this should be put into the hands of the local hierarchies was warmly received. Fr. Congar comments as follows:

Almost all the bishops rejoiced that this Schema proclaims, in its very first paragraph, that it should be handed over to the episcopal conferences of each country to decide the programme of studies and the training of future priests. We ourselves, who taught from 1931 to 1954, can bear witness to the difficult and serious inconvenience which arose from the fact that the teaching was obliged to follow a programme imposed and controlled by Rome, where the Congregation of Studies is known to be one of the least progressive.[9]

No doubt the feelings which Fr. Congar here expressed were felt by many of those who had the task of preparing men for the ministry all over the world.

(2) How far should the future priest be segregated from his fellows and cut off from the world? This was a matter of considerable importance. In the past the tendency has been to get the boy as soon as possible into the pipe-line out of which he will one day emerge as a priest. This means that, from the age of eleven, he would be put to a course of study designed to prepare him, during the course of the next twelve years, for the priesthood. The question was: Is this segregation healthy? Does it enable a man to win souls for Christ?

Many of us would feel very doubtful about this. In the Anglican Communion the tendency is to let the future priest go through a fairly normal course of education until three or four years before the end, when he will be living among fellow-candidates for the ministry and spending his whole time in the necessary preparation for it. This means that the Anglican ordinand attends the ordinary schools and universities where he mixes with other students—Anglicans and non-Anglicans,

[9] Yves Congar, O.P., *Le concile au jour le jour: Troisième session* (Paris, 1965), p.110.

Christians and non-Christians, friendly and hostile, docile and argumentative. This, we feel, is a valuable preparation for his future ministry. It encourages him to stand up for the faith that is in him and gives him the opportunity of learning something about the sort of people among whom he will one day have to minister. In the Roman Catholic Church the tendency is all the other way; and those who have read the *Diary of a Soul* by Pope John XXIII will know both the good and the bad elements in a policy of professional training which starts at the age of eleven. Visitors to Rome will have noted the contrast between the students of the Gregorian University, in their cassocks and clerical collars, and the more normal-looking young men who are studying at the state university of Rome, and will have wondered whether it is wise to keep these two groups so much apart.

The decree on Priestly Formation accepts the principle of segregation, though a good many of the bishops were doubtful of its value. Such doubts were certainly shared by the delegate observers, many of whom had, at one time or another, had experience in training men for the ministry. It was generally felt that a man is most likely to be effective in proclaiming the Christian faith if he has rubbed shoulders with his fellow-men and has learnt something about their ways of thought. Writing in the *Heythrop Journal* about Pope John's *Diary of a Soul*, I drew attention to the way in which the young Angelo Roncalli had completely cut himself off from the world at a very tender age.

How far this was a strengthening of his character it is hard to say. 'By their fruits ye shall know them'; and there is no doubt about the fruit which he bore or the blessings which he gave to the world. But to those of us who were trained in a different tradition it seems a rather narrow, over-heated world. The natural man disappears under the cassock at a very early age, and the priest becomes a man separated from the rest of humanity. It is perhaps interesting to recall, in this connexion, an address given by a great trainer of Anglican clergy to a group of priests about to start a Clergy Training College immediately after the First World War. Speaking to this group, Canon B. K. Cunningham said: 'Let the order of the growth be "first that which is natural and afterwards that which is spiritual".... Perhaps the greatest weakness of the Church of England clergy today is not that there are a few men who ought never to have been priests, but that there are many priests who have never been men.'[10]

If this is true of the Anglican clergy, how much more true must it be of those segregated at an earlier age?

(3) How far should the training of the priest be dominated by scholastic philosophy, especially the writings of Thomas Aquinas? To many of the Council Fathers the *Summa Theologica* was clearly the only possible basis for any philosophical and theological training. Others very naturally wished to carry out an *aggiornamento* in the seminaries and bring the teaching much more into line with modern thought and modern method. On this issue the Council was very much divided, and a lively debate took place on what was felt by all to be a matter of great importance. Cardinal Léger of Montreal objected to the phrase 'philosophia perennis', which suggested that the conclusions of thirteenth-century philosophers of one particular school were infallible and irreformable. 'The important thing', he said, 'is to recommend not so much the doctrinal ideas of St. Thomas as his scientific and spiritual approach which was to use the ideas of his day to illustrate and extol the Gospel.' But any attempt to dislodge St. Thomas from his place of supremacy was bitterly opposed by men like Cardinal Bacci and Archbishop Staffa who were clearly unable to foresee any curriculum which was not firmly based on the *Summa*. In the end it was the followers of Cardinal Léger who won the day, for the final text of the decree speaks merely of seminarists studying philosophy 'under the guidance of St. Thomas'. On the other hand, much emphasis is placed on the study of the Bible (where possible in the original languages), of patristics, of moral theology, of comparative religion, of ecumenism and of the world in which we live. By so doing, the decree has a pleasantly modern and intelligent look which was reinforced by its clear and insistent teaching on the importance of proper training in the arts of teaching and preaching, in the conduct of public worship, in spiritual direction and in psychology and sociology. Suggestions

[10] *Heythrop Journal*, vol. vi (October, 1965), p. 404.

that the more pastoral element in the training for the ministry should be given in the parishes brought the text more into line with Anglican customs, since every Anglican student spends the year of his diaconate not in the seminary but under the care of a parish priest.

4. Deacons

The Council produced no decree on deacons, though there is a paragraph about them in the Constitution on the Church.

Problems concerning the ministry of deacons have exercised the Church for a long time. In the primitive Church they clearly had a function to perform, but by the Middle Ages this had more or less died out, and the diaconate had become one of the orders through which a man passed on his way to the priesthood. This remains true of the Roman and Anglican Churches today, though, in the Orthodox Churches, a few permanent deacons are still to be found.

The diaconate, being one of the three major orders which had developed by the end of the first century, was obviously intended to fulfil some specific function in the ministry of the Church. This ministry was closely linked with the ministry of Christ and was shared out among various officers. The sacrificial ministry was clearly something which was continued by bishops and priests, who alone had the power to present the Eucharistic sacrifice at the altar. The teaching ministry was again largely in the hands of the higher ranks of the clergy who alone had the necessary qualifications. In more recent years, however, this ministry has been shared by teachers of many different kinds including readers, catechists, and schoolmasters. The healing ministry of Christ was somewhat neglected by the Church after the first few years, though hospitals owe their origin to ecclesiastical foundations and medical missions play an important part in the developing countries. Finally, the serving ministry of Christ is something in which the whole Church must share, clergy and laity alike. But, since diaconate means service, there is a sense in which those who do this work on behalf of Christ, in all its various forms, should hold office as deacons.

The Council had to discuss the question as to whether the Church should restore a permanent diaconate, and so have, as part of its ministry, a body of men dedicated and commissioned for the service of mankind. This is a question which the Anglican Church has also had to consider. At the Lambeth Conference in 1958 some attention was given to the place of deacons in the Church; but the feeling was that the work originally done by deacons was now largely performed by laymen acting as part-time workers. After speaking of the excellent work done by readers and catechists, the Report says: 'As a result of this development the fact must be faced that in most areas of the Anglican Communion the traditional functions of a deacon may all, under episcopal authority, be fulfilled by a reader or by a catechist.' It then goes on to say that it would prefer to see greater encouragement and status being given to these laymen rather than the establishment of a permanent diaconate.[11]

Before deciding whether or not to revive an order of men working permanently and full-time as deacons, the Church must decide what the functions of a deacon are. These are defined in the Anglical Ordinal as follows:

It appertaineth to the office of a deacon, in the church where he shall be appointed to serve, to assist the Priest in Divine Service, and specially when he ministereth the Holy Communion, and to help him in the distribution thereof; and to read Holy Scriptures and Homilies in the church; and to instruct the youth in the Catechism; in the absence of the Priest to baptize infants; and to preach, if he be admitted thereto by the Bishop.

It then goes on to say that the deacon must visit the sick and poor so that relief can be given to them. It thus assumes that the deacon shall be attached to a particular church and that he will devote the best part of his time to his ministry.

In the Constitution on the Church the functions of a deacon are similarly set out.

It is the duty of the deacon, [it says] according as it shall have been assigned to him by competent authority, to administer baptism solemnly, to be custodian and dispenser of the Eucharist, to assist

11 *The Lambeth Conference 1958* (London, 1958), pp. 2, 106–7.

at and bless marriages in the name of the Church, to bring Viaticum to the dying, to read the Sacred Scriptures to the faithful, to administer sacramentals, to officiate at funeral and burial services.

It will be seen that this assigns to the deacon more than is given to him in the Anglican Church, which permits him to baptize only 'in the absence of the priest' and disallows him from officiating at weddings since this involves the giving of the blessing. But, on the whole, the Anglican and Roman Catholic Churches are more or less in agreement on what a deacon should do.

The two matters which really divided the Council were (1) whether a permanent diaconate should be revived, and (2) whether such deacons should be allowed to be married men. These two questions are closely related, for if the Church is to impose on deacons the discipline of celibacy there seems little point in preventing them from being priests.

The demand for a permanent and, if necessary, married diaconate came mostly from those parts of the world where there is an acute shortage of clergy. Bishops who were struggling with large dioceses, which they had to administer with very slender resources, welcomed the idea of increasing their manpower by the creation of permanent deacons. These men, by visiting the sick, teaching the children, taking the sacraments to those unable to attend church, officiating at weddings and funerals, could relieve the priests of much of their pastoral work and thereby enable them to cover wider areas for the specific functions for which only a priest will suffice. But, if an adequate number of men is to be found to do this work, then it would seem natural to allow them to marry. Otherwise, far fewer men will be available, and there would seem no particular point in refusing them the priesthood. Others, however, pleaded very strongly that the rule of celibacy should not be relaxed for any who were in major orders. Should this be done, they foresaw many men accepting the diaconate but refusing to go forward to the priesthood so that they could marry and have children.

The question of the diaconate was made one of the five 'guiding votes' put to the Fathers on 30 October 1963. The fifth question was framed thus: 'Is the *schema* to be drawn up in such a way that consideration is given to the opportunity for the restoration of the diaconate as a distinct and permanent degree of the sacramental ministry in accordance with the needs of the Church in various regions?' This was carried by 1,588 votes to 525. The Commission, therefore, put into the draft text the following words. After referring to the duties of the deacon (as given above), it says:

Since these duties, so very necessary to the life of the Church, can be fulfilled only with difficulty in many regions in accordance with the discipline of the Latin Church as it exists today, the Diaconate can in the future be restored as a proper and permanent rank of the hierarchy. It pertains to the competent territorial bodies of Bishops, of one kind or another, with the approval of the Supreme Pontiff, to decide whether and where it is opportune for such deacons to be established for the care of souls. It is within the competence of the Supreme Authority to decide whether this diaconate can be conferred upon men of mature age, even living in matrimony, or even upon suitable young men upon whom the law of celibacy will not be imposed, or whether on the contrary the law of celibacy should remain firm even for this type of deacons.

This, however, came under considerable fire, especially the last part about allowing men to be made deacons without imposing upon them the law of celibacy. So strong was the opposition that eventually this sentence had to be rewritten, and it now reads as follows:

... With the consent of the Roman Pontiff this diaconate can in the future be conferred upon men of mature age, even upon those living in the married state. It may also be conferred upon suitable young men for whom the law of celibacy must remain intact.

The Council has thus accepted a compromise: permanent deacons may be appointed; if they are older men and already married, this will be no bar; but if they are young men they must, like priests, accept the vow of celibacy.

It is still too early to say how this is likely to work out; but experiments are already taking place in certain parts of the world. In the Diocese of Rottenburg in Germany, where there is an acute shortage of priests, married deacons, whether full-time or part-time, are to be appointed. Their chief function will be to lead the worship of the congregations on Sundays, preach sermons, and distribute the Eucharist from the tabernacle. By so doing they will make it possible for smaller places to have a service every Sunday, even though no priest is available. If this becomes general, it will greatly alter the whole concept of worship in the Church. It will certainly not be popular; but the alternative is that, in time, villages may be able to have any sort of Eucharistic worship only on those rare occasions when a priest is able to visit them.[12]

5. *Religious*

It is difficult for anyone outside the Roman Church to realize what an enormous part the religious orders play in the life of that Church; indeed, much of its work would break down if it were not for the vast number of men and women who have devoted themselves to a life of discipline and self-renunciation and have offered their services to the Church to be used as and where she wills. Not only are there a great many orders, many of them devoted to some particular kind of ministry, but some of them are very large. The three branches of the Order of St. Francis, for example, contain at least fifty thousand brethren besides large numbers of sisters. In teaching, nursing, care of children, and in the mission field the Church depends very largely on its 'religious'.

In the past the religious life has had a very strong appeal and has influenced the Church profoundly. It was the Benedictine Order which largely saved both the Church and Christian civilization in the West when the Roman Empire fell to pieces; it was the Order of St. Francis which did so much for the renewal of the life of the Church in the Middle Ages and inaugurated missionary enterprise both in the east and in the west; at the same time it was the Order of St. Dominic which helped to save the Church from heresy and intellectual torpor; and it was the Society of Jesus which contributed so much to

---

[12] *Herder Correspondence*, April 1966, p. 101.

the strength of the Church in the sixteenth century and carried the Gospel into the newly-discovered countries. So it has always been. Whenever there has been work which needed a considerable number of wholly devoted and dedicated men and women, the religious orders have never failed.

Because of their high standards, their special type of vocation, and their renunciation of the world, there has always been a tendency for the religious orders to be regarded as something in the nature of a 'Church within a church'. Many congregations are exempt from episcopal control and take their orders either from the Holy See or from their own superiors in Rome. As a result they have tended to be self-conscious, traditional, conservative, jealous of their independence and resentful of criticism.

But criticism there has been. Everyone knows that all members of religious orders are subject to the threefold vow of Poverty, Chastity, and Obedience; these are the people who have renounced the world and all its allurements and pleasures and like to regard themselves as living in a 'state of perfection'. But the rest of the Church has sometimes doubted whether the abnegation and austerity of their lives is, in fact, quite so sacrificial as it appears. Does the vow of Poverty really mean that the members of the religious orders are so much poorer than many of the secular clergy, or of the laity? Does the vow of Chastity demand more than is expected of every secular priest, and, indeed of some lay people whose work makes it impossible for them to marry? Does the vow of Obedience impose on them greater discipline than many people outside the monasteries impose upon themselves for the sake of their calling? Such questions as these are being asked, and the Council realized that, if the religious orders were to keep the respect of the world there was need for renewal of their life. The Council also realized that if the orders were to play their part in the total life of the Church there was need for change and adaptation in some of their more antiquated customs. It was as a result of this that the decree which dealt with the members of the religious orders came to be called a decree On the Adaptation and Renewal of the Religious Life.

As with other decrees, the basis of all this was a chapter in the Constitution on the Church. This tries to set out the basis of the religious life, founded on the three evangelical counsels and on the whole of the teaching and example of Christ. From small beginnings this way of life has grown into a great organization, the 'militia Christi', composed of men and women who, having given up all for Christ, were ready to serve Him wherever they were needed. But, although these men and women were dedicated to the service of God 'on a new and special warrant' (*novo et peculiari titulo*), it was important that they should be closely integrated into the life of the Church, so that 'the way of life which the Son of God accepted on entering into this world ... might be more accurately exemplified and perpetually made present in the Church'. This was the ideal; but, if it was to be achieved, then the orders must be carefully guided, either by the Holy Father or by the local bishops, who must see not only that the men and women involved are faithful to their ideals, but also that they are not so much cut off from the world as to lose touch with its problems or become themselves 'inhuman'.

On the basis of these general principles, a *schema* was drawn up. It was at first entitled *De Religiosis* and was in the form of a series of propositions which were presented to the Council during the Third Session in November 1964. These propositions were of a practical nature, calling for reform of the orders and suggesting ways in which this could be carried out. As such they came in for a good deal of adverse criticism. Many felt that the religious orders, which had such a splendid history and had done so much for the Church, deserved something rather better than this. 'Poor, barren, dry, juridical' was how Cardinal Döpfner described the *schema*, and many of the Fathers supported him in pleading for something a little more inspiring. If the religious orders were really to find the bases of a spiritual renewal, they needed something better than this, something more scriptural and devotional. Many of the Fathers felt that if the religious orders were to find real renewal it would be by becoming far more integrated into the life of the Church. As usual, Cardinal Bea had some wise things to say. 'Religious', he said, 'should draw their inspiration from the purest founts of doctrine, namely Sacred Scripture and the Liturgy. They need also to develop the missionary spirit and the ecumenical spirit. The riches of the Church are placed in evidence by the variety of the religious institutes. But the present text is lacking in that spirit which can give it new force. It is essential for religious to remember that, besides being members of their institutes, they are also members of the Church with the obligation to live its life and to co-operate with the Church as she renews herself through the Council.'[13]

All this was good; but much was said on the other side. Some of the Fathers were afraid that, if the religious orders became too much involved with the life of the Church, they would lose some of their special features which could only develop by withdrawal from the world. Others thought that too little had been said about the work done by the contemplative orders, who, if these propositions were passed, would look as if they had cut themselves off from the main stream of the Church's life. Cardinal Spellman of New York saw the danger of religious being hindered from fulfilling their own special vocation if they were to be regarded as available for every kind of job that the Church wanted done.

As a result of two days' debate it was generally felt that these nineteen propositions would not do, and the Commission was asked to prepare a longer and more comprehensive document. This was presented to the Council in 1965 as a decree On the Adaptation and Renewal of the Religious Life, and was solemnly promulgated on 28 October. This is a much more satisfactory document, far more worthy of a fine body of men and women, to whom everyone felt that justice had now been done.

Apart from the two brothers from Taizé, to whom the whole discussion was of great interest, many of the observers found this debate rather remote, since it dealt with a subject of which they had no immediate experience. We who represented the Anglican Communion were more involved as we now have a number of religious orders, though their numbers are

[13] Daily Bulletin, 11 November 1964.

infinitesimal compared with those in the Roman Catholic Church. When Cardinal Landázuri-Ricketts of Lima, Peru, told us that there were eight hundred thousand men and one million two hundred thousand women, all members of religious orders working in the mission field alone, it gave us some idea of the vastness both of the resources and of the problems involved. It is no wonder that this short debate was taken with the greatest seriousness, since the lives of so many people were likely to be affected by it and since nearly one third of the Council Fathers were themselves members of one or other of the religious orders. The final document is not one of the great texts which Vatican II has produced; but it was generally thought that it would help the orders both in the renewal of their inner life and in their adaptation to the needs of today.

6. *The Laity*

No series of documents on 'the Church' or on 'ministry' would be complete nowadays without serious consideration being given to the place of the laity in the mission of the Church. Christians everywhere are now discussing this problem. The days of sacerdotalism and priestcraft are regarded as belonging to the past, and much thought is being given both to the theology of the laity and to practical ways in which the laity can play their part in the work and witness of the Church as a whole. The laity, the *laos*, form the 'people of God' which must include both those who are ordained and those who are not. There is now a general feeling that the Church must act as one if it is to fulfil its divine mission. No longer can one talk of 'going into the Church' or demand that 'the Church' should do certain things. We now realize that we are all in this together, sharing in a common responsibility and exercising our own *charismata* in promoting the cause of Christ in the world. There is, therefore, a revolt against clericalism, against the idea that it is the clergy who 'run' the Church and expect the laity to do what they are told— 'to pray, pay and obey', as is sometimes said. In the Anglican Communion there is a breakaway from the older conception of the parson as an autocrat and the clergy as a separate caste while we develop and discuss plans for 'synodical government', 'training of the laity for mission', and so forth. In other Churches the laity have traditionally more power, whether as elders in the Church of Scotland or as lay members of committees which organize the work of the Free Churches.

The Roman Catholic Church is naturally more priest-ridden than other Churches since much of the modern movement towards lay co-operation has passed it by. But it was essential, if the Council were to carry out any form of *aggiornamento*, for it to try to balance its theology of the hierarchy and priesthood with some theology of the laity.

This was done in the Constitution on the Church. In its first form (1962) there was a short chapter on the laity which began with a quotation from *Pastor aeternus* of Vatican I in 1870, describing the Church as being composed of all the faithful, and then went on to say that the honourable task (*onus honorificum*) of proclaiming the Gospel to all men rests upon the whole Church, clergy and laity alike. Quoting from Exodus 19. 6, where the children of Israel are described as 'a kingdom of priests and a holy nation', it pointed out that, although some men are set aside for special ministerial functions, all the faithful are called upon to share in the mission of the Church. By prayer, example, sacrifice, and word, as individuals, or as groups, their task is to build up the Church of God and to consecrate the world.

All this was good so far as it went; but there was a feeling that the whole passage was too slight and superficial. It hardly needed a conciliar document to tell people that it was their duty to be witnesses to their faith. What was needed was something more theological, something which would deal with such difficult phrases as 'a royal priesthood' or the common, though unbiblical, expression about 'the priesthood of all believers'. The new form of the *schema*, therefore, tried to go a little deeper, explaining that, as part of the People of God, the laity shared in the priestly, prophetic, and kingly office of Christ —priestly by the sacrifice of themselves and their lives to God, prophetic by witnessing to their faith, kingly by enlarging the Kingdom of God in the world.

As with other subjects, this was meant to serve as a theological basis for a decree on The Apostolate of the Laity, the draft of which was laid before the Council in 1964. This begins by saying: 'The holy Council Vatican II has proposed as its principal aim the development of a deeper spiritual life and more intense involvement on the part of all members of the Church', and went on to say that, in these days, there was special need for the laity to exercise their apostolate in such things as scientific and technical progress, the problems of the population explosion, the struggle against secularism, the right use of modern means of communication, the shortage of clergy or the fact that in some countries they were not allowed to function, and the general alienation from religious and moral influences of certain areas of human life. After this it contains twenty-one paragraphs outlining the ways in which the laity can play their part in the work of the Church.

This *schema* was debated during October 1964 when it came in for a good deal of criticism.[14] Many speakers felt that it was too clerical, and more than one pleaded for some attempt to treat the laity not as children but as adults. A complaint that the laity had not been consulted in drawing up the *schema* led to some of the lay auditors at the Council being invited to attend meetings of the Commission as *periti*, while one of them, Mr. Patrick Keegan, addressed the Council on 14 October from the *pulpitum*.[15] Much time was spent in discussing the work of the organization known as Catholic Action, and the suggestion was put forward that a new Secretariat for the lay apostolate should be set up in Rome.

As a result of this fairly long debate, lasting six days, the *schema* was considerably revised and rewritten before it was put to the vote in the following year. In its final form it is considerably enlarged, containing a Procemium and six chapters dealing with the Vocation of the Laity and the Apostolate, the Objectives, the various Fields and various Forms of the Apostolate, the maintaining of proper relationships with the hier-

[14] X. Rynne, *The Third Session* (London, 1965), pp. 69–84.
[15] His speech is printed in *English Bishops at the Council: Third Session*, ed. D. Worlock, pp. 111–14.

archy, and the Training of the Laity for their work. Many subjects are touched on—the share of the laity in the three-fold ministry of Christ, the example of the Blessed Virgin, the necessity for charity and relief work, the responsibility of the Christian in his family, in the social milieu and in national and international affairs, the place of Catholic Action and other associations in the Church, the advisability of setting up the equivalent of what we in the Church of England call Parochial Church Councils, Ruri-decanal Conferences, Diocesan Conferences, and the Church Assembly, and the need for a new Secretariat in Rome to encourage and conduct the apostolate of the laity.

The decree has, therefore, made an attempt to be comprehensive; yet in many ways it is a disappointment. The language and thought are still somewhat archaic; it never really comes to grips with the problems of fulfilling the Christian law in a modern secular society, nor with the conflict of loyalty which can so easily be set up in a mind which has a dual responsibility to both Church and State. In spite of what is said, both here and in the Constitution on the Church, the whole subject of the lay apostolate has never really been adequately dealt with, and the document formally promulgated on 18 November 1965 is unlikely to stand out among the decrees which have done so much to renew the life of the Church.

5 Ecumenism

HOWARD E. ROOT

Professor of Theology in the University of Southampton

I

Historians may one day agree that the debate on the Decree on Ecumenism, during the second Session of the Council,[1] was in some ways more important than the final text of the decree itself. It raised far more questions than the decree answers, but it opened doors which no decree could close. Even after the words and initiatives of Pope John in the years preceding the opening of the Council (he had more than once said that Christian unity would be one of the main concerns of the Council), and despite those dramatic events in the first Session which led to so much hope, there were still many who doubted that the Church of Rome could ever take ecumenism seriously. No one can say that there were no grounds for this scepticism. Even if we keep to the modern period and go no further back than 1928 and the encyclical *Mortalium Animos*,[2] Rome's attitude to the ecumenical movement had ever been (to put it as gently as possible) distinctly chilly. And how could it not be? How could a Church making Rome's claims ever be willing to enter into serious dialogue with churches which she said were no churches at all? There was at least a consistency in the older attitude. The Church of Rome is the one and only true church of Christ. Therefore any so-called reunion will be nothing more or less than a return of the schismatic, dissident communities to the one true fold. Could Rome remain consistent

---

[1] 18–22, 25–29 November, 2 December, 1963.

[2] In this encyclical Pius XI effectively suggested that unity would only be possible by a return of all Christians to Roman obedience and forbade the participation of Roman Catholics in conferences on unity. Those who still maintain that the Church of Rome never changes would find a stimulating exercise in comparing this encyclical with the Decree on Ecumenism.

and at the same time espouse ecumenism? Would not an openness to dialogue either compromise her claims or else lead to contradiction?

It is one of the paradoxes of the Council that the text of the Decree on Ecumenism does not answer these questions, even though it raises them, and even though Rome now behaves or assumes a stance which would suggest that those questions had not only been raised but perfectly and harmoniously resolved. It is the Council itself rather than the text of any of the decrees which has made this stance possible. It may or may not be stable. We shall not know about that for a long while. What we feel certain of now (without anything like compelling evidence) is that a return to the spirit of *Mortalium Animos* or to anything like the pre-Council official attitude to ecumenism is unthinkable, or even impossible. Psychologically if not juridically Rome has in some sense passed the point of no return in the matter of her relations with other Christians. (And other matters too, even more fundamental to her self-understanding.) What the future holds is not predictable (and the present period of confusion and rapid zig-zag changes is no proper basis for prediction) but we still feel no hesitation in saying that whatever the future does hold, it will be very unlike the past, that era which stretches from the Counter Reformation and the Council of Trent through the First Vatican Council of 1870 and down to the election of John XXIII in 1958 and the opening of Vatican II in 1962.

In 1963 these things were not so clear, or not so strongly felt. During the first Session there was an enormous struggle, or series of struggles, to decide whether this was indeed to be a Council of bishops deliberating freely and working through to decisions of their own, or merely a large meeting of bishops which would listen to some admonitory words from curial Cardinals and then do what they were told to do and go home. Perhaps it was only Pope John's intervention and personal charism which gave the bishops the chance to become a Council. This was another of the Council's paradoxes (and it was to be repeated in later Sessions). Only the personal intervention of the Supreme Pontiff, as it were turned against the Council's machinery, could ensure that the majority of the bishops would gain its will over the minority. The machinery was heavily weighted in favour of the minority, and Pope John is alleged to have said on one occasion, 'But what can I do? I'm only the Pope.'

By the end of the first Session in December 1962, it looked as though there was a good fighting chance for the bishops. They were not prepared to give even a collegial rubber-stamp approval to the drafts of the preparatory Theological Commission. They had thrown out the *schema* On the Sources of Revelation, and they went home determined (or so one hoped) to destroy forever the image of a church dominated by the trinity of devils that Bishop de Smedt of Bruges openly named as clericalism, juridicalism, and triumphalism. This was one of the Council's classic speeches and will be remembered far longer than many words in most of the decrees.[3]

But that was 1962, and before the second Session was to begin in September 1963, Pope John had died and been succeeded by Cardinal Montini, Archbishop of Milan, as Paul VI. It was widely supposed that Pope Paul was as dedicated to the cause of *aggiornamento* as his predecessor, and he had spoken words which supported this view, but no one really knew what kind of a pope he would be or what would happen to Pope John's Council under Pope Paul's hand. He was a very different kind of man. Not necessarily weaker, but very different: intellectual, reserved, perhaps introspective, a man who had long worked with Pius XII and in manner somehow reminded one of Pope John's predecessor—but perhaps without his decisiveness.

On 29 September 1963, therefore, before the service inaugurating the second Session, the atmosphere was thick with speculation and tension. This would be Pope Paul's first appearance before the Bishops in Council as Supreme Pontiff. Everyone wondered whether his allocution would give a clear-cut picture of his intentions for the Council. The observers wondered just as actively as the bishops and *periti*. For by the grace of Pope John's original invitation the observers had come to feel them-

[3] Xavier Rynne, *Letters from Vatican City* (London, 1963), pp. 217-19.

selves not only involved in but also somehow committed to the Council. We were not just spectators, least of all disinterested spectators.

In the event Pope Paul's allocution by no means answered all the questions people were asking—an impossibility in any case. It was, like all his statements, very carefully balanced, unexaggerated, evidencing the deepest kind of sense of the difficulty and delicacy and complexity of the problems which the Council was raising for the Church, not only by its deliberations but (implicitly) by its very existence less than a century after the door-closing definitions of Vatican I. But near the end of the speech a warmth and passion (which is always there beneath his surface calm and poise) broke through. The Pope looked directly at the observers and in a voice throbbing with emotion said:

Our voice trembles and our heart beats the faster both because of the inexpressible consolation and reasonable hope that their presence [the observers'] stirs up within us, as well as because of the deep sadness we feel at their prolonged separation.

If we are in any way to blame for that separation, we humbly beg God's forgiveness and ask pardon too of our brethren who feel themselves to have been injured by us. For our part, we willingly forgive the injuries which the Catholic Church has suffered, and forget the grief endured during the long series of dissensions and separations. May the heavenly Father deign to hear our prayers and grant us true brotherly peace.[4]

Even now it is difficult to realize the staggering significance and impact of those words. The Supreme Pontiff of the one and only and indefectible Church speaking in terms of a blame which might attach to his Church, and of forgiveness and pardon needed. So far as the observers were concerned, there could be no doubt now that the Church of Rome was going to take ecumenism seriously, however gravely this might strain her post-Tridentine and post-Vatican I theological resources, and disquiet many of her faithful members. The observers along with the bishops had studied the *schema* on ecumenism which would be debated in this second Session. From 29

[4] Quoted in Xavier Rynne, *The Second Session* (London, 1964), p. 358.

September onwards, that was the debate they wanted to hear.

This brings us back to the suggestion that the 1963 debate on the draft decree on ecumenism might in some sense have been more important than the final text of the decree itself. In this brief chapter it is not possible to recount the full history of the decree and its various revisions. That story has already been told more than once and is readily available to those who have special interest in the way that the decrees of Vatican II took shape.[5] Here we can do no more than give a very brief account of how the text developed.

Before the opening of the first Session of the Council in 1962, and as part of the general preparation for the Council, no less than three separate documents on Church unity had been drafted for submission to the Fathers. One was the work of the Preparatory Commission for the Eastern Churches and therefore dealt exclusively with the question of unity with the Orthodox Churches of the East. A second had been prepared by the Theological Commission, as the final chapter in its *schema* on the Church. The third was produced by the Secretariat for Promoting Christian Unity, but unlike the other two it never even got as far as distribution to the Fathers. In this situation it was not surprising that during the first Session a good many disquieted voices complained about the apparent lack of co-ordination, at the preparatory stage, on so central a subject as unity and ecumenism.

By the end of the Session it was therefore agreed that the Secretariat for Unity should produce a new *schema*, combining the three, for submission to the second Session. By the summer of 1963 (i.e. between the first and second Sessions) an agreed draft of the first three chapters of this new *schema* was approved by the Co-ordinating Commission. It was distributed to the Fathers before the Session opened in September. The titles of these chapters were as follows: 1. The Principles of Catholic Ecumenism; 2. The Implementation of Ecumenism; 3. Christians separated from the Catholic Church (I the Oriental Churches, II Christian Communities arising after the

[5] See Note A at end of this chapter.

sixteenth century). It is important to take careful note of these titles. They were not to remain unchanged before a final text was approved in 1964, and the changes were significant.

The fate of these three chapters in the second Session was complicated (and some thought imperilled) by another factor. Soon after the opening of the Session it became known that the Secretariat for Unity proposed to add two further chapters: 4. On the Jews, and 5. On Religious Liberty. These were not in fact distributed until 8 and 19 November. For obvious reasons the general debate on the *schema* (which began on 18 November) was seriously affected by the addition of these chapters. Both were highly controversial (though for very different reasons), and they probably received more attention from the press than any other part of the work of the Council. The chapter on religious liberty raised quite fundamental problems for Roman Catholic theology and practice, and bishops from predominantly Roman Catholic countries were profoundly troubled about its consequences for them. The chapter on the Jews aroused great anxiety in the minds of Eastern Fathers, most of whom live in Arab and Moslem countries. To their mind any kind of statement about the Jews would be interpreted in their own lands as some kind of official approval for the principles of Zionism and the policies (and existence) of the State of Israel. (See Chapter 8a for a discussion of the final text of the Declaration on Non-Christian Religions.)

For our immediate purposes, the most important result of the addition of these two chapters was the way it distracted attention from the first three chapters, which were in fact the more significant part of the *schema* as a document directed to Christian unity. In the end it was quite properly decided that these two chapters did not really belong in this decree. Each was finally to become the subject of a separate Declaration quite distinct from the document on ecumenism. At the same time it might be argued that the controversial nature of the chapter on religious liberty so drew the fire of the more conservative bishops that the earlier chapters escaped fairly lightly.

In retrospect it is still a matter for astonishment that the debate on those three chapters was accomplished in no more than eleven days. Much to the surprise of the Secretariat, the *schema* was often criticized for being too cautious.[6] They had expected that the *schema* would be charged with indifferentism —and of course it was—but they had little expected that a majority of the Fathers would not only go along with their draft but would be willing to go further still. According to Father Stransky, the Secretariat had to work its way through 1,063 pages of suggestions from the Fathers in redrafting the text. He says, 'In preparing the *schema*, the Secretariat had underestimated the influence of Pope John's actions and words upon the ecumenical pulse of the episcopal body and thus had misread its beat. The new draft for the third Session, consequently, became much bolder.'[7]

It is not possible here to summarize even the major speeches given during these eleven days of debate. The story is vividly told by Xavier Rynne.[8] Our attention will have to go to the final text, and in perfect fairness it should be said that only the expert would detect the import of the differences between the 1963 and 1964 versions. To historians and theologians the differences are of course very interesting, not least in showing how the Secretariat was able to respond to criticisms from various quarters. But it would be absurd to suggest that there was some major or wholly unexpected new departure in the revised text which reflected a substantial change in thinking on the subject between 1963 and 1964. To the non-Roman-Catholic (who perhaps also underestimated Pope John's influence) either text would have been considered a wonder as coming from the highest authority of the Roman Catholic Church. In some respects the final text is less guarded than its immediate predecessor, but when compared with a document

[6] See T. F. Stransky's remarks in *The Decree on Ecumenism* (Glen Rock, N. J., 1965), pp. 9–10.

[7] ibid.

[8] Xavier Rynne, *The Second Session* (London, 1964), pp. 216–91. There is no doubt that Rynne's four volumes (one on each Session) comprise the best available account in English of what actually happened at the Council and what it meant. This pseudonymous writer (or group of writers?) combines a knowledge of the historical and theological issues, a shrewd understanding of Vatican politics, and a lively style.

like *Mortalium Animos*, both equally belong to a quite different world.

In accordance with the Council's ordinary procedure, the revised draft was not debated again (i.e. in the third Session) but simply voted upon. Near the end of the Session, however, and before the final vote on the decree as a whole, Pope Paul introduced some nineteen changes into the text. (Or should we say, the Secretariat for Unity accepted some nineteen changes in the text proposed by Pope Paul? It is by no means clear which is the correct form of words. That there is a difference is obvious, and one of potentially immense significance.) The story of this intervention by the Holy Father has been recorded in many places, and in not quite consistent versions.[9] It is enough to say here that at the time the incident caused something of a furore amongst bishops, *periti*, observers, and journalists. Father Stransky says, 'No one questioned the right of the Holy Father, as the highest authority within the Council, so to act; but many bishops were perplexed by the procedure.' While this is strictly speaking true, it hardly brings out the impact of the incident or gives adequate reason for the degree of distress that was quite openly expressed on so many sides. Notice that Father Stransky very carefully refers to the Holy Father as 'the highest authority within the Council'. This, one suspects, was just the problem. The Fathers were beginning to feel very collegial, and there were those who felt that the Pope's action was not an exercise of authority *within* the Council but outside it or over against it. Although this was scarcely articulated in so many words one cannot doubt that the degree of frustration and resentment can only be understood along these lines. This becomes all the more clear when one looks carefully at the actual content of these nineteen alterations.[10] With one possible exception (I do not myself believe it is an exception) none of these alterations is of any major theological significance whatever. They do not weaken the text, ecumenically, in

[9] Cf. Stransky, *op. cit.*, pp. 10–12; Rynne, *The Third Session* (London, 1965), pp. 263f.; Leeming, *op. cit.*, pp. 251–4.

[10] Stransky gives and comments on each one as it occurs in the text. Leeming collects them all together, with comment, in an Appendix.

any sense at all. Some of them are merely stylistic. Others usefully add to clarity. The furore is inexplicable if it is thought to have to do with the actual content of these changes. But then, one feels, it was not about content, theology or ecumenical principles. What was resented was simply the fact that the Pope had seen fit to exercise authority in this way by tampering with a text which the Fathers had in principle already approved. It seemed (to some, if by no means to all) an unfortunately uncollegial sort of action. And, even more mysteriously, why should the Pope at this particular moment risk that kind of reaction over a series of minor, inconsequential changes in this decree? We can only guess. The changes themselves are really not worth the time that has already been spent on them.

All of this, however, was at the end of the story, in 1964, before the final text was promulgated. Before we look more closely at some of the features of that text we must retrace our steps and return to the 1963 debate on the earlier version of the *schema*. We cannot deal at any length with that debate, but one feature of it is of particular interest to Anglicans.

We noticed before that in the 1963 *schema*, Chapter 3 was called 'Christians separated from the Catholic Church' and divided into two sections: I The Oriental Churches, II Christian Communities arising after the sixteenth century. It was a somewhat curious, though well-meant chapter. The intention was simply to give some account of the variety of Christian bodies not in communion with Rome. It was natural that, from a Roman standpoint, a fundamental distinction between the Orthodox churches of the East and the reformed churches of the West would be emphasized. But it was widely recognized (not least by some of those who had been responsible for drafting the text) that it was impossible to do justice to the historical and theological subtleties of the present situation. Moreover, an inadequate account—and nothing short of a lengthy volume could begin to be adequate—would be bound to open old wounds and arouse old suspicions. Unless the various churches could find themselves described in this chapter as they saw and understood themselves they might seriously question Rome's intentions and conception of ecumenical dialogue. In other words, the chapter was attempting the impossible. The *schema* had to say something about the different Christian churches, but in the space of a few paragraphs it could not possibly do so without running the risk of giving offence to somebody or other and thereby undermining the whole purpose of the decree.

In this delicate situation the Anglican observers were very much aware of their own responsibilities. The observers from all churches were encouraged by the Secretariat for Unity to express their views on the *schema* (as they were in connexion with all the *schemata* debated by the Council). The Anglicans could scarcely help noticing one feature of this difficult third chapter. It divided all churches into two groups, the Orthodox churches of the East and the churches in the West which 'arose or began in the sixteenth century'. If this division was taken at face value the Anglican Communion, at least according to its own self-understanding, was not included in the *schema* at all. Manifestly it is not one of the Eastern Churches, but neither does it see itself as having begun in the sixteenth century. The claim to continuity with the ancient and undivided Church had always been a central part of Anglican self-understanding. The Anglican observers, therefore, both individually and collectively, could hardly overlook this matter in their discussions with the Secretariat.

As the general debate on the *schema* was to show, it was by no means only the Anglican observers who had noticed this point. In the course of the debate two French Fathers specifically asked for some special mention of the Anglican Communion and its particular place (Bishop Bernadin Collin of Digne and Archbishop Paul Gouyon of Rennes). Others, like Bishop Jean Rupp of Monaco, referred to the need for some explicit attention to Anglican witness and tradition. Bishop Ernest Arthur Greene of Port Elizabeth, South Africa, firmly maintained that the whole question of Anglican orders should be re-examined. The only voice from Britain raised on this question was that of the then Abbot of Downside (Dom—now Bishop—Christopher Butler), and his was an eloquent appeal for the inclusion of some direct appreciation of the honourable traditions of Anglicanism. All of these speeches were made in the very last days of debate, but they were not lost on those who had the task of revising the draft. When the new draft came before the Council in 1964 the Anglican Communion was specifically mentioned, the only non-Roman-Catholic Church to be mentioned by name in the decree.[11]

One ought not to over-emphasize the significance of this whole episode. However interesting to the Anglican observers, it was by no means a major issue in the great 1963 debate on ecumenism. Many more fundamental and far-reaching matters were confronting the Fathers, indeed the whole question of how the Church of Rome could understand and embrace the principles of ecumenism. The story was worth recounting here for two reasons. First, it is a good example (and one among countless others) of how the various parts of the decree took their final shape. Second, it shows the remarkable sensitiveness of the drafting bodies to points made in the debate, and also to the feelings of other churches as expressed by their observers. Anglicans can certainly take it as a gesture of the greatest courtesy and genuine brotherly concern. It was the kind of thing which helped make possible the historic visit of the Archbishop of Canterbury to the Pope in March of 1966 and their decision to initiate official dialogue between the two churches at the highest level.[12]

We must now move from general considerations and background material to the contents of the Decree on Ecumenism finally promulgated by the Pope and Council on 21 November 1964. One thing which is likely to strike the general reader when he looks at the text itself is its brevity. It is only 4,790 words in length. In the paperback edition of all the documents of the Council[13] the whole decree, with copious editorial footnotes, only occupies twenty-five pages, no more comparatively than a chapter or two in a paperback novel or travel book. It could, in other words, be read through in a few minutes. This seeming short-windedness is not to be put down to any desire

---

[11] See Note B at end of this chapter.
[12] See Note C at end of this chapter.
[13] ed. W. M. Abbott (London, 1966). See note 4 above.

on the part of the Council to deal with ecumenism as quickly as possible. Conciliar decrees lose their point and pastoral effectiveness if they expand to the size of theological treatises. Further, no new theological definitions or dogmas are put forth in this decree. It is only properly understood if it is taken as a very general statement by the Roman Catholic Church on the problems of Christian unity, the ways in which that church can engage itself in ecumenical activity, and the ways in which its present self-understanding must set limits to that engagement.

Beyond this there is another limitation to the decree which must be stressed. On any reckoning the Decree on Ecumenism is not one of the most central acts of the Council.[14] It is subsidiary, and subsidiary in particular to the Constitution on the Church (*Lumen Gentium*).[15] Since the conclusion of the Council it has more than once been said that the Constitution on the Church is, even ecumenically, more important than the Decree on Ecumenism. In a sense this is plainly true and no paradox. The introduction to the latter decree says that it will be giving 'guidelines, helps and methods' for Roman Catholic participation in ecumenical activity. But these practical suggestions and aids must have some theological foundation. And such foundation, if it is to be found at all, will be in the doctrine of the church, ecclesiology. This has all along been the Roman Catholic problem about ecumenism. How could Rome take ecumenism into its system, seeming to abandon (or actually abandoning) its theology of the Church—a theology which simplified matters by the handy device of so defining the nature of the Church that only Rome qualified for the title?

How far, then, does this Constitution on the Church (*Lumen Gentium*) provide a theology of the church which can take the strains of ecumenical encounter? That document is dealt with in chapter 3 of this volume and repetition is to be

---

[14] It would be generally agreed that the central decrees of the Council are those on Liturgy, Revelation, The Church, and The Church in the Modern World.

[15] This relationship between the decrees is made explicit in the final paragraph of the Introduction (no. 1) of the Decree on Ecumenism.

avoided, but one or two remarks will raise the appropriate questions. In no. 8 *Lumen Gentium* declares that the unique Church of Christ 'subsists in the Catholic Church, which is governed by the successor of Peter and by the bishops in union with that successor, although many elements of sanctification can be found outside of her visible structure. These elements, however, as gifts properly belonging to the Church of Christ, possess an inner dynamism toward Catholic unity.'[16] Later in no. 15, this theme is amplified. 'The Church recognizes that in many ways she is linked with those who, being baptized, are honoured with the name of Christian, though they do not profess the faith in its entirety or do not preserve unity of communion with the successor of Peter.'[17] The section then goes on to specify some of these links which connect other churches (in one degree or another) with Rome: reverence for Scripture, belief in The Triune God, baptism, recognition and reception of other sacraments, the episcopate, the Eucharist, devotion to the Virgin Mother of God. It continues, 'likewise we can say that in some real way they are joined with us in the Holy Spirit, for to them also He gives His gifts and graces, and is thereby operating among them with His sanctifying power.'[18]

It must be admitted that these passages do not take us very far away from traditional Roman ecclesiology. And by themselves they would hardly constitute any massive theological reorientation providing a new basis and encouragement for ecumenism. The tone is genuinely charitable and ought not to be taken as condescending. (The stilted language suggests condescension, but this is a universal failing in ecclesiastical pronouncements and one has somehow to pretend that it's all in

[16] Abbott, op. cit., p. 23. (The final sentence in this passage is not without disquieting overtones. In criticizing the traditional Roman Catholic view, Magdalen Goffin puts it like this: 'While it should be remembered how much even Christians divided from her in good faith share in the grace-gifts which flow from our redemption, and borne in mind that elements of aids to salvation are found outside the Church, these elements are still "things of the Church", ecclesiastical property, so to speak, which has got into unauthorized hands.' In *The Future of Catholic Christianity*, ed. M. de la Bedoyere (London, 1966), p. 69.)

[17] ibid., pp. 33–34. (Is there then some sense in which it *is* possible to 'profess the faith in its entirety' and yet not be in 'communion with the successor of Peter'?)   [18] ibid., p. 34.

some alien tongue which has to be translated into a living, human language.) But when people speak of the ecumenical importance of *Lumen Gentium* they are not really referring so much to the words in that Constitution on Christians not in communion with Rome. They are thinking more about the general spirit and atmosphere of the document, things which to some extent reveal themselves more in the structure of the document. For a Roman Catholic utterance of this degree of authority it is markedly free from a legalistic, scholastic, triumphalist temper. It is much more pastoral, open, and in that sense ecumenical. One has the sense of doors being opened (e.g. in the discussion of the relation of bishops and Pope) and new developments allowed to begin.

To some this will all seem very vague. It is all very well to talk about tone, atmosphere, and temper. But where precisely are the differences between the old and the new look in Roman ecclesiology? In what way exactly does *Lumen Gentium* provide solid theological underpinning for a decree on ecumenism? These questions are impossible to answer to the satisfaction of the man who will distrust Roman Catholic utterances unless they repudiate their own past and contain unambiguous evidence of conversion to the man's own standpoint. This the documents of the Council do not do. It would of course make our ecumenical life much easier if in describing Council documents we had not so often to fall back on phrases like 'general temper', 'spirit behind the words', and so on. But this is perhaps another of the Council's paradoxes, that in a sense the Council itself moved far beyond the literal contents of any of its promulgated texts, and that by the time they appeared all were seriously out of date as a reflection of the actual state of Roman Catholic thinking and theology. For the time being this is a quite unprovable assertion. We shall have to see whether, now that more doors are open, more people actually pass through them. And it is only in this sense that we can speak of *Lumen Gentium* as possessing great importance in work towards the restoration of Christian unity. We may have a moral certainty that a line of development has begun and is not likely to be deflected, but there is no use asking for compelling evidence of this, chapter and verse, in all the Council's acts. It is either not there at all or is a good deal short of compelling.

It is in the light of this ambiguity between letter and spirit, promise and achievement, hope and fulfilment that we must see the Decree on Ecumenism. It does not make the exegetical job an easy one, but it does at least at times bolster one's confidence when the text itself is not wholly promising.

II

The Introduction begins boldly, 'The restoration of unity among all Christians is one of the principal concerns of the Second Vatican Council.' It then goes on to say that the Christian division so obvious in the world 'openly contradicts the will of Christ, scandalizes the world, and damages that most holy cause, the preaching of the Gospel to every creature.' This is perhaps not a very startling or original beginning. But it does carry with it the implicit admission that the witness of the Roman Catholic Church itself is compromised and hampered by the fact of division. An earlier apologetic impulse might have been to point to division as no more than evidence of the wilful sin of heretics and schismatics. Here at least there is recognition of involvement in the painful cost of division to the whole Christian cause.

Chapter I is called 'Catholic Principles of Ecumenism.' (In the 1963 text the title had run, 'Principles of Catholic Ecumenism'. One need not labour the significance of this change.[19]) It is probably the most important chapter of the decree because it attempts to set out, in the broadest way, the general principles which govern and inform Roman Catholic engagement in work for Christian unity. It breaks new ground because it not only sanctions but encourages Roman Catholic participation in that ecumenical movement which has for so long been a primary concern of other churches.

The chapter begins by declaring that God's will, as expressed in the Incarnation, is to unify the whole human race. Christian unity, in the form of a single reunited Church is not, in other

[19] ibid., p. 343, no. 9.

words, an end in itself. Such unity is, as it were, only a stage on the way towards the unity of all men. In one sense this is an obvious point, but in discussions of unity it has often fallen very much into the background.

It then goes on at once to describe the Eucharist as the sacrament 'by which the unity of the Church is both signified and brought about' and to stress that it is the Holy Spirit who is 'the principle of the Church's unity'. There follows, not unexpectedly, a straightforward statement of the specifically Roman and Petrine claims. 'In order to establish this His Holy Church everywhere in the world till the end of time, Christ entrusted to the College of the Twelve the task of teaching, ruling and sanctifying. Among their number He chose Peter . . . determined that on him he would build His Church . . . and entrusted all His sheep to him to be confirmed in faith and shepherded in perfect unity.' 'It is through the faithful preaching of the Gospel by the Apostles and their successors— the bishops with Peter's successor at their head . . . that Jesus Christ wishes His people to increase, under the action of the Holy Spirit; and he perfects its fellowship in unity.' . . . 'The Church, then, God's only flock, like a standard high lifted for the nations to see it, ministers the Gospel of peace to all mankind. . . .'

Needless to say, biblical references are given throughout this section, and they do no more than reflect or repeat the traditional Roman use of Holy Scripture as a support for the claims about the Petrine primacy, apostolic succession, and the hierarchical nature of teaching authority and pastoral oversight in the Church. No account is taken (and it would have been unrealistic to expect it) of the enormous body of critical and historical biblical scholarship which at least puts a question mark against this kind of use of scriptural texts. Of course a conciliar decree cannot provide a conspectus of the current state of biblical scholarship, but some will no doubt find it disheartening that the very first paragraphs of the decree take so confidently for granted a number of things which, at the level of pure scholarship, are by no means universally accepted. Issues of this kind are bound to play an important part in Anglican–

Roman Catholic dialogue. However strongly Anglicans adhere to the historic episcopate (or even to the symbolic and continuing importance of the place of Peter amongst the Apostles) they would find it very difficult to find adequate scholarly basis for this kind of exegesis.

The next section (no. 3)[20] moves on to the candid statement that 'In this one and only Church of God from its very beginnings there arose certain rifts . . . for which, often enough, men of both sides were to blame.' This reference to mutual responsibility did not appear in the 1963 text, and there can be little doubt that Pope Paul's words at the inauguration service (which we quoted earlier) provided the drafters with every reason for adding it here. But then, having admitted this much, how is one to account for these divisions and provide some theological explanation for them? In a sense this is the fundamental problem of the whole decree, and given the absolute claims made at the beginning it is by no means easy to handle. The decree makes a brave try.

This section (no. 3) is crucial for an understanding of how the try was conceived, as these quotations show. 'One cannot charge with the sin of separation those who at present are born in these [separated] communities and in them are brought up in the faith of Christ, and the Catholic Church accepts them with respect and affection as brothers. For men who believe in Christ and have been properly baptized are brought into certain, though imperfect, communion with the Catholic Church.' We are then told that many obstacles, in doctrine and discipline, still hinder full communion. 'But even in spite of them it remains true that all who have been justified by faith in baptism are incorporated into Christ.' We notice here, and throughout the decree, that the term or concept of church 'membership' is strictly avoided. In one way this is probably an advantage. Theological opinion at the Council was certainly not in a position to give a straightforward answer to the question of who, precisely, is a 'member' of the church. But the

[20] The whole decree is numbered in 24 sections which run continuously through the three chapters. Here reference will be given only to these numbers without added designation of chapter.

emphasis upon baptism and on 'certain, though imperfect, communion' plainly allows for theological development. In fact, one feels, development in one direction or other is not only possible but actually made necessary by the terms used. As they stand they cannot really be defined at all and are therefore unstable.

In line with *Lumen Gentium* the text then mentions several elements and gifts which can be found outside the visible Roman Catholic communion. But it goes even further. 'The brethren divided from us also carry out many liturgical actions of the Christian religion. In ways that vary according to the condition of each church or community, these most certainly can truly engender a life of grace, and, one must say, can aptly give access to the communion of salvation.' This is one of the most startling as well as promising declarations in the decree. It is as though the writers were trying to find some way out of the more rigid categories of liturgical and sacramental 'validity'. If it is true that the 'liturgical actions' of a separated church can *engender* a life of grace (even though technically these have no validity from the Roman standpoint) then some kind of concept of efficacy and value as distinct from technical validity is being hinted at. The language is of course vague and can again only lead to some kind of future theological development. As it stands it is only too delicately and painfully balanced between incompatible notions.

Having gone so far, the final paragraphs in no. 3 quickly reaffirm the Roman claims to uniqueness. The means of salvation found outside the Roman communion 'derive their efficacy from the very fullness of grace and truth entrusted to the Catholic Church.'[21] Furthermore, it is straightforwardly said that 'our separated brethren ... are not blessed with that unity which Jesus Christ wished to bestow on all those to whom He has given new birth into one body ... For it is through Christ's Catholic Church alone, which is the all-embracing means of salvation, that the fullness of the means of salvation can be obtained.' One could say that this section contains in itself all that ambiguity or tension which is characteristic of the decree as a whole.

[21] Cf. the quotation from Mrs. Goffin in note 16 above.

The next section (no. 4) deals with the ecumenical movement throughout Christendom and commends the enterprise of dialogue. It speaks of the need for wider co-operation between churches in the service of man and also envisages common prayer, 'where this is permitted'. It looks forward to a future, obstacles overcome, when 'all Christians will be gathered, in a common celebration of the Eucharist, into the unity of the one and only church, which Christ bestowed on His Church from the beginning. This unity, we believe, subsists[22] in the Catholic Church as something she can never lose, and we hope that it will continue to increase until the end of time.' Once again there is this two-sided approach which requires the balance of a tight-rope performer. The Roman prerogatives are there, but there is something else as well. All Christians, in this vision, will be gathered into the unity of the one and only church. The unity has 'really' been there all the time, a possession of the Roman Catholic Church which indeed she can never lose. And yet, there is expressed the hope that this unity will increase. And if it is possible for something to increase it must be the case that a truly perfect fullness is not there now. This is an enormously subtle and pregnant formulation, and its precise meaning may well already be a matter of controversy within the Church of Rome itself.

We are next told (no doubt to allay the suspicions of some of the Council Fathers) that ecumenical activity is quite distinct from, and not opposed to 'the work of preparing and reconciling those individuals who wish for full Catholic communion', i.e. individual 'conversions'. In the 1963 debate more than one reference was made to this question, and there was worry in the minds of some that a wholehearted ecumenism might undermine an activity which they were not happy to see die. If one has always thought in terms of Rome as the one and only church then the task of gaining individual converts—proselytism in any licit form—will seem fundamental. Practically, this was certainly a disturbing problem for bishops who had never before been confronted with or had to think out the implications of ecumenism. The decree does not really solve their

[22] See Note D at end of this chapter.

problem, but it could help them to see it in a new perspective. From the point of view of other churches the brief statement in this section is quite unexceptionable even if it does not break any new ground. The practical dilemma, in one form or other, remains for everyone.

There are other things in this section of greater significance. There is a strong admonition to Roman Catholics to get on with the work of renewal and purification so that the true radiance of their church may become more perceptible to others. And then there is a reminder of what in Anglican terms would be called the positive value of comprehensiveness. 'While preserving unity in essentials, let everyone in the Church, according to the office entrusted to him, preserve a proper freedom in the various forms of spiritual life and discipline, in the variety of liturgical rites, and even in the theological elaborations of revealed truth. In all things let charity prevail.' It could hardly be better put, even though the delimitation of 'essentials' is (wisely) left undone. (Some privately dreamed of a day when this sentence, as it stands, might be engraved on the walls of offices of officials in the Roman Curia.)

The section and chapter conclude with further words about other Christians and churches, an instruction to be ready to learn from them. 'Whatever is truly Christian is never contrary to what genuinely belongs to the faith; indeed, it can always bring a more perfect realization of the very mystery of Christ and the Church.'

Finally, a remark which while still balanced between incompatibles seems to give a fairly clear indication of how development could go. 'The divisions among Christians prevent the Church from realizing the fullness of catholicity proper to her in those of her sons who, though joined to her by baptism, are yet separated from full communion with her. Furthermore, the Church herself finds it more difficult to express in actual life her full catholicity in all its aspects.' It is but tautology to say that the full realization of [Roman] catholicity is not possible in those separated from Rome. It is a much bolder thing to go on and say that the [Roman] Church herself is hindered in expressing full catholicity by the fact of divisions. This kind of recognition, however carefully worded, is full of implications for the whole theology of the church. Some will be more anxious than others to follow up those implications.

Chapter II is called 'The Practice of Ecumenism' and is meant to indicate at least the first steps in the implementation of the principles outlined in Chapter I. There is, however, a certain amount of overlapping. More general principles are given here, even as practical steps had been commended in the preceding chapter. No. 6 forcefully returns to a theme already introduced, i.e. that the Church is always called 'to that continual reformation of which she always has need . . . Consequently, if . . . there have been deficiencies in moral conduct or in church discipline, or even in the way that church teaching has been formulated—to be carefully distinguished from the deposit of faith itself—these should be set right at the opportune moment and in the proper way.'[23] There is of course no specifying of particular issues where there may have been deficiencies in the formulation of teaching, but the very fact that such a possibility is so squarely allowed for will no doubt have an immensely liberating effect upon many theologians. It may only be the herald of struggles to come—the kind of struggles which Anglicans have been living with since the last century. It will be no easier for Roman Catholics than for any of the rest of us to reach clear-cut distinctions between the true substance and its expression. But it will often be consoling to know that we are all involved in the same exacting business.

The next sections (7–8) return to the need for inward conversion and repeat, almost verbatim, Pope Paul's words asking pardon and promising forgiveness for anything that has been amiss. And just in this context the need for common prayer is underlined so that 'in prayer services "for unity" and during

[23] This is very near a quotation from Pope John's allocution opening the first session of the Council. He said, 'The deposit of faith is one thing, the way that it is presented is another; for the truths preserved in our sacred doctrine can retain the same substance and meaning under different forms of expression.' (Quoted by Stransky, op. cit., p. 60.) This principle was obviously basic to Pope John's sense of how the Council should conceive its task. The widespread bewilderment about the intention of Pope Paul's encyclical on the Eucharist (*Mysterium Fidei*) was its seeming departure from this principle.

ecumenical gatherings, it is allowable, indeed desirable that
Catholics should join in prayer with their separated brethren.'

The further problem of 'worship in common' (*communicatio
in sacris*) poses much greater problems. The main principle
enunciated is that '*communicatio in sacris* is not to be considered as a means to be used indiscriminately for the restoration of unity among Christians.' (Taken at face value this is far
from a categorical prohibition, a point which has so far not
been very widely manifested in practice.) Two considerations
are then adduced to explain this principle. First, common
worship, from one standpoint, ought to be the expression of an
actual unity. Therefore if in particular cases there were
genuine grounds for fearing that a false impression would be
given, such worship should be avoided. Second, from another
standpoint worship in common would simply be a sharing in
means of grace. In such circumstances this kind of worship
could well be commended. It is then left to local episcopal
authority or Bishops' Conferences, unless Rome has made
specific rulings, to take decisions on the permissibility of such
occasions of worship. Here the text really does provide room for
as much liberty as anyone could ask. The only obvious reasons
why permission should be withheld would be in cases where it
led people to believe that full unity had already been achieved.
People so easily misled would be a rare breed. As a matter of
actual fact those Christians, in all churches, who long most for
opportunities of worship in common are precisely those most
acutely conscious that full unity is only too far away. Whether
the bishops, individually or in national conferences, will make
use of the liberty here given remains to be seen.

There follow (9–10) some admirable practical suggestions,
quite as applicable to Anglicans and others as to the Roman
Catholic faithful to whom they are addressed. The aim is to
get to know those from whom we are separated. 'Catholics . . .
need to acquire a more adequate understanding of the respective doctrines of our separated brethren, their history, their
spiritual and liturgical life,[24] their religious psychology and

[24] As a matter of speculation, how (one wonders) could a Roman Catholic
gain a deeper understanding of Anglican liturgical life unless he were permitted

cultural background.' To this end, theological discussions 'on an equal footing' are specially commended. But perhaps even more important for the future is the further recommendation about the teaching of theology and related subjects—not least to seminarians. Theology should be taught, we are told, 'with due regard for the ecumenical point of view ... not polemically, especially with regard to those aspects which concern the relations of separated brethren with the Catholic Church' (no. 10). We all have a very long way to go in this direction. The decree not only gives encouragement to a particular attitude toward the teaching of theology, but it would seem to lead logically to much greater collaboration in theological education, whether at university or seminary and theological college level. Or, at least, it is hard to see (given the sense and spirit of this section of the decree) how Roman Catholic leaders and educators could not positively welcome the prospect of this kind of collaboration and begin now to see that it is effectively put into practice.

The need for non-polemical teaching of theology leads to a connected point in no. 11. 'The manner and order in which Catholic belief is expressed should in no way become an obstacle to dialogue with our brethren. It is, of course, essential that the doctrine be clearly presented in its entirety. Nothing is so foreign to the spirit of ecumenism as a false irenicism ...' Surely both factors in this instruction would be as important to an Anglican. In the 1963 debate there had been a good deal of use of this phrase 'false irenicism', so much so that as a cliché it became something of a joke. It was generally heard on the lips of those for whom ecumenism itself, as a matter of definition, was false irenicism. There are still those who hold this view, and some Anglicans as well as Roman Catholics. But though the cliché has stuck it is possible to wonder whether the phenomenon exists. And if so, where and among whom?

Possibly the most notable part of no. 11 deals with a distinct but connected matter. After speaking of the need for dialogue

to attend Anglican eucharists? Not, of course, as a communicant, but nonetheless to attend them? With this specific recommendation in the decree one may now compare the terms of the Directorium (no. 59), in Appendix II, below.

and for a joint search 'with love for the truth, with charity, and with humility' a rather new principle is set forth. 'When comparing doctrines with one another, they should remember that in Catholic doctrine there exists an order or "hierarchy" of truths, since they vary in their relation to the foundation of the Christian faith.'[25] In itself the notion of a hierarchy of truths is not novel in Roman Catholic theology. But none the less its appearance at this juncture is intriguing. It can be taken in connexion with two themes already brought out in the decree: the admitted need for some kind of comprehensiveness still loyal to 'essentials', and the distinction drawn between the substance and the expression of theological truth. Though plausibly related to these ideas, the concept of an order or hierarchy of truths seems to suggest something more. It needs careful elucidation, but one can imagine it playing a very important part in future dialogue. It may also be symptomatic of a very important process now going on (and still in its early stages) within Roman Catholic thinking. It is not, in other words, a concept which (in this context) would have been very congenial to the post-Tridentine or post-Vatican-I theological mind. It is another example of one of those inconspicuous seeds planted in this document which may never germinate but which under certain conditions might grow to extraordinary proportions, astonishing even those who planted them.

Before leaving this second chapter on 'The Practice of Ecumenism' a further point should be registered. From even this selective account it is plain that this chapter does not take us very far in the direction of practical applications. Principles may be admirable, but they are of necessity stated in such general terms that unwilling or uncomprehending administrators can frustrate their implementation indefinitely. (Or, if you prefer, foolish ones might try to do everything overnight.) During the course of the third Session (1964) of the Council it became known that after the promulgation of the decree a Directorium would be published giving in greater detail the

[25] Stransky (*op. cit.*, p. 64, no. 30) comments: 'This sentence was added as a result of the *modi* [written suggestions from the Fathers]. It may be the most important change made during the fourth [*sic*] session development of the text.'

ground rules for ecumenical activity throughout the world. It was never quite clear what authority this Directorium would possess, but that no doubt would be revealed at its publication. Presumably it would be drawn up in the first instance by the Secretariat for Christian Unity and then be subject to approval by higher (or at least other) authority. Nor was it ever made clear just how precise this compendium of practical rules would be, or whether it would be universally binding, or partially binding, or of only advisory character. (Although in some sense a kind of appendix to the Decree on Ecumenism it could hardly possess the authority of a conciliar decree since it would not be the work of the Council.) That such a Directorium was needed no one would challenge. But it was needed urgently and Part I did not appear until Pentecost 1967. For those authorities not entirely wedded to the principles of ecumenism this delay meant a splendid (but lamentable) reprieve. For until it did appear such authorities were able to continue in a state of ecumenical moratorium, pleading that they lacked proper authorization to do anything. Even now, it is incomplete. Fortunately, however, there are parts of the world where local Roman Catholic authorities have not felt so inhibited and have found quite enough concrete content in the Council's decree to set them to work in earnest. [For a note on the Directorium, see Appendix II, p. 241, below.]

Chapter III is devoted to 'Churches and Ecclesial Communities separated from the Roman Apostolic See.' It should be regarded, as we have suggested before, as a kind of appendix to the main body of the decree. It attempts, in only slender detail, to say something about the origins and characteristics of those churches, Eastern and Western, not in communion with Rome. In the 1963 text the title was 'Christians separated from the Catholic Church'. The alteration was more important and more promising than might at first appear. An earlier Roman Catholic habit had been to speak of 'other Christians' simply as individual baptized people, giving no serious recognition to their claim to be not just individuals but members of churches, or indeed as members of the Church. (In Anglican practice people are not baptized into—or ordained to the sacred ministry of—the *Anglican* Church, but simply in the Church of God.) The original title of this chapter seemed to perpetuate this habitual usage. It was a point which disquieted observers seriously, for implicit in the usage they saw a denial of any truly 'church' character or status to their own communions. (A denial which, to many, was itself implicit in the Roman claim to be the one and only 'Church'.) As the debate progressed it was clear that not a few of the Fathers were themselves aware of this anxiety and sensitivity and would be glad to see a change in the formula. The result is the title as it now stands. The term 'ecclesial community' was not introduced to make an invidious distinction between bodies which (from the Roman standpoint) had a claim to the title church (e.g. the Orthodox Churches) and others with no such claim. The wording of the title and of the chapter itself leaves it an open question as to which Western communions should be called 'churches'. This is perfectly reasonable because there are Western communities (like the Quakers) who do not choose to call themselves a church.

The introduction to this chapter (no. 13) simply records the difference between the 'dissolving of ecclesiastical communion between the Eastern Patriarchates and the Roman See' and those divisions which 'stemmed from the events commonly referred to as the Reformation.' It is in this brief section that the Anglican Communion is said to occupy a special place.[26] The next sections (14–18) deal with 'The special position of the Eastern Churches.' No. 14 recalls the 'brotherly communion' which for so many centuries existed between East and West and urges the need for a deeper study of the subsequent development of the Eastern traditions. We are then given a list of elements, both in doctrine and practice, which Rome and Orthodoxy still share (no. 15). These include a love for the Liturgy, a veneration for the Blessed Virgin Mary, and the offering of homage to the saints. It then declares, 'these churches, although separated from us, yet possess true sacraments, above all—by apostolic succession—the priesthood and the Eucharist, whereby they are still joined to us in closest

[26] Cf. Note B below, for the background and wording.

intimacy. Therefore some worship in common (*communicatio in sacris*), given suitable circumstances and the approval of church authority, is not merely possible but is encouraged.'[27]

The remainder of this part of the chapter reinforces attitudes taken earlier in the decree (now with special reference to the Orthodox) towards the rightfulness of a 'diversity of customs and observances' within a Catholic church. It also allows that there can well be a legitimate variety 'in theological expressions of doctrine' which 'are to be considered often as complementary rather than conflicting.' There is finally an admirable quotation from Acts 15. 28 to underline the principle that in restoring unity one must 'impose no burden beyond what is indispensable'. The tone of the whole discussion is modest and conciliatory and one can but hope that in due time it will provide the basis for substantial approaches by Rome to the Orthodox Churches. A symbolic beginning to this dialogue was undertaken in Pope Paul's meeting with the Ecumenical Patriarch of Constantinople in Jerusalem and in the documents later signed by Pope and Ecumenical Patriarch nullifying their predecessors' sentences of excommunication.

The second part of Chapter III discusses 'The Separated Churches and Ecclesial Communities in the West' (nos. 19–23). We move at once into a rather different theological atmosphere. In dealing with the Orthodox Churches things held in common were stressed and differences remained in the background or were unmentioned. Often it is the same set of features which are mentioned now, but while similarities were emphasized in discussing the Eastern Churches, it is the differences which receive more attention when the decree turns towards the West. There is no lessening of the spirit of charity, but the complexity of the situation in the West obviously set

[27] In this connexion close attention should be given to another act of the Council, the Decree on Eastern Catholic Churches (*Orientalium Ecclesiarum*). As the title indicates, this decree is specifically addressed to the so-called Uniate Churches of the East (those in communion with Rome) rather than to those more generally known simply as Eastern Orthodox. But the question of *communicatio in sacris* receives special attention. The translation provided by Abbott (op. cit.) is followed by an interesting comment from an Orthodox theologian, Fr. Alexander Schmemann.

special problems. The variety in doctrine and practice which abounds in Western non-Roman-Catholic Churches made it impossible to deal with them in the simple way that was possible for a statement about the Orthodox Churches. Of course there are ties, as no. 19 admits, which naturally proceed from the many centuries of relationship before the divisions took place. But 'there are very weighty differences not only of an historical, sociological, psychological and cultural character, but especially in the interpretation of revealed truth.' 'We are indeed aware that there exist considerable differences from the doctrines of the Catholic Church even concerning Christ the Word of God made flesh and the work of redemption, and thus concerning the mystery and ministry of the church and the role of Mary in the work of salvation' (no. 20).

This is all perfectly fair, as those with any experience of ecumenical discussions will know. Perhaps it could be said that sociological, psychological, and cultural factors are not really greater here than they are in the East-West division. In fact, it is really the other way around. To fabricate an example, American Roman Catholic and (say) Presbyterian theologians speak the same language in a way that they do not speak the same language with theologians from the Eastern Patriarchates. There is considerable lack of realism, not least among Anglicans, on this matter. Despite all our affection for Orthodox traditions, the Anglican tradition belongs to the Latin West. Not only in terminology but in our whole way of thinking we are in this sense much nearer Rome than to Constantinople. It is a kind of romantic illusion to think otherwise. No doubt in the quest for unity both Rome and Canterbury will have to take the Eastern tradition much more seriously, and this will help to draw us together. But our starting place is Western, and this means Latin. Perhaps it would be realistic for Rome too, despite all the elements she shares with the East at one level, to recognize that she is in many ways nearer the so-called reformed churches. Even where there is disagreement it is disagreement in the same language.

The following sections deal circumspectly with things held in common, for example reverence for Holy Scripture (even

though there are differences in interpretation and in the understanding of the relationship of Scripture and Church).[28] Baptism, though constituting a bond, 'is only a beginning, a
point of departure, for it is wholly directed toward the acquiring
of fullness of life in Christ . . . toward a complete profession of
faith, a complete incorporation into the system of salvation such
as Christ himself willed it to be, and finally, toward a complete
integration into eucharistic communion' (no. 22). In other
words, the separated communities 'lack the fullness of unity
which flows from baptism' and 'have not preserved the proper
reality of the eucharistic mystery in its fullness, especially because of the absence of the sacrament of Orders . . .' The best
that can be said about these defective eucharistic celebrations
is that they in some way have to do with 'life in communion
with Christ'. The drafters of these paragraphs were obviously
faced with an insuperable problem: to find words which
would state the received Roman Catholic position without
giving offence to other churches. That they could not succeed
was, as it were, built into their problem. It is at this point that
a great many Anglicans will feel the greatest difficulty in the
whole decree. For they know that so long as Leo XIII's *Apostolicae Curae* remains in force, Roman Catholics must hold
Anglican orders to be null and void and Anglican eucharistic
celebrations to be no true eucharists at all. Anglicans totally
reject these judgements, but both theologically and historically
it would be absurd to pretend that they have not created enormous psychological barriers. The problem of Anglican orders
is, properly speaking, not an Anglican problem at all but only a
Roman one. The kind of theology which lay behind *Apostolicae Curae* (it appeared in 1897) is now much less fashionable in
Roman Catholic circles, but it has left its mark and the vestiges
are there to be seen in this section of the decree. The most
promising thing here (little comfort though it will give to some)
is the definite statement that 'the doctrine about the Lord's
Supper, about the other sacraments, worship, and ministry in

---

[28] It is in this section (no. 21) that the most widely publicized addition
by Pope Paul to the final text occurs. We do not feel that it merits yet more attention here, and a full and fair account can be found in Stransky, op. cit., p. 79.

the Church, should form subjects of dialogue.' In Anglican-Roman-Catholic dialogue there is no doubt that they will.

The next paragraphs allude to positive virtues like devotional practices and practical work for social and educational causes. Problems about the moral application of the gospel are therefore proposed as subjects for dialogue, for 'in moral matters there are many Christians who do not always understand the Gospel in the same way as Catholics, and do not admit the same solutions for the more difficult problems of modern society . . .' (no. 23). Some might think this a quite extraordinarily mild and irenic statement. It is arguable that some of the most intractable issues which divide Rome from other churches are moral ones.

Chapter III, and therefore the decree as a whole, ends with an appropriate call for faithfulness and obedience to God's will. 'This Council . . . realizes that . . . the reconciliation of all Christians in the unity of the one and only Church of Christ transcends human powers and gifts. It therefore places its hope entirely in the prayer of Christ for the Church, in the love of the Father for us, and in the power of the Holy Spirit.' (no. 24).

III

There are two very general types of questions which might be asked about this decree as a whole. The first would be questions of characterization and assessment. How is one best to describe, understand, and evaluate this act of the Council? In the preceding summary and analysis we have already found ourselves touching these questions at several points, but there may still be place for a more general comment. The second type of question would be more interested in predictions of the future. Where will this decree actually take us in the restoration of Christian unity? How and how far will it be implemented? These are questions for a prophet, but perhaps some possibilities suggest themselves more strongly than others.

More than once in the foregoing pages we have claimed that the document is marked by tensions, ambiguities, ambivalences. As a product of the religious history of our time this adds to its fascination but at times makes it all but impossible to say precisely what it means or how it will be interpreted in thirty days or thirty years. The ambivalences cluster round the fact that the decree set out to do something which it was impossible for Roman Catholic theology to do, given its actual resources and state of development in the 1960s. The church which has claimed uniqueness and indefectibility in the way Rome has traditionally done so cannot suddenly embrace other churches or engage in genuine dialogue simply, as it were, by changing gear on the same old machine. So much that seems equivocation is simply the outcome of this effort to make a certain theological apparatus do things for which it was never designed and which in the end only strains it to the breaking point. The illustrations are obvious. The problem of who is a 'member' of the church cannot be satisfactorily handled—and must therefore be avoided—if one's traditional theology leads in one direction whereas present insight and desire lead in the opposite direction. In the years 1962–5 Roman Catholicism did not possess the theological apparatus to do consistent justice to the insight and inspiration of a John XXIII, or even the sentiments of his bishops.

This may seem an oversimplification—and of course it is—but it does provide some kind of key to the paradoxes and enigmas of this decree and the whole Council. Why should there be such cloudiness about whether baptism truly makes one a member of *the* church? What exactly does it mean to be in a 'certain, but imperfect, communion' with the church? In what sense can technically invalid liturgical actions in any way engender a life of grace? How can those totally deprived of valid sacraments in any way participate in the gifts which Christ promised? The juridical mind of Rome, though much challenged and chastened by the Council, is not something which can be transformed in four years. This mind has for centuries used a theology which not only suited its purposes but raised those purposes to the status of immutable truth. A good many Roman Catholic theologians now not only admit but rejoice in the fact that this theology (and mind) has had its day and can no longer truly express the richness of Catholic thought and faith. But it is one thing to recognize that a particular theological mode is no longer adequate, and quite another to replace it overnight by some different mode or modes. This Decree on Ecumenism is a perfect example of the transitional character of present Roman Catholic theology and mentality. Over and over again the juridical hand still asserts itself (as though to remind us that no successor has supplanted it) even when the overall intention and spirit of the decree cries aloud for a very different handling.

In terms of structure this battle of mind is especially obvious when the decree attempts description and evaluation of other Christian communions. The standard of measurement is almost wholly quantitative. It is as though one could give numerical marks to the various churches out of the 100 per cent. possessed by Rome alone. So many marks for communion with the Holy See (this is where the handicap begins); so many for valid sacraments deriving from valid orders; so many for devotion to Our Lady and the Saints; and then finally (where everybody can collect a few marks), so many for things like reverence for the Bible and Christian behaviour in the world. Measured like this Rome wins the race (although, ironically, by a margin of points rather than absolutely). The Orthodox come second (if a poor second because of their initial handicap on the Roman primacy), and then come all the rest without too many points between them. Anglicans may have a slight edge because they at least believe they have preserved certain 'catholic structures' even though Rome has elsewhere pronounced that belief erroneous. All of this, of course, is caricature, utterly foreign to what we believe to be the fundamental spirit of the decree. But then the quantitative (or quasi-quantitative) valuations which so often obtrude themselves invite this kind of caricature.

For our own part we believe that this aspect of the decree is of only secondary importance—the vestiges of that juridical mind which no longer faithfully serves the church it so long dominated. The primary importance of the decree lies in its many moments of warmth, charity, and longing for a restoration of unity in truth. That charity and longing cannot be expressed in the theological language and apparatus which dictate much of the structure of this decree. One could give numerous examples of words and concepts which, in the true spirit of the decree, now call for re-examination and re-statement in a theological language consonant with present Roman Catholic insight. What, for example, about the notion of 'validity' in relation to the sacraments of Holy Orders and the Eucharist? What about the notions of 'defective' or 'imperfect' states of communion with (or within) the Church? What about the full implications of baptism as the sign of 'membership' in the one, holy, catholic and apostolic Church? What about the use of Scripture (or scriptural texts) as unexamined proof for points at issue, without regard to the whole corpus of biblical scholarship?

These are only random examples and even in themselves provide material for essays far beyond the scope and purpose of this book. It is not for an Anglican to prescribe or even suggest the future course of development in Roman Catholic theology. But there are passages in the Decree on Ecumenism which not only suggest but necessitate a development in Roman Catholic thinking. Necessitate, that is, from the point of view of the integrity and vitality of that thinking. This decree alone provides the impetus for wide-ranging developments. Developments there must be, but their direction cannot be charted as easily as their necessity.

This brings us to the point where prophecy must take over from description and analysis. How will the decree be implemented and what difference will it make to local situations? No one can say. Some Roman Catholic authorities will move quickly; others slowly. Much will depend upon the completion and full study of the Directorium mentioned above. Some bishops and episcopal conferences will need no prodding from any Directorium; others will hesitate until they are sure that they are truly and firmly directed to say Yes to this and No to that. This feature in the situation will be disconcerting to many Anglicans. They have been long accustomed to think (wrongly) that the Roman Catholic Church speaks identically everywhere on all matters. The debates in the Council proved otherwise, but it will take some time before Anglicans re-adjust their thinking to that Roman comprehensiveness which is a true glory of any church called Catholic. This is an impatient age, and Christians are now everywhere displaying their impatience by manifestations of discontent with those divisions which were not of their doing and contradict their deepest feelings. For them—Roman Catholic, Anglican, or whatever—it is not enough to point out that academic theology lags far behind not only their own feelings but also those of many who are charged with their pastoral oversight. Rome, Constantinople, Canterbury, and Geneva cannot be forced or rushed by feelings and impatience of their faithful adherents. Theological questions matter, not because they give jobs to theologians but because they are at once the symbols and symptoms of divergencies which must in some way be resolved before we can give to God that united praise, sacrifice, and thanksgiving which He wills us to give in the one body of His Son.

Finally, the most important point of all. This book is a volume of essays by Anglicans and is in the first instance directed to an Anglican public. Much has been said here in criticism of the Vatican Council's Decree on Ecumenism. In particular (in the later pages) much point has been made of the conflict between the old theology and a new theology which is struggling for acceptance. It is still impossible to define old and new with any kind of precision, simply because there is no hard and fast distinction. The one grows into the other as the child grows into the man. Christian theology is not static. It has advances and reverses even as every Christian man knows ups and downs in his own spiritual life. We have contended that Roman Catholic thought and theology have reached a crucial point in this decree. They have. What still remains to be seen is how future developments will confirm or negate our analysis. It could go either way. We can imagine a development which would call old categories of thought into question. We can also imagine a retrenchment of thought. The decree itself is patient of at least these two interpretations. Whatever an Anglican observer might wish to say about his own impressions, the future remains open. But it is open too in other churches.

Anglicans are no less wedded to certain words and concepts than are Roman Catholics, and they are in no less need of a theological *aggiornamento*. Perhaps, despite all differences, Anglicans need exhortation even more than Roman Catholics. Anglican immobilism and triumphalism are no less a hindrance to final unity than Roman Catholic counterparts. Like the Roman Catholic Church, we have no theological apparatus at hand to help us overcome the difficulties. We are equally imprisoned in our categories of thought. The challenge to dialogue can generate fear on both sides, but it can also generate hope. There is now no Christian communion in the world which has a theological language adequate to express a true *consensus fidelium* on the urgency of recovering unity. Anglicans and Roman Catholics have much in common, not only in the theological languages they speak but also in the theological modes which they could now—without sacrifice to truth—develop together. The future lies in that dialogue where each not only learns from the other but also learns how he can develop in concert with the other a new theological idiom in which to speak truly of those things which he treasures most. For Rome, unity will be best served by that internal cleansing and renewal which the decree commands. This is no less true for the Anglican churches. In our common task of renewing and cleansing we shall find not only our true selves but also the basis of our unity. That unity for which our Lord prayed was in itself a simple thing. In these distracted and historically burdened days it will take even more than our present common resources to rediscover that simplicity. But the spirit of the decree makes clear our common intention. Whatever the difficulties we cannot rest until we find again that unity and communion which God in Christ willed for his Church.

NOTES TO CHAPTER 5

Note A (page 116). *The Genesis of the Decree: Translations*

A condensed but faithful account will be found in Fr. Bernard Leeming's book, *The Vatican Council and Christian Unity* (London 1966), pp. 19–30. Fr. Leeming's book, although written very near the events, is in general a masterful account of the background and contents of the Decree on Ecumenism. It is also written from the standpoint of one who has personal knowledge and understanding of the Anglican position. A further (and in many ways similar) account of the history of the text can be found in Fr. T. Stransky's edition of *The Decree on Ecumenism* (Paulist Press, Glen Rock, New Jersey 1965.) Fr. Stransky is a member of the staff of the Vatican Secretariat for Promoting Christian Unity and therefore has the closest possible knowledge of the complicated history of the text. Additional information from this source can be found in an interview with Fr. Stransky published in *The Clergy Review* of January, 1966. It contains information not otherwise easily available in English.

Concerning English translations of the final text it must be emphasized that there is no official English translation. The only official text is the one in Latin promulgated by the Pope and the Bishops on 21 November 1964. A number of English translations are in circulation. The one in the Paulist Press edition mentioned above is probably the most useful. It was the work of Fr. Stransky and Fr. J. Long, both members of the Secretariat, and was originally published by the Vatican Polyglot Press. It is also the basis of the translation to be found in *The Documents of Vatican II*, ed. Walter M. Abbott, S.J., (London, 1966.) At many points Fr. Leeming's own translation (in the book mentioned above) is particularly helpful and will commend itself to those who have a strong sense of the differences between British and American usage of the English language. For the sake of uniformity, quotations in this chapter are from the Stransky-Long translation. At the same time it should be urged that anyone with a keen interest in the decree should go to the official Latin text before making any judgments on the basis of unofficial translations or paraphrases.

Note B (page 122). *The Anglican Communion*

In the penultimate version the reference was as follows: 'Among these [Churches and Communities separated from Rome in the sixteenth century], in which Catholic traditions and structures continue to subsist in part, the most outstanding is the Anglican Communion.' ('Inter eas, in quibus traditiones et structurae catholicae ex parte subsistere pergunt praeeminet Communio anglicana.') In the final text this was changed to read, 'Among these ... the Anglican Communion occupies a special place.' '... locum specialem tenet Communio anglicana.') It was understood that this alteration (which does not really affect the intended substance of the comment) was made to avoid giving any possible offence to the Old Catholic Churches. This was not an unreal issue. The 1963 text, in speaking of the separated churches of West, contained a statement which was generally assumed to refer to the Old Catholics. It read, '... yet one must not forget that even in parts of the West there are Communities that also rejoice in the means of salvation deriving from a valid priesthood.' ('... immo obliviscendum non est, in Occidentis quoque regionibus adesse Communitates quae etiam mediis salutis, e sacerdotio valido promanantibus, gaudent.') This statement (not in any case of markedly ecumenical tone) dropped out entirely in the 1964 revision. It could be said that the new reference to the Anglican Communion took its place.

Note C (page 122). *Dialogue*

This dialogue was begun by a Joint Theological Commission, appointed to prepare the way for dialogue, which met at Gazzada in Northern Italy from 9 to 13 December, 1966. At the conclusion of this meeting, the Commission began its statement to the Press with these words: 'After four hundred years of separation between the Roman Catholic Church and the Anglican Church, the official representatives of the two Churches have taken the first steps towards the restoration of unity.'

Note D (page 130): ' ... *subsists in*'

Some have made much of this use of the phrase 'subsists in', in place of a simple equation of the Church of God with the Church of Rome. (cf. the similar passage in *Lumen Gentium*, n. 15 above). It may be behind the remark (attributed to Professor Hans Küng) that the most important achievement of the Council was an allowance of some distinction between the Church of God and the visible Roman Catholic Church. I think it would be rash to make too much of the use of a single word. What we find unacceptable as scriptural exegesis can be just as dangerous in the exegesis of conciliar documents. At the same time there must have been some reason for using this word, and we are none the sorrier if it is patient of more than one interpretation.

6 The Liturgy

MASSEY H. SHEPHERD Jr.

Professor of Liturgics, The Church
Divinity School of the Pacific, Berkeley, Cal.

The *Constitution on the Sacred Liturgy* was the first of the several documents (*schemata*) considered by the Council to be debated, amended, approved, promulgated, and implemented by concrete reforms.[1] It therefore established a pattern for the entire work of the Council, and a promise of things to come. Now that the Council's labours are ended, optimists and pessimists may formulate their respective prophecies, whether the enormous effort and expense of the Council were fruitful or wasted. We who belong to the Anglican Communion, with our well-known attachment to liturgical worship, should be counted with the optimists. We may agree with a Protestant commentator that 'it is no exaggeration to say that if the Council had produced nothing else, the *Constitution on the Sacred Liturgy*, promulgated on 4 December 1963, would have made it all worthwhile. This document is ... one of the finest achievements in the long history of Church councils, and ... ranks as the most significant statement the Roman Church has made since the Council of Trent.'[2]

The Constitution consists of a Preamble and seven chapters, divided into 130 sections. The first chapter—about one-third of the entire text—opens with a magisterial synopsis of the wondrous works of God for our salvation, which are celebrated and made present to us by grace in the liturgy, largely documented by salient citations from the Scriptures and from the

[1] For texts, translations, and commentaries on the Constitution, see the appended Bibliography.

[2] Lewis A. Briner, 'A Protestant Looks at the New Constitution on the Sacred Liturgy', *Yearbook of Liturgical Studies 5* (1964), 7–8. The Yearbook, edited by John H. Miller, C.S.C., and now published by The Liturgical Press, Collegeville, Minn., gives full coverage of articles and books on the Council's work on the liturgy.

liturgy itself. It then proceeds to outline basic principles and norms for the promotion of liturgical renewal in seminaries, dioceses, and parishes, with guide-lines for specific revisions and reforms. Succeeding chapters take up *seriatim* the principal parts of the liturgy, with brief rationale of their meaning and significance, and suggest specific aspects of their present form or observance that need review and alteration: The Eucharist; The Other Sacraments and the Sacramentals; The Divine Office; The Liturgical Year; Sacred Music; and Sacred Art and Furnishings.

A brief chronological summary of the progress of the Constitution in the Council may be useful:

1. Following the organization of the Council and establishment of its procedural policies, the *schema* on the Liturgy was debated from 22 October to 13 November 1962, and approved in principle, subject to amendments by the Liturgy Commission of the Council, by a vote of 2,162 to 46, with 7 abstentions.[3]

2. Before the end of the first session, some 28 amendments to the Preamble and Chapter I were voted, and ratified on 7 December by 1,922 to 11, with 5 abstentions.

3. At the second session, 1963, amendments were approved for Chapters II–VII; and the entire Constitution was ratified by vote of 2,147 to 4 and promulgated by Pope Paul VI at the final congregation on 4 December.

4. On 25 January 1964 (Feast of the Conversion of St. Paul), Pope Paul issued a *Motu proprio* ('Sacram Liturgiam') that directed immediate norms for carrying out certain provisions of the Constitution.

5. Detailed changes and reforms in the liturgy were issued in an *Instruction*, dated 26 September 1964, by joint authority of the Congregation of Rites and the conciliar Commission on the Liturgy, with the approval of the Pope—'to be diligently observed' not later than the First

[3] René Laurentin said of this vote: 'The result surpassed all predictions . . . more than 97 per cent approval. . . . Suddenly, and in striking fashion, we were out of the tunnel. *Conciliar unanimity* had been achieved beyond all expectations.' See 'Vatican II: Report on the First Session', *Cross Currents 13* (1963), 414.

Sunday in Lent, 7 March 1965. Meanwhile other directives have been and are being published, with authority of the several national or regional conferences of Bishops; and more of them are expected in the near future.[4]

It is fair to say that the scope of liturgical re-formation now in progress in the Roman Catholic Church is only comparable to three other revisions of the Latin rite in the history of western Catholicism: (1) The sixth century revisions of Sacramentaries and other liturgical books that culminated in the work of Pope Gregory the Great (590–604); (2) the ninth century Romano-Frankish revisions initiated and sponsored by Charlemagne, under the direction of Alcuin of York; and (3) the reforms inaugurated by Pius V in the *Missal* of 1570, in response to the Reformation and Counter-Reformation movements.[5]

1. *Background of the Constitution*

In his address at the conclusion of the first session of the Council, Pope John remarked that 'it was not by chance that the first *schema* to be considered was on the sacred liturgy, which defines the relationship between man and God.'[6] His reflection was apt, especially in view of his inspiration in calling the Council, and his positive direction of its labours towards a pastoral and missionary orientation. The Constitution itself affirms that 'the liturgy is the summit toward which the activity of the Church is directed; at the same time it is the fount from which all its power flows'(1. 10). Pope John did not wish the Council to argue old doctrines or formulate new ones, but to elucidate the continuing validity of the Church's traditional teaching, 'through the methods of research and the

---

[4] In the United States, the latest collection of approved texts is incorporated in *The Book of Catholic Worship* (Washington: The Liturgical Conference, 1966).

[5] The standard history is J. A. Jungmann, *The Mass of the Roman Rite*, 2 vols. (New York: Benziger Brothers, Inc., London, 1951–55), especially I, 49–167. For a brief, popular account, see Theodor Klauser, *A Brief History of Liturgy* (Collegeville, Minn.: The Liturgical Press, 1953).

[6] Xavier Rynne, *Letters from Vatican City*, Vatican Council II: (First Session): Background and Debates (New York: Farrar, Straus and Co., London, 1963), p. 275.

literary forms of modern thought', for an age of revolutionary change—a time uncertain and insecure about the issues of its technical progress, and tense with the conflicting aims of how to promote peace and happiness among all races and peoples.[7]

Christianity is at once both a religion and a gospel. As religion, its essence is worship; as gospel, its obligation is mission. Worship informs its mission, and fulfills its mission. But mission leads to worship, and mission loses relevance without worship.

How are men to call upon him in whom they have not believed? And how are they to believe in him of whom they have never heard? And how are they to hear without a preacher? And how can men preach unless they are sent? (Rom. 10.14–15; *Constitution* 1.9.)

Both the worship and the mission of the Church, however, are dissipated in effectualness by the disunity of Christians. Hence Pope John summoned the Council not only for an inner pastoral renewal as its proximate goal. Its ultimate hope was nothing less than 'the great mystery of unity, which Jesus Christ invoked with fervent prayer from His heavenly Father on the eve of His sacrifice'—unity among Catholics themselves; unity among separated Christians who serve one common Lord; unity in esteem and respect between Christians and those who follow non-Christian religions; and finally, unity among all men.[8]

The Council responded to the Pope's vision—ambitious, bold, difficult, and adventurous, as it was—in its *Message to the World* (20 October 1962),[9] and in more succinct terms in the Preamble of the *Constitution on the Liturgy*:

This sacred Council has several aims in view: it desires to impart an ever increasing vigor to the Christian life of the faithful; to adapt more suitably to the needs of our own times those institu-

[7] See the address of Pope John at the opening of the Council on 11 October 1962; Rynne, op. cit., pp. 262–72.

[8] ibid., pp. 269-70.

[9] An English translation may be found in Yves Congar, *Report from Rome*, On the First Session of the Vatican Council (The Christian Living Series; London: Geoffrey Chapman, 1963), pp. 106–9. For the background of the Message, see Rynne, op. cit., pp. 88–92.

tions which are subject to change; to foster whatever can promote union among all who believe in Christ; to strengthen whatever can help to call the whole of mankind into the household of the Church.

Time alone will tell us whether the striving after this vision has been fruitful or barren. No one can fault either the Pope or the Council Fathers for engaging themselves to a great endeavour. 'With God all things are possible' (Matt. 19. 26).

There is a logical reason, over and beyond the guidance of Divine Providence, why the liturgy should have been the first order of business of the Council. The Roman Catholic Church does take worship seriously. The canonical regulations for the attendance of the faithful at Mass and the daily recitation of the Divine Office by the clergy and religious—with all the threatened penalties for their neglect—are a marvel to non-Catholics who consider such duties a matter of free choice.

Every Observer at the Council will testify that the daily Mass which opened each congregation of the Council was no mere routine of 'opening exercise' or preliminary devotion. It was part and parcel of the day's business, taking roughly one-fourth or more of the precious time allotted to each day's corporate session of speeches and voting. Yet it always seemed 'meet and right so to do'. The profound sense of prayer that pervaded the whole great nave of St. Peter's was very real indeed. It carried over into the spirit of all that followed. One asks inevitably if the devotions that precede the official meetings of other Christian bodies have the same effect upon their business.

The daily Council Mass was a corporate act, an experience of the Bishops in corporate liturgical participation—at least on the days when the liturgy was celebrated in Latin. Once a week, however, the daily worship was according to one of the Eastern rites; and the Bishops were dependent upon external aids, written or oral, for following them. The point was not missed. As one missionary bishop said to the author of this essay, 'It is good for the Bishops to be forced to participate in a form of worship which they do not understand. It helps them realize the problem of the laity in the Church's worship!'

As matters turned out, there was a good tactical reason for placing the Liturgy *schema* first on the agenda. It raised no doctrinal problem, as for example the *schemata* On Revelation or On the Church. Its issues were very practical, and therefore served admirably as a testing of Pope John's pastoral aims. It is understandable that much of the prolonged debate revolved about the question of the use of the vernacular, concelebration, and communion in both kinds.[10] Such reforms, if carried out, would immediately affect the devotion of every worshipping Catholic, whether priest or layman. They would be indicative of how far-reaching the 'up-dating' desired by the Pope would go.

The discussion served an important subsidiary purpose by allowing the Bishops to test procedural policies and manoeuvres, to sound out one another's points of view and to listen for 'the sense of the meeting'. In so large an assembly, where so few had intimate personal knowledge of one another or any personal experience of precedent to guide them, it was crucial to discover the focus of power that might control the direction of the Council. Pope John at a very early stage made it clear that he had no intention of dictating to the Bishops or of manipulating them. It was then a question of the relative strength of so-called 'conservative' and 'progressive' forces within the Council itself. The overwhelming consensus reached in the vote on the Preamble and First Chapter of the Liturgy *schema* was decisive. Not only were the Bishops in control of their own assembly, but their predominant mood looked to reform. The Liturgy *schema* became a foundation for all that was to follow in successive sessions of the Council.[11]

---

[10] The best account in English of the substance of the debate will be found in Rynne, op. cit., pp. 95–139; see also Laurentin, op. cit., pp. 411–14, 463–64; William J. Wolf, 'Rome and Reunion', *The Episcopalian*, vol. 128, no. 1 (January 1963), pp. 2–6.

[11] The danger of overly hasty predictions is illustrated by the widespread expression of disappointment over the one 'reform' established by the end of the first session—and that not by vote of the Council, but by the Pope's unilateral decision to insert St. Joseph's name in the Canon of the Mass. It seemed a strange way to begin the renewal of the Church. Rynne, op. cit., p. 129, gives a touching story of the reasons that motivated the Pope in this action. Wolf, op. cit., p. 5,

Another reason given for the priority of the Liturgy *schema* in the Council schedule was its more finished state of preparation. The pre-conciliar Commission which had drafted it, and the conciliar Commission which guided its progress and amendment were not dominated by the conservative mentality of the Curia. They included bishops and experts of wide knowledge and experience in the Liturgical Movement, especially in Germany and France. Behind their work was a massive accumulation of suggestions, studies, and experiments, which began in the liturgical principles and innovations of Pius X (1903–14), and which found concrete expression and application in the encyclicals and reforms of Pius XII (1939–58).[12]

In fact, one could make a plausible argument that the liturgical reforms set in motion by the Council were but a catalyst. They would have taken place, without the Council, by a natural process of evolution. Many of the specific recommendations of the Constitution were already in effect in various regions of the Catholic world.

All historians agree that official papal support of liturgical renewal dates from Pius X's *Motu proprio* on Sacred Music, issued 22 November 1903, three months after his elevation to the pontificate. He gave the foundation principle: 'the true Christian spirit' of the faithful is acquired 'from its foremost and indispensable fount, the active participation in the most holy mysteries and in the public and solemn prayer of the Church'. The saintly Pope gave concrete direction to his principle by encouragement of frequent communion within the context of the Mass celebration itself, and by his initiation of revisions of the Breviary looking towards a more effective devotion of the clergy in their daily prayer.[13]

has suggested that it was a tactic to please the 'more conservative forces', so that they might 'find it easier to accept the much more liberal reforms of the liturgy'.

[12] An account of the preparation of the Constitution is given by P. M. Gy, 'Esquisse historique', in the special issue of *La Maison-Dieu*, No. 76 (1963), pp. 7–17, devoted to the Liturgy Constitution. English translation of his essay in *Vatican II: The Liturgy Constitution*, edited by Austin Flannery, 4th ed. (Dublin: Scepter Books, 1965), pp. 11–19.

[13] The texts of papal documents on the liturgy, beginning with Pius X, have

The ideals of Pius X were taken up, first by the Benedictines, then by an increasing number of pastors, in a far-ranging campaign of education and nurture in liturgical principles, which in the course of a generation overcame innumerable obstacles of indifference and misunderstanding, if not at times outright hostility. But Pius XII set a seal on the reformers' efforts, in his two magisterial encyclicals: *Mystici corporis* (1943), on the Church as the Mystical Body of Christ, and *Mediator Dei* (1947), on the Liturgy.

Pius XII was himself an ardent disciple of his papal namesake, whom he canonized in 1953. But his liturgical reforms rested on a foundation that would have scandalized his admired predecessor—namely, the approval of critical investigation and interpretation of the Bible, as outlined in his revolutionary encyclical letter *Divino Afflante Spiritu*, dated 30 September 1943. In this brief document Pius XII simply removed the shackles from Catholic Biblical scholars under which they had laboured since Pius X's condemnation of 'Modernism'.

It is well known that a major influence in the forming of this significant document on Biblical studies was the distinguished German Jesuit, Augustin Bea, at the time head of the Pontifical Biblical Institute in Rome, a close adviser of the Pope and later his confessor. The fame of this great man is now known in all the Churches. Pope John made him a cardinal in 1959 and placed him in charge of the new Secretariat for Promoting Christian Unity created in 1961. As such, Cardinal Bea was official host and guide—and a most gracious one indeed—to all the Observers at the Council.

What specific influence Cardinal Bea may have had in the preparation of the *Constitution on the Sacred Liturgy* cannot as yet be assessed. According to Father Gy, Bea was a principal member of a special commission created by Pope Pius XII in the forties for study of liturgical reform. There is no question of Cardinal Bea's preeminence, among all the 'Eminences' of the Council, in guiding the Fathers to a responsible attitude

been collected by A. Bugnini, *Documenta pontificia ad instaurationem liturgicam spectantia (1903–1953)*, Bibliotheca "Ephemerides Liturgicae" Sectio Practica 6 (Rome: Edizioni liturgiche, 1953).

towards and critical use of the Holy Scriptures in all the conciliar texts. Surely the solid Biblical foundation given to the Liturgy Constitution must owe much to him. As one American archbishop remarked to the present writer, 'God raised up Cardinal Bea in His providence for the work of this Council. His whole life has been a preparation for it.'

The encyclical *Mediator Dei* had a certain ambiguity, which evoked contradictory responses. Yet there can be no question about its basic approval of Liturgical Movement principles; otherwise one cannot explain the Pope's later liturgical reforms. The encyclical did endeavour to put a brake upon certain advanced experiments and ideas which were being promoted, especially in the northern European countries. A good motto for the encyclical would be *Festina lente*, 'Make haste slowly'. But by 1948 the Pope had set up his special commission on liturgical reform to work with the Congregation of Rites. A series of international conferences or study weeks on the subject was launched in 1951—the first one appropriately held at the Abbey of Maria Laach, famed pioneer in liturgical renewal. Distinguished churchmen and scholars from all over the world discussed needed revisions in worship and sent their findings to the Vatican. Pius XII himself received the members of the fifth of these conferences, which was held at Assisi in 1956.[14]

Against all this background one must understand the liturgical revisions of Pius XII's last years: the simplification of rubrics, the relaxation of the Eucharistic fast, the extensive permissions for evening Masses, the approval of vernacular forms in sacraments other than the Eucharist, and above all the reconstruction of the rites of Holy Week. Pope John promulgated other reforms that had been prepared under Pius, such as the instructions on church music and the revisions of the liturgical calendar.

A perceptive Protestant scholar in Italy, Valdo Vinay, has suggested that the Council's Constitution is not so much a ratification of Pius XII's encyclical, as it is a reply to it. This

[14] Of course, many of the cardinals and bishops active in these conferences were leaders in the Council for liturgical reform; and a large number of the non-episcopal participants were accredited *periti* at the Council.

may be an exaggeration. But he is right in insisting on the Biblical emphasis of the Constitution as an advance upon Pius' exposition. He says of the *schema*:

It reveals a notable shift of emphasis in the sense of an evangelical comprehension of worship. It concentrates attention on the presence of the Lord and gives to it rightly the greatest importance, in that worship appears to be essentially a work of the Lord, since in its action the Lord unites to Himself the Church. The Lord speaks by means of the Holy Scriptures. The Lord praises God the Father. The Lord continues and completes the work of salvation by means of the sacraments. The Lord offers Himself in the sacrifice of the Mass, even though by mediation of the priestly minister. In the Encyclical, the subject of liturgical action is always the Church. ... The Church renders worship to God the Father in union with Jesus Christ—not the Lord associating the Church with Himself. ... The *schema* evidently wishes to correct something in the ecclesiology of the Encyclical.[15]

2. *Significance of the Constitution*

All readers of the Constitution, both inside and outside the Church of Rome, will doubtless bring to it varying perspectives and interpretations. Yet all will be impressed by the absence of theological polemic. The text is positive and inclusive, based upon Biblical foundations that all Christians share in common. Anglicans should find little or nothing in the Constitution, so far as theology is concerned, which is unacceptable.[16] Issues so

[15] Valdo Vinay, *Il Concilio Vaticano II in una visuale protestante italiana* (Piccola collana moderna, 6; Torino: Claudiana Editrice, 1964), p. 13. Mr. Vinay's point can be evaluated by comparing the definition of the liturgy in Pius XII's encyclical, and the definition of the Constitution, which definitely depends upon it. *Pius XII:* 'The sacred liturgy comprises the public cult which our Redeemer, the Head of the Church, renders to the heavenly Father, and which also the community of Christian faithful renders to its Creator and through Him to the eternal Father; in short ... it comprises the whole public cult of the mystical Body of Jesus Christ, both in its Head and members' (Sec. 20). *Constitution:* 'The liturgy is ... an exercise of the priestly office of Jesus Christ. ... In the liturgy the whole public worship is performed by the mystical Body of Jesus Christ, that is, by the Head and His members' (1. 7).

[16] The only phrase in the Constitution that is at variance with the theology of the Prayer Book is that concerning the commemoration of martyrs and saints: '... through their merits she [i. e., the Church] pleads for God's favors' (V. 104). No doubt some Anglicans would have no objection to this phrase. Certainly,

hotly debated at the Reformation are not argued. This is not
to say that they are forgotten or ignored. They are simply left
open for constructive dialogue and discussion.

The Real Presence of our Lord in the Eucharistic species is
affirmed (1. 7), but there is no reference to Transubstantiation.
Yet in the same context reference is made to Christ's presence
in Baptism, in the word of Scripture, and in the gathering together of two or three in His Name. The exact nature of the
'sacrifice of the Mass' is never defined (cf. 1. 7; 2. 47). It is
balanced by reference to the Sacrament as a 'banquet' that
gives pledge of our future glory. If it is said that 'the immaculate victim' is offered through the hands of the priest, it is said
in the same sentence that the people also offer with the priest,
and that they should learn to offer themselves through Christ
the Mediator (2. 48). Certainly many Anglicans find this doctrine in their Prayer Book; and if not there, they sing it in their
hymns at Eucharistic and other liturgical assemblies.

The Constitution removes what Pope John once called one
of the 'old quarrels' that has divided Anglicans and Roman
Catholics since the Reformation. There are, to be sure, obstacles other than liturgical worship which have separated us:
theological and institutional differences, not to speak of psychological and cultural variances of temper and behaviour. Yet
we have both set first and foremost always, in the obligation of
Christ's Church, the public and corporate worship of God by
his faithful people. We have both affirmed and experienced
through the liturgy that unity of faith in the bond of peace
which is the peculiar treasure of the Missal and Breviary on
the one hand, and of the Book of Common Prayer on the
other. Now it seems possible to envisage a reconciliation in
worship, which derives not only from a common origin, but
from agreement in basic principles.[17] This common liturgical

the Anglican Churches are in communion with Churches that hold to this
doctrine—namely, the Old Catholics and the Philippine Independent Church.

[17] In an appended note, we give some parallel phrases that illustrate our
common principles, taken from the Preface of the First Prayer Book of 1549
and the Liturgy Constitution. Doubtless many others could be drawn from a
more thorough comparison of the two texts—texts which in no way have any
literary connection.

tradition of Roman Catholics and Anglicans has, of course, always been recognized by all those who have given any attention to the history of worship and comparative liturgics. What is so exciting now is that this community of worship can be more easily grasped by any worshipper in the two respective Communions—not only because of the increasing use of the vernacular in the Roman liturgy, but also by reason of current changes in structure of the rites that are taking place in both traditions. The unitive pattern is becoming more and more evident.

The unitive pattern is not, however, merely one of external liturgical structure. The Constitution provides a substantial theological principle for it: namely, the reference of the whole liturgy to its *fons et origo* ('fount and origin') in the Paschal Mystery. The phrase occurs three times in the opening chapter of the Constitution (1. 5, 6), with an additional citation from the Easter post-communion: 'the paschal sacraments' (1. 10). The chapter on the Eucharist describes the sacrament as 'a Paschal banquet' (2. 47), and in the chapter on the Liturgical Year, Sunday is defined as the day when 'the Church celebrates the Paschal Mystery' (5. 106). The most incisive and comprehensive reference occurs in the chapter on the Sacraments and Sacramentals: 'the stream of divine grace which flows from the Paschal Mystery of the passion, death, and resurrection of Christ, the fount from which all sacraments and sacramentals draw their power' (3. 61).

The term 'mystery' takes us to the heart of the Gospel. It is not a matter of esoteric rites and ceremonies. On the contrary it is 'revelation'—the manifestation of God's plan (hitherto 'secret', to be sure), in the redemptive event of Christ and the opening of the Kingdom of heaven to all believers. It is unfolded in the proclamation of the Word, in the celebration of the Sacraments, in the new communion of saints of all sorts and conditions of men of all times and places. The 'Mystery' is 'hidden' only to the unbelieving world; to the community of the redeemed it is an inexhaustible fount of wisdom and life revealing the consummation of all things in Christ. Gospel, Mystery, Liturgy: the three are inextricably woven together in the indissoluble bond of Christ with His Church, and their union in worship and mission.

The Constitution thus provides in the 'Paschal Mystery' a new principle and concept that opens creative perspectives to theology in all its Biblical, historical, and philosophical inter-relationships. It suggests a new foundation for both the theory and practice of Christian worship—expressed in the familiar phrase *lex orandi lex credendi*[18]—that bypasses and transcends so much of the sterile polemic between Catholics and Protestants concerning the exact number of the Sacraments, the distinction of Sacraments of the Gospel and of the Church, the separation of Word and Sacrament, the contrast of cultic and spiritual worship, or the respective internal and external authority of the liturgy. It gives us a Biblical and dynamic principle, affording flesh and blood to the dry bones and skin of scholastic and abstract arguments.

The adoption of the key phrase 'Paschal Mystery' may be taken also as a seal upon the fruitful insights of the so-called 'Mystery-theology' developed during the past generation, more especially by the Benedictine 'school of Maria Laach' and its outstanding interpreter, the late Dom Odo Casel. This is not to say that the Constitution in any way canonizes any peculiar or specific historical and theological exegesis of this school of thought, which has had such a wide influence throughout the currents of liturgical renewal in all of Christendom. Yet it does point, as Father Louis Bouyer puts it, to the 'freshness' of 'a view of Christianity possessed by the Fathers of the Church, both Greek and Latin, Eastern and Western. It means, once again, that faith is not just an intellectual assent to a series of dogmatic propositions, but the awakening consciousness of a divine and human history, which should become, and may actually become, our own history. It is the sacred history of salvation.'[19]

[18] Cf. the remarks of Pius XII, *Mediator Dei*, 45–47.

[19] *The Liturgy Revived* (University of Notre Dame Press, 1964), pp. 13–14. For English-speaking readers, Dom Casel's work is now available in *The Mystery of Christian Worship and Other Writings*, edited by Burkhard Neunhauser, O.S.B. (Westminster, Maryland: The Newman Press, 1962). The editor's preface provides important bibliographical references to the discussions of Dom Casel's

A principal thrust of the Constitution concerns the restoration of corporate, responsible participation by the entire liturgical assembly, laity as well as clergy. This emphasis is characteristic of the modern liturgical renewal in all the Churches. It is not a peculiar problem of the Roman Catholic Church alone. Clerical domination of worship is all too familiar in all Churches, whether their ministers think of themselves chiefly as priests or as prophets.

The root of the problem lies in our need for a clearer doctrine of the Church, as a community of members one of another in the Mystical Body of Christ, each and every one endowed with *charismata*, gifts of the Spirit, for ministry to and edification of the whole. The liturgy must exhibit this truth if the Church is to manifest its proper character in its mission to the world. All ecumenical discussion of the past generation has come to this focus: our differences stem from our lack of common understanding of the nature of the Church—its divine and human structure, its ministries, its mission, its relation to God's Kingdom and to His world, its authority and its terms of obedience. No ecumenical council of past ages made any definition of the Church—as it did, for example, of the Trinity and the Incarnation. There is no ecumenical theology of the Church.

Despite Pope John and the Council's disclaimer of formulating new doctrines, it was inevitable that Vatican II had to supplement, and if possible complete, the unfinished business of Vatican I, by expounding more fully the relation of the hierarchy, the priesthood, and the laity, to the papal primacy. This task was not, of course, the primary purpose of the Liturgy Constitution. It was spelled out more systematically and

position. Fr. Bouyer has given a more detailed critique in his earlier work, *Liturgical Piety* (University of Notre Dame Press, 1955), pp. 86 ff. It is interesting to note that Pius XII in *Mediator Dei* avoids the phrase 'Paschal Mystery', though he speaks of the 'Paschal solemnities' and in general of the 'mysteries of Jesus Christ' in his exposition of the Christian Year—see sections 149 ff. Note especially 162: 'His bitter sufferings constitute the principal mystery from which our salvation arises ... and it is the very center of divine worship, since the Eucharistic Sacrifice daily represents and renews it, and since all the Sacraments are united in the closest bond of the Cross.'

thoroughly in the Constitution on the Church, and in other documents on the Pastoral Office of Bishops, the Apostolate of the Laity, and the Decree on Ecumenism. But the Liturgy Constitution laid important groundwork, building on the encyclicals of Pius XII on the Church and on the Liturgy. Specifically, the Constitution on the Liturgy underscored three aspects of the Church:

(1) Its visible and invisible, human and divine, temporal and eschatological nature and situation (Preamble 2).
(2) Its corporate priesthood in Christ, which embraces all the baptized (1. 7, 14).
(3) The manifestation of this corporate priesthood in the 'full active participation of all God's holy people in these liturgical celebrations, especially in the same Eucharist, in a single prayer, at one altar, at which there presides the Bishop surrounded by his college of priests and by his ministers' (1. 41).

The Constitution was therefore concerned primarily with a restoration of the principle of 'Order', as this is exhibited in an ideal liturgical assembly. Each Order—Bishop, Priest, Deacon, Layman—has his own ministry and function to perform, according to his spiritual gift and calling, and 'in different ways, according to their differing rank, office, and actual participation' (1. 26). The laity are as responsible as the clergy for the fulfillment of worship. They are not merely passive spectators and recipients of clerical ministrations.

The implication of all this opens far-reaching horizons. It stresses the priestly and pastoral, as over against the purely administrative and juridical, function of the Bishop. It asserts the normative position of Masses celebrated with the people on Sundays and feasts of obligation, as over against the private Mass (which, however, is not ruled out or condemned). It commends 'that more perfect form of participation in the Mass whereby the faithful, after the priest's communion, receive the Lord's Body from the same sacrifice' (2. 55).

Two corollaries are drawn from these principles. One is the direction of decentralization of authority in liturgical matters to national or regional groups of bishops. Its implementation is already at work, especially as regards the use of the vernacular in the liturgy. How far the process may go yet remains to be seen—i.e., the control of the Holy See over local and regional autonomy in liturgical usages. But it is clear that the Roman Church has abandoned the principle of strict uniformity in rite and ceremony and observance—a principle so dear to the sixteenth century, both in the Roman Catholic and the Anglican churches. The principle is acceptance of what is now basic in ecumenical thinking about worship—the quest for unity without uniformity.

Though the regulation of the Constitution is, for the present, an internal matter of discipline within the Roman Catholic Church itself, it does allow for a recognition of the validity of other liturgies than that of the Latin rite—the more so, since the Council affirmed unequivocally the privileges and values of the Eastern rites, and acceptance of 'legitimate variations and adaptations' of worship according to the 'genius and talents of various races and peoples' (Preamble, 3–4; 1. 37–38). Anglicans may hope, on immediate reading of the Constitution, that it might imply a recognition of the Anglican rite as a legitimate tradition, somewhat comparable to the Eastern rites. Such a hope would perhaps be overly optimistic. The Anglican liturgy is a revision and reform of the Latin rite; it is not, as are the Eastern liturgies, an independent development of an ancient, common tradition, stemming from the patristic age.[20]

Yet there is a basis for optimism, if only in the fact that both Roman and Anglican liturgies are once again in a state of flux and experimental innovation. Each is bound to exert influence upon the other—in structure, in language, and in the perspectives of a commonly shared Biblical theology of the 'Paschal Mystery'. The real test will come when the Roman

[20] We do not mean to ignore the influence of ancient Eastern liturgies upon the formulation of the Anglican rite—not only from Archbishop Cranmer's knowledge of them in his work of Prayer Book compilation, but more especially from the studies of the Scottish Non-Jurors. The Liturgy of St. James has profoundly affected the formularies of the Scottish Prayer Book, and from it, those Anglican rites influenced by it, beginning with the American Prayer Book of 1789.

Canon of the Mass is revised and translated into the vernacu-
lars, and then laid alongside the Anglican Prayer Book's
'Prayer of Consecration'.

Another extension of the principle of 'Order' in the Constitution is the promotion of experiment with Concelebration on
occasions when many priests are present, with or without their
Bishop. There are obscurities in the origin and interpretation
of concelebration in the ancient Church. But its custom has
survived in the Eastern Churches, and in an attenuated way
in the Ordination Masses of the Latin Church. During the
Council sessions, a number of concelebrations were held, often
with the Pope as chief celebrant. Detailed norms are again a
matter of experimental regulation. But it is clear that the
ancient practice is being revived, fostered and developed. It
makes sense, if the Eucharist is indeed a Sacrament of unity. It
exalts the 'conventual Mass' as over against a diffusive and
individualistic private celebration where ordained clergy live
in community. It allows clergy to fulfil their ministry whenever
they are present in the liturgical assembly.

Anglicans have done very little experimentation in this
direction. They have tended to follow either the situation obtaining at the Reformation period, or modern Roman practices. Here the Anglican Communion has much to learn from
the reforms of the Constitution. Nothing in Anglican law or
tradition forbids the practice.[21]

Many other concerns of the Liturgy Constitution can be
mentioned only briefly. They will evoke both enthusiastic response from Anglicans, and also, it is hoped, a careful searching by Anglicans of their own traditions. Basic to all of these
concerns is the principle of simplification:

The rites should be distinguished by a noble simplicity; they
should be short, clear, and unencumbered by useless repetitions;

[21] For a good general introduction, with copious bibliography, see Jean
Carroll McGowan, R.S.C.J., *Concelebration, Sign of the Unity of the Church* (Herder
and Herder, 1964); Hendrik Manders, C.SS.R., 'Concelebration', *The Church
and the Liturgy*, Liturgy Vol. 2 (Concilium; Glen Rock, N. J.: Paulist Press, 1965),
pp. 135–51. A history of concelebration in Anglicanism is a *desideratum*; to date
the principal study has been that of Basil Minchin, *Every Man in His Ministry*
(Worship in the Body of Christ; Longmans, Green and Co., 1960).

they should be within the people's powers of comprehension, and normally should not require much explanation (1.34).

No doubt many Anglicans would place first and foremost in this simplification the use of the vernacular (1. 36; 2. 54; 3. 63; 4. 101). They forget that vernacular translation, whether of substance or of style, presents a very different problem from that of the sixteenth century. Archbishop Cranmer, genius that he was, had advantages that modern translators do not have: an English vernacular in a limited geographical area, which had no fixed precedents of liturgical language; an opportunity of moulding religious language in a way that would affect the usage of the vernacular generally; and a situation in which Church and State were closely bound, indeed inseparable. His remarkable achievement is a constant wonder of the English-speaking world. But today it is in fact a museum piece, which for all its clarity and beauty does not reflect the literary or spoken English that is now one of the international languages of mankind.[22] Roman Catholic translators today must work with a very different set of categories—whatever the jarring results may be to Anglican sensibilities, so long attuned to an archaic vernacular, which even Anglicans themselves find increasingly needs interpretation and simplification.

The vernacular is to serve, above all else, as the instrument of communication of the Word of God in the liturgy. The Constitution puts great emphasis here:

more reading from Holy Scripture . . . more varied and suitable . . . the treasures of the Bible are to be opened more lavishly; preaching is to be fulfilled with exactitude and fidelity, . . . from scriptural and liturgical sources . . . a proclamation of God's wonderful works in the history of salvation, the mystery of Christ, . . . it should not be omitted except for a serious reason. (1.35; 2.51–52.)

[22] See the important study of Stella Brook, *The Language of The Book of Common Prayer* (André Deutsch, London, 1965). The Roman Catholic Church has an 'International Committee on English in the Liturgy', under the chairmanship of the Archbishop of St. Andrews and Edinburgh, Scotland, which is at work on common vernacular forms in English, with assistance from English scholars, theologians, translators, and musicians, and advisers from non-Roman Catholic Communions.

There can be no controversy about these directives. The exhortation is to all of us. An important implementation expected soon is a richer and more comprehensive lectionary for the Mass 'in the course of a prescribed number of years' (2. 51). Both Anglicans and Lutherans have been living, with our Roman Catholic brethren, with a lectionary drawn up in the sixth and seventh centuries, which, though modified here and there in detail, has had no major review of its adequacy or coherence. Except for the most important holy days, the Eucharistic lections we have inherited show little if any intelligible rationale, except perhaps to antiquarian researchers.

It is a great boon that the Roman Church now plans to give us a lead in lectionary revision, which we trust will exhibit the best insights of modern Biblical criticism and understanding of the whole 'history of salvation, the mystery of Christ'. Other Churches should certainly welcome a convincing project of this kind, and be ready to join in the use of it. At the same time, the Constitution's recommendation of 'Bible services' (in the same context, 1. 35) should give assurance to the more non-liturgical traditions that freedom in the use of the Word of God is not opposed to regular, prescribed lectionaries which are more comprehensive in scope.

Closely related to these reforms are the striking suggestions in the chapter on the Divine Office. In some ways, this chapter will be the most surprising and the most welcome to Anglicans. For the Constitution looks towards such a restructuring of the Office as we have known in our own Anglican tradition (and for that matter also in the Lutheran); and we can testify to its tremendous impact upon the spirituality of both clergy and laity. The Constitution, in effect, asserts the primary importance of Lauds and Vespers as 'the two hinges on which the Daily Office turns; hence they are to be considered as the chief hours' (4. 89). Much shortening and flexibility is envisioned, especially for clergy not bound to communities that are obliged to the choral office. The Psalter is to be redistributed over a longer period. More Scripture is to be included, with elimination of legendary readings from the lives of the saints. Hymns are to be revised to remove 'whatever smacks of mythology or ill accords with Christian piety' (4. 93). Above all, the laity are to be encouraged to recite the Office 'either with the priests, or among themselves, or even individually' (4. 100). Much of this sounds very similar to Cranmer's Preface to the 1549 Prayer Book! It certainly brings in much closer relation the pattern of the Daily Office in the Roman Communion and in those Churches of the Reformation who preserved and continued its basic treasures.

If Anglicans are tempted to think that the reforms of the Daily Office are merely a 'catching up' to what we have known for several centuries, we should on the other hand note the very important reform in the Liturgical Year—specifically the restoration of Sunday as 'the original feast day' and the directive that 'other celebrations, unless they be truly of greatest importance, shall not have precedence over the Sunday, which is the foundation and kernel of the whole liturgical year'. (5. 106). Actually this reform came into effect before the Council, in the new rubrics and calendar for the Breviary and Missal, promulgated by Pope John XXIII in July 1960—another example of the fruit of long and patient planning for reform in the later years of Pope Pius XII.[23] For Anglicans, this restoration of the true dignity and meaning of Sunday points at the least to a reconsideration of its own calendrical Tables of Precedence in the Prayer Book; for Protestants, it certainly should be provocative of a new look at the corrosive effect of community and secular concerns that have intruded themselves into their Sunday worship. The revival of a theological approach to Sunday is one of the more hopeful ecumenical signs: not only because Sunday observance is one of the few ancient traditions preserved by almost all Christian bodies, but because the new factors of our secular way of living are creating unprecedented problems in maintaining the obligation of Sunday worship.

On the subject of Sacraments, other than the Eucharist, the Constitution is not so radical, though in every case where it calls for change, we can detect a movement in closer har-

---

[23] A convenient English edition is: *Rubrics of the Roman Breviary and Missal* ... Translated from *Acta Apostolicae Sedis*, LII (1960). (Collegeville, Minn.: The Liturgical Press, 1960.)

mony with Anglican perspectives. The document does not enter very much into the thorny and at present debated problem of Christian initiation. It limits itself principally to an appeal for a revised rite of Confirmation that exhibits the 'intimate connection' this sacrament has with Baptism. Unction is no longer merely 'extreme unction'; it is recognized for what it was in the ancient Church—a liturgy for the beginning of sickness, no less than for the end of it. And the burial rites are to receive a new spirit and emphasis by expressing 'more clearly the Paschal character of Christian death'. (See 3. 71, 73, and 81 respectively.)

The final chapters of the Constitution, on music and art, are not a mere appendix, but are integral to the whole programme of renewal. It is worth remembering that official promotion of the Liturgical Movement began with Pius X's *Motu proprio* of 22 November 1903 (the feast of St. Cecilia) 'On Sacred Music'. Pius XI took up the theme again in his Apostolic Constitution, *Divini cultus*, of 20 December 1928. And Pius XII gave repeated exhortations and instructions on the subject: in *Mediator Dei*; in an encyclical *Musicae sacrae disciplina* (25 December 1955); and in what may be considered his final will and testament, the Decree of the Congregation of Rites, dated 3 September 1958, on Sacred Music and the Liturgy.

It is relatively easy to lay down principles of dignity, beauty, integrity, and the fostering of piety in matters of religious and liturgical art. It is another matter to discern philosophical guidelines in aesthetics that can form bases for judgments regarding the appropriateness of specific applications. Individual tastes, emotional reactions, and varieties of experience constantly clash one with another when it comes to acceptance or rejection, as conducive to or repugnant to piety and devotion, in concrete cases of artistic works. Moreover there is a disputed boundary regarding what may be in and of itself religiously effective, and what may be suitable and proper to the setting of the liturgy as a corporate act of many sorts and conditions of faithful people. In no area of Christian devotion is it more difficult to enforce standards of value and of taste.

On the whole, Roman Catholics and Lutherans have been

more adventurous officially, and more experimental unofficially than have Anglicans in this nervously tense area of concern. Of course, many Anglicans have shared fully in the new currents of liturgical art. Individual dioceses, and provincial commissions and departments have given advisory leadership and educational guidance. But at the official, canonical level, Anglican Churches have done little more than produce authorized Hymnals, which generally include approved though not prescribed 'service music'. There is no document to which Anglicans can point as an authoritative statement in the field of liturgical arts. (It would be interesting, though perhaps unfortunate, if the Lambeth Conference were to make the subject part of its agenda.) Many may well consider this lack a blessing, in view of the many pitfalls and dangers inherent in regulating what is after all a very unpredictable gift of the Spirit.

Yet discernment of spirits in the prophetic charisma of art is no less important than in the prophetic charisma of utterance. The communication of the Gospel is by sign as well as by word and deed. In our generation we are more aware than ever of the power of symbol, of visual (as well as auditory) aid, of the depths of response to 'archetypal images'. For many people, whatever their education or sophistication, a picture or a melody is a much more potent communication of meaning than a discourse or instruction. An icon says more about the nature and person of our Lord than a sermon. A musical setting conveys more of the joy and glory of the Eucharist than the verbal formularies of the liturgy. Despite its generalities, the Constitution on the Liturgy should provoke us to a more earnest consideration of the importance of art in the communication of truth and in the stirring of a living faith.

APPENDED NOTE

Preface of 1549 Prayer Book
There was never any thing by the wit of man so well devised, or so sure established, which (in continuance of time) hath not been corrupted: as (among other things) it may plainly appear by the common prayers in the Church . . .

The ancient fathers . . . so ordered the matter, that all the whole Bible (or the greatest part thereof) should be read over once in the year: intending thereby that the clergy . . . be stirred up to godliness themselves, and be more able also to exhort other by wholesome doctrine. . . . And further, that the people . . . should continually profit more and more in the knowledge of God, and be the more inflamed with love of his true religion.

But these many years passed, this godly and decent order of the ancient fathers, hath been so altered, broken, and neglected, by planting in uncertain Stories, Legends, Responds, Verses, vain Repetitions, Commemorations, and Sinodalls, that commonly when any book of the Bible was begun, before three or four Chapters were read out, all the rest were unread.

Constitution on the Liturgy
The liturgy is made up of immutable elements divinely instituted, and of elements subject to change. These not only may but ought to be changed with the passage of time if they have suffered from the intrusion of anything out of harmony with the inner nature of the liturgy or have become unsuited to it. (1.21).

In sacred celebrations there is to be more reading from Holy Scripture, and it is to be more varied and suitable. Because the sermon is part of the liturgical service . . . the ministry of preaching is to be fulfilled with exactitude and fidelity. The sermon, moreover, should draw its content mainly from scriptural and liturgical sources, and its character should be that of a proclamation of God's wonderful works in the history of salvation, the mystery of Christ, ever made present and active within us, especially in the celebration of the liturgy. (1.35.)

Sacred Scripture is of the greatest importance in the celebration of the liturgy. . . . Thus to achieve the restoration, progress, and adaptation of the sacred liturgy, it is essential to promote that warm and living love for Scripture . . . (1.24.) Readings from sacred Scripture shall be arranged so that the riches of God's word may be easily accessible in more abundant measure. Readings excerpted from the works of the fathers, doctors, and ecclesiastical writers shall be better selected. The accounts of martyrdom or the lives of the saints are to accord with the facts of history. (4.92.)

And moreover, whereas Saint Paul would have such language spoken to the people in the Church, as they might understand, and have profit by hearing the same, the service ... (these many years) hath been read in Latin to the people, which they understood not: so that they have heard with their ears only, and their hearts, spirit, and mind, have not been edified thereby.

Both texts and rites should be drawn up so that they express more clearly the holy things which they signify; the Christian people, so far as possible, should be enabled to understand them with ease and to take part in them fully, actively, and as befits a community. (1.21.)

Since the use of the mother tongue, whether in the Mass, the administration of the sacraments, or other parts of the liturgy, frequently may be of great advantage to the people, the limits of its employment may be extended. (1.36.)

And furthermore, notwithstanding that the ancient fathers have divided the Psalms into seven portions ... now of late time, a few of them have been daily said (and oft repeated) and the rest utterly omitted.

So that it may really be possible in practice to observe the course of the Hours ... the Psalms are no longer to be distributed throughout one week, but through some longer period of time. (4.91.)

Moreover the number and hardness of the rules ... , and the manifold changings of the service, was the cause ... that many times, there was more business to find out what should be read, than to read it when it was found out.... It is ... ordained nothing to be read, but the very pure word of God, the Holy Scriptures, or that which is evidently grounded upon the same: and that in such a language and order, as is most easy and plain for the understanding, both of the readers and hearers. It is also more commodious, both for the shortness thereof, and for the plainness of the order, and for that the rules be few and easy.

The rites should be distinguished by a noble simplicity; they should be short, clear, and unencumbered by useless repetitions; they should be within the people's powers of comprehension, and normally should not require much explanation. (1.34.)

BIBLIOGRAPHICAL NOTE

Constitutio de sacra liturgia. 4 December 1963.

A Latin and English edition of the Constitution was published by the Liturgical Press, Collegeville, Minn., 1964. An English version, with discussion outline and bibliography was produced by the National Catholic Welfare Conference, Washington, D.C.; and a Study-Club Edition, with a Commentary by Gerard S. Sloyan, was issued by the Paulist Press, Glen Rock, N.J.

Instructio ad exsecutionem Constitutionis de sacra liturgia recte ordinandam. 26 September 1964.

An English translation was published by the National Catholic Welfare Conference, Washington, D.C.

The following books, articles, and commentaries in English on the Constitution are selected from the larger bibliography of publication:

Bouyer, Louis, *The Liturgy Revived.* A Doctrinal Commentary of the Conciliar Constitution on the Liturgy. University of Notre Dame Press, 1964.

Crichton, J. D., *The Church's Worship.* Considerations on the Liturgical Constitution of the Second Vatican Council. Sheed and Ward, 1964.

Flannery, Austin (ed.), *Vatican II: The Liturgy Constitution.* 4th ed. Dublin: Scepter Books, 1965. (Contains also a translation of the Constitution and Instruction, with a bibliography.)

Franzen, P., 'The Theological Implications of the Discussions of the Liturgy at the Second Vatican Council', *Scottish Journal of Theology* 16 (1963), 1–20.

Lindbeck, George A., 'Liturgical Reform in the Second Vatican Council', *Lutheran World* 10 (1963), 161–71.

McManus, Frederick R., 'The Constitution on Liturgy Commentary', *Worship* 38 (1964), 314–74, 450–96, 515–65.

Moorman, John, 'An Observer Looks at the Schema on the Liturgy', *The Thomist* 27 (1963), 440–50.

Sheppard, Lancelot C., *Blueprint for Worship.* With a Foreword by John B. Mannion. The Newman Press, 1964.

Tierney, Dom Mark, *The Council and the Mass.* Dublin, Clonmore and Reynolds Ltd., 1965.

The Church and the Liturgy. Liturgy Vol. 2. (Concilium Theology in the age of renewal). Glen Rock, Paulist Press, 1965.

*The Commentary on the Constitution and on the Instruction on
the Sacred Liturgy.* Edited by Annibale Bugnini, and Carlo
Braga. Translated by Vincent P. Mallon. New York, Benziger
Brothers, 1965.

The Liturgy of Vatican II. A Symposium, in two volumes. Edited
by William Baraúna. English edition by Jovian Lang. Chicago:
Franciscan Herald Press, 1966.

7 Religious Liberty

WILLIAM J. WOLF

Professor of Theology,
Episcopal Theological School,
Cambridge, Mass.

If the Declaration on Religious Liberty had not been promulgated by the Council or if it had been passed in an unsatisfactory way, the result would have been almost fatal for Pope John's reform and renewal. The liturgical renewal and the deepening of the Roman Catholic Church's theological concept of the Church would have developed on their own, although without as much influence on other Christian Churches as there will now be. The Decree on Ecumenism, however, would have become a dead letter and the Declaration on the Non-Christian Religions an empty statement. In other words, the claim is here being made that the Declaration on Religious Liberty is properly the presupposition to many of the other decrees and to the potential influence of them all. At the same time this claim can be rendered paradoxical by asserting that the Declaration on Religious Liberty has simply brought the Roman Catholic Church to the point reached generations ago by the best secular thought and by most of the other churches. John Cogley, a distinguished Roman Catholic layman, has written: 'On some questions, like religious liberty, the church is merely catching up belatedly with developments that the secular world by and large accepted long ago.'[1]

Not only is the Declaration the presupposition to the new ecumenical orientation of the Roman Catholic Church; it exhibits also the actual reality of ecumenical dialogue in its development more than any other single document. The actual wording of the document in places and many of the changes in the course of its many revisions within the Council owed much to the representations of the Observers in Rome both in their

[1] *New York Times*, 19 October 1965.

discussions with the Secretariat for Promoting Christian Unity and in their individual discussions with the Council Fathers. An even greater ecumenical influence was the work of the World Council of Churches' Secretariat for Religious Liberty headed by Dr. A. F. Carrillo de Albornoz who kept abreast of each stage of revision and offered at all points the experience and point of view of the World Council of Churches in its many studies of and declarations about religious freedom.

The Declaration had greater difficulties than any other document, even including the controversial Declaration on the Jews, in getting through the Council. The sheer drama, not to say at times melodrama, of its passage will attract for generations the studies of the historian. On few other points was the confrontation between the conservatives and the progressives so clear, sharp, and decisive. It has been called by some of the Council Fathers 'the American decree' and the 'vindication of Father Murray'. This is a tremendous oversimplification, but it is true that the American hierarchy made this decree their special interest. For a hierarchy that had been noted before for its docility and passivity towards Rome it brought a startling reversal of role when near the end of the Third Session a petition to the Pope to overrule the questionable ruling of Cardinal Tisserant was spontaneously agitated on the Council floor. It was not, however, 'an American decree' for it was strengthened and supported by progressives especially from French-speaking Catholicism. Father John Courtney Murray did draft a considerable part of the document. It is true that he had been disciplined from Rome for writing throughout a dedicated lifetime on religious liberty in a way that aroused curialist opposition, but the document is by no means his alone. It emerged as a genuine consensus ('Murray Europeanized' as someone put it!) with a tremendous debt on the part of us all to the tireless work of Cardinal Bea and the staff and membership of the Secretariat for Promoting Christian Unity.

The Two Views on Religious Liberty

When the Council met the Roman Catholic Church was already divided by an internal debate on religious liberty. The matter can be somewhat oversimplified by calling the two views the conservative and the progressive. On religious liberty the polarization was somewhat different from the usual positions of 'conservative' and 'progressive'. For example, Cardinal Spellman who had been very 'conservative' on the subjects of the liturgy and ecclesiology was a 'progressive' on religious liberty. The descriptive terms are differently used in different contexts. The confusion is also compounded when it is seen that there were many positions in between the so-called opposites and that the debate prior to the Council was more of an affirmation of positions arising out of quite different premises, questions, and historico-geographical bases rather than one that could presuppose some common affirmations, but difference in conclusions. It would be necessary therefore to secure some agreement on what the issue was really all about; there would have to be some common metaphysical or philosophical shape given to the problem before the distinctive theological insights of the Council could be usefully reconciled.

This lack of agreement on the basic problem itself could be symbolized by three pre-council 'situations':

(1) It was widely believed that Cardinal Ottaviani, the Head of the Holy Office, had been responsible for the restraints placed upon Father Murray.

(2) Cardinal Ottaviani had developed the conservative position of thesis–hypothesis in an address at Rome in 1953 that defended the Spanish conception of the confessional state as the ideal.

(3) It was widely believed that Pope Pius XII's address in 1953 to a convention of Catholic jurists was really a rebuke to Cardinal Ottaviani and a support for religious liberty as a valid principle.

The Conservative view might be summarized as follows. Error has no rights. The Roman Catholic Church alone possesses the truth. Therefore, she demands for herself of the state full religious liberty for her sacred mission. It is the duty of a Catholic state to aid this mission by suppressing other religious groups that disagree with the Catholic Church, for error has not the same rights as truth. The aim of Vatican diplomacy should be to establish this thesis where possible by concordats with Catholic states. The one with Ecuador has often been used as an illustration of the 'ideal'.

The Catholic Apostolic Roman religion shall continue to be the single [*unica*] religion of the Republic of Ecuador, and it shall always be maintained in the possession of all the rights and prerogatives which it ought to enjoy according to the law of God and the dispositions of canon law. In consequence, no other dissident cult and no society condemned by the Church can ever be permitted in Ecuador.[2]

But the idyllic Ecuadors are diminishing in the modern world! Therefore, the conservative had recourse to 'hypotheses' in dealing with situations that fell short of the ideal. The 'hypothesis' constitutes concessions that may have to be made to circumstances. States which already had guarantees of religious liberty might be accepted on grounds of realism. Denial of religious liberty in such a situation might produce public unrest which would be unfortunate. An oath to support such a constitution might be taken in good faith by a Roman Catholic.

Non-Roman Christians in the United States were always disturbed by reading in John Ryan's and Frances Boland's *Catholic Principles of Politics*:

Suppose that the constitutional obstacle to proscription of non-Catholics has been legitimately removed and they themselves have become numerically insignificant: what then would be the proper course of action for a Catholic State? Apparently, the latter State could logically tolerate only such religious activities as were confined to the members of the dissenting group. It could not permit them to carry on general propaganda nor accord their organization certain privileges, etc....

Therefore, we shall continue to profess the true principles of the relations between Church and State, confident that the great majority of our fellow citizens will be sufficiently honorable to respect our devotion to truth, and sufficiently realistic to see that

[2] Concordat with Republic of Ecuador, 26 September 1862.

the danger of religious intolerance toward non-Catholics in the
United States is so improbable and so far in the future that it
should not occupy their time or attention.[3]

It must clearly be stated, however, that the proponents of
the conservative view upheld the traditional Catholic teaching
that there must be no forcing of conscience by persecution or
external pressure. The conservatives, moreover, seemed to have
the Popes of the nineteenth century on their side. Had not,
they asked, Leo XIII condemned 'religious liberty'? Had not
Gregory XVI called it a 'delirium' and Pius IX as 'supremely
fatal for the salvation of souls'? Their catena of papal passages
seemed impregnable. They often taxed their Catholic opponents with near-heresy for teaching on points 'already decided' by the supreme magisterium.

In the light of all this and of the discrimination against
non-Catholics practised in Italy, Spain, and some areas of
Latin America it was difficult for the non-Roman Christian
to realize that there was an alternative position on religious
liberty that was evolving and emerging in the Church. He
could not have had the assurance that it would triumph in the
coming Council, but he hoped it would.

The position of the progressives could be found in writings
by John Courtney Murray, Karl Rahner, Maritain, Léonard,
Hartmann, Pribilla, Journet, and others. It could be seen corporately (although not often theologically articulated) in statements by national hierarchies clearly accepting the particular
position of their country's constitution. In general, this position
could be described as accepting without reservation universal
religious freedom as 'thesis' or as principle. The approach
claimed to be realistic as against the 'abstractionism' and 'juridicalism' of its opponents. It addressed itself to the concrete
historical situation of modern man increasingly conscious of
his right to religious liberty as part of his human dignity and
to the actual facts of constitutional guarantees of freedom. It
had an uphill battle to fight in its exegesis of the nineteenth
century Popes, but took the line that those seeming verbal
denials of religious liberty were really not against the reality as

[3] Ryan and Boland, *Catholic Principles of Politics*, pp. 320–1, edition 1947.

such, but against a religious liberty falsely based on indifferentism or religious relativism. By such exegetical norms as 'a law of continuity' and 'a law of progress' the main emphasis came to rest on the twentieth-century papacy with tremendous help from John XXIII's *Pacem in Terris*.

One of the clearest pre-conciliar statements of this progressive position can be found in Father Augustin Léonard. It is fascinating to see how each of his points would be picked up in the Council Declaration.

Can the state approve the principle of religious freedom in the civil sphere, or does Catholic doctrine compel it, in theory (thesis) if not in practice (hypothesis), to grant the Catholic Church a position of privilege?

The only answer which is fully in keeping with the free nature of faith is the promulgation of religious freedom, not as a lesser evil, to be borne out of unwilling tolerance, or as a relative good as long as we are living in the state of 'hypothesis', but as a principle, permanently and finally established. This principle is not based on a superficial opportunism that seeks to adapt itself to political changes in the modern world, but constitutes an enhancement of the psychological structure of faith, its implanting in the human individual and its freedom, no less than its supernatural transcendency, while in other ages the emphasis had been placed rather on the connection between faith and its object.

Religious freedom, if it is to be effective, should be included in the constitution of states and confirmed by legal statute. . . . Even supposing the faith were to know again a time of triumph, religious freedom would nevertheless continue to be a sacred duty.[4]

The difference between the two views can be described as that between the categorical, abstract, propositional and scholastic type of approach, and the concrete, historically-conscious, and person-centred approach.

The intramural debate between the conservatives and progressives, moreover, was influenced by the world situation with respect to religious freedom. The following factors would be obvious as the Council met to do its work and to resolve the differences on this question:

---

[4] Augustin Léonard, *Tolerance et Communauté Humaine*, pp. 146–7, 1952.

(1) A clear and present danger was manifest in many of the emerging nations. There was a tendency to reject Christian missions as a vestige of colonialism and to build a confessional state emphasizing the national heritage and to exclude others as 'foreign'. This could be seen particularly in many Islamic areas, as for example in the Sudan. Appeal to religious freedom might be called disloyalty to the state.

(2) There was the problem of the Christian Church in Communist countries ranging from imperfect constitutional guarantees and practice in the Soviet Union through confused church-state relationships with Eastern European countries to outright persecution in Communist China.

(3) There was the problem of the freedom of the secularist and atheist to have no religion. If the Roman Catholic Church wanted dialogue here, this question would surely be asked.

(4) There were the differing historical and social experiences of Roman Catholics in different countries. The American hierarchy felt that the vitality of its churches was directly related to the First Amendment to the Constitution that 'Congress shall make no law respecting an establishment of religion, or prohibiting the free exercise thereof.' It felt that the 'separation' of Church and state was 'fortunate'. Elsewhere, especially where the French Revolution had brought a persecuting rationalism, the word 'separation' meant something 'unfortunate'. In Spain, 'religious freedom' expressed the very essence of a hated 'Liberalismo' that would destroy the unity of Church and state.

(5) There was a clear definition of religious liberty in the Universal Declaration of Human Rights of the United Nations. The Commission of the Churches on International Affairs had had considerable influence in bringing the ecumenical wisdom of the churches to bear here in the interests of a less restricted definition than earlier proposed versions. Article 18 read:

Everyone has the right to freedom of thought, conscience and religion: this right includes freedom to change his religion or belief, and freedom, either alone or in community with others and in public or private, to manifest his religion or belief in teaching, practice, worship and observance.

The Evolution of the Declaration and the Conciliar Debate

It was an uphill struggle all the way. There had been no preparation before the Council met of any document on religious liberty, although some seventy *schemata* had been prepared in advance.

The first version of the Declaration on Religious Liberty appeared originally as Chapter V of the Decree on Ecumenism. Printed as a separate booklet, it was distributed to the Fathers very late in the Second Session on 19 November 1963.

The lateness was due chiefly to Cardinals Ottaviani and Michael Browne, the president and first vice-president of the Theological Commission, who were opposed to the progressive text that Cardinal Bea's Secretariat for Promoting Christian Unity had submitted to the Commission in June 1963. The conservatives had prevented the printing of the document. It was widely reported that Cardinal Ottaviani had failed in an effort to influence Pope Paul to have the document deferred. He was directed to have his Theological Commission meet and vote on the document. Some time before this Cardinal Spellman had presented a petition to the Pope from a majority of the American hierarchy requesting consideration of religious liberty in the Second Session.

Cardinal Léger's subcommittee of the Theological Commission had recommended unanimously the release of the document to the Fathers. At the meeting of the Theological Commission itself John Courtney Murray, who had been 'disinvited' to the First Session, was invited to speak. Cardinal Ottaviani after many delaying tactics had to put the matter to a vote. It passed 18 to 5 with one invalid vote.

General discussion of the Decree on Ecumenism with some of the Fathers speaking on Chapter V took place from 19 to 21 November. Bishop de Smedt of Bruges, one of the great orators of the Council, introduced the subject with a masterful interpretation of the nineteenth-century papacy leading up by the law of continuity and the law of progress to *Pacem in Terris* with its 'clearer distinction between errors and the person who errs in good faith. While on the one hand errors must always be rejected, on the other hand the man in error does not cease to be endowed with human nature, nor does he ever lose his dignity as a person, due consideration of which must always be maintained.'[5]

Cardinal Ritter supported the document, Cardinal Bueno y Monreal of Spain made his position utterly clear: 'It should not be forgotten that only the Catholic church has the right and duty to evangelize.'

On 21 November the Moderators announced an immediate vote on the acceptance of Chapters I–III of the Decree on Ecumenism as a basis for discussion. Secretary-General Felici announced a vote on Chapters IV and V within a few days. Actually these chapters never reached a vote in the Second Session. As late as the next to the last day of debate Bishop Helmsing of Kansas City–St. Joseph courageously suggested an immediate vote, but the Moderators did not respond. Over the week-end the American bishops learned that the Pope had decided to postpone a vote. This was confirmed by Cardinal Bea's expression of regret that there had not been time, but his assurance that 'what is put off is not put away' was made more concrete by an invitation to the Fathers to forward their written comments on these chapters to the Secretariat before the middle of February.

Robert McAfee Brown expressed the feeling of many of the Council Fathers and of the Observers when he wrote:

It is true that the majority of the Council fathers wished to adopt a statement affirming religious liberty. But it is also true that they were not permitted to do so. . . . The setback is only a temporary one, but it is disturbing all the same. Believers in religious liberty must see to it that session three does not indulge in further equivocation on this issue, which as Cardinal Ritter so rightly pointed out, is a precondition for any genuine trust in ecumenical life.[6]

In the Third Session of the Council debate on religious liberty began on 23 September following an introduction again by the relator, Bishop de Smedt. He referred to 380 suggestions that had led to a text which he felt was an improvement over

---

[5] *Council Speeches of Vatican II*, edited by Küng, Congar, O'Hanlon, p. 246.
[6] Robert McA. Brown, *Observer in Rome*, pp. 247–8.

the previous one circulated, but not formally debated in Session Two. Cardinal Ruffini presented the old line of approach, fearing religious indifferentism, and urging that the name of the document be changed to 'Religious Tolerance'. A similar basic position was taken by the Spanish Cardinal Quiroga y Palacios of Santiago de Compostela who said the document was apparently designed only for Protestant countries and would be harmful and revolutionary in Spain.

Strong support for the need of a statement came from the American Cardinals Cushing, Meyer, and Ritter. After many interventions the Council agreed to terminate discussion on 25 September. On 28 September there were five more speeches on this subject, each representing according to Council rules the views of at least seventy bishops. Archbishop Heenan of Westminster described the benefits that had come in England since the principle of religious liberty had won acceptance. There was no discrimination against Roman Catholics even if the Church of England was established. Roman Catholics received the same support from the state for education that other Churches did. He warned against possible abuses in too broad recognition of the right of the state to intervene in religious matters for 'the common good'. Bishop Colombo, the Pope's private theologian, was naturally listened to with great interest. 'Unless we have this declaration there can be no dialogue with men of good will.' He said that a general statement would not be enough, that it must be grounded theologically, on a number of points, one of which was man's right to search for truth. Cardinal Montini had emphasized this in his speech near the close of the First Session.

Secretary-General Felici attempted in early October to side-track the normal procedure for developing a document which provided that the commission which had presented it should remain in control of the text until final promulgation. In a letter to Cardinal Bea, sent with the authority of the Cardinal Secretary of State Cicognani but apparently without the knowledge of other members of the Coordinating Commission including the Moderators, Archbishop Felici wrote of the Pope's desire that the text be reworked by a new special mixed commission. Archbishop Felici then appointed in addition to Bishop Colombo three members known to be opposed to the very concept of religious liberty. The subsequent development of what many Council Fathers called by a pun 'the infelicitous plot' is too complicated for analysis here. A letter signed, it is said, by seventeen progressive cardinals was presented to the Pope expressing concern over the move and the threat it posed to Council rules and procedure. It started with the phrase *magno cum dolore* (with great sorrow).

By action of the Pope the Declaration on Religious Liberty remained under the jurisdiction of the Secretariat for Promoting Christian Unity, but with suggestions for improvement from a new mixed commission of twenty members appointed in terms of Article 58 of the rules of conciliar procedure.

On 17 November the newly Revised Text was handed out to the Fathers together with a report of the Secretariat on the observations sent to them. The Secretary-General announced that a vote would be taken on 19 November. On 18 November, however, the Secretary-General towards the end of the session announced that the Council Presidents and Moderators had decided to heed a petition that had been submitted to them by about 200 conservatives asking more time to consider a document which they felt had been so revised as practically to constitute a new text. They would, therefore, on 19 November allow a preliminary vote on whether to proceed at once to the balloting already scheduled.

Late on the morning of the nineteenth when the Council Fathers were beginning to become restless because the vote on religious liberty had not been called, Cardinal Tisserant arose to say that after mature deliberation it seemed to the Presidency Council that business touching on Council procedure could not properly be decided by a vote of the General Congregation and that it had therefore been decided that the Fathers would not vote on the *schema* in that session, but that they might submit written observations before 31 January 1965.

An uproar followed. Bishops swarmed from their places. Two moderators and seven of the ten council presidents left their places to cluster around the confession of St. Peter's. A telephone call from the Pope ordered Secretary-General Felici to the Pope's apartment. Spontaneously a petition was drawn up with signatures finally totalling about 1400.

Your Holiness:

With reverence but urgently, very urgently, most urgently (*instanter, instantius, instantissime*) we request that a vote on the declaration on religious liberty be taken before the end of the session of the Council, lest the confidence of the world, both Christian and non-Christian, be lost.

Cardinals Meyer, Ritter, and Leger carried the petition to His Holiness. The Pope received them kindly, but pointed out that since Cardinal Roberti, the Council's legal expert, had ruled that Cardinal Tisserant's action was within his power the Pope would not interfere. He guaranteed and repeated the promise in his address two days later that the Declaration would be the first order of business at the Fourth Session.

Two hundred and eighteen written interventions were later examined by the Secretariat for Promoting Christian Unity, and after plenary meeting it decided upon the 'Re-revised Text' in March 1965. Then in April members of the Theological Commission contributed seventeen written opinions. The Secretariat further modified its text and on 11 May, the Commission for Coordinating the work of the Council decided to submit the Re-revised Text with its report to the Council Fathers.

Lively debate followed the presentation in September 1965 of the Re-revised Text to the General Congregation. It was clear that the two sides were about as far apart as before. Following five days of debate with sixty-two speeches on the subject the Fathers voted to end debate. The chief speakers against the document were Cardinals Arriba y Castro of Spain, Ruffini of Palermo, Siri of Genoa, and Spanish-born Bishop Velasco of Amoy, China, whose anger was evident as he charged that 'the glorious minority' was being ignored although they were witnessing to Catholic truth on the subject.

Cardinal Arriba y Castro restated the case for the conservatives: 'Only the Catholic Church has the duty and the right to preach the Gospel, and therefore proselytism by non-Catholics among Catholics is illicit and must be obstructed not only by the Church but by civil authority itself to the extent the common good requires it.'

Three tireless opponents of freedom will enter history by their concise formulations:

(1) 'As the truth is one, so also the true religion is one, and to it alone properly belongs the right of liberty.' (Cardinal Ruffini on 15 September.)

(2) 'Truth and falsehood cannot have equal rights. The text proposes solutions which are contrary to the common doctrine of the Church.' (Cardinal Ottaviani on 17 September.)

(3) 'Equal rights cannot be given to all religions. The right to spread false doctrine in Catholic countries cannot be given.' (Cardinal Browne on 20 September.)

The Fathers were warned of grave dangers to come by Bishop Gasbarri: 'The *schema* leaves the door open to liberalism, laicism, indifferentism, existentialism, irenicism, situation ethics . . .'

The chief defenders of the document were Cardinals Cushing, Spellman, Ritter, Shehan of the United States, Cardinals Heenan of Westminster, Conway of Armagh, Frings of Cologne, Alfrink of Utrecht, Urbani of Venice, and Silva Henriquez of Santiago, Chile.

Cardinal Cushing said: 'I have only two things to say about the amended *schema*. First, its doctrine about the right of man to religious liberty is solidly founded and totally Catholic . . . (No shades of subjectiveness or juridic positivism may be found in the *schema*) . . . Secondly, the promulgation of this doctrine is of prime necessity today for the whole world.'

Cardinal Heenan attempted to cut the ground from under the conservatives: 'We must be clear on this: it is completely absurd to say that error has no rights and that only the truth has them. Rights are rooted in persons, not in things.'

Cardinal Silva Henriquez, in his own person a distinguished refutation of the claim that Hispanic cultural orientation was totally against religious liberty, sensed an evangelical power in the Declaration: '[It] introduces a new spirit into the apostolate of the Church in that it reinforces a sensitivity for the

Spirit, liberty and responsibility in whoever preaches the Gospel.'

It has been reported that by a narrow margin it was decided by the appropriate organs of the Council not to ask the Council to vote positively or negatively on the text as a basis for future revision, but to ask a series of questions on the most disputed points as was done on 'collegiality' in *De Ecclesia*. It has been further reported that early on Tuesday morning, 21 September when the voting would take place, Pope Paul after consulting Cardinal Tisserant, Archbishop Felici, and Bishop Colombo ordered instead a general vote with the following special formula:

Do the Fathers judge that the revised text on religious liberty can serve as a basis for a definitive declaration which will be perfected in the light of the Catholic teaching on the true religion and according to observations proposed by Fathers during the discussions and which will be approved later according to the regulations of the Council?

Undoubtedly this special phrasing made it possible for many with reservations to vote affirmatively. The result was a great victory for the progressives. Of the 2,222 voting, 1,997 said Yes; 224 said No, and one vote was null. Pope Paul would now go to the United Nations with a firm conciliar approval in principle of religious liberty.

On 26 October the Council again voted on a new preface to the document proposed to meet the pressure of the conservatives. Just why a reassertion of traditional Roman Catholic doctrine of the 'one true Church' should preface a document on religious liberty remains a debatable issue with Observers predicting that it would seriously limit the ecumenical significance of the statement and many Roman Catholics arguing that the traditional assertion was out of place in this connexion.

On 19 November came the historic and decisive vote with 1,954 in favour and 249 against. This hard core of opposition had actually increased by twenty-five over the earlier draft voted in October and raises in retrospect the value of having tried to reduce opposition by an accommodation. On the other hand, the vote of one against to about eight in favour shows the declaration must be a strong one. It is possible that a few liberals voted negatively. The negative vote is almost identical in number with that cast against the Declaration on the Jews in the context of the Declaration on the Relations of the Church with the Non-Christian Religions.

The course of the debate revealed an interesting fact that should surprise no one. One's theology is partly the expression of his social-historical context. Thus the American hierarchy seemed to many others to be standing for 'the American way of life' rather than theological principle in their practically unanimous support and pressure for the Declaration. The American view itself was ably stated by Cardinal Cushing: 'I am sure that the experience of the Church in the United States is destined in the providence of God to make its contribution in the deliberations of the Second Vatican Council for the best formulation of the Christian principles that should govern the relations between Church and State.'[7]

The bishops in Communist countries were also extremely articulate in their support of the Declaration. For many of them it was a matter of life and death for the Church. Their position of being discriminated against today gave them a commitment to the principle and a sense of penitence for the past. Cardinal Beran of Prague made this clear:

Experience shows that every action undertaken against liberty of conscience is pernicious, morally speaking... Thus, in my country it seems that the Catholic Church is today expiating the defects and the sins committed in her name against religious liberty in past centuries, such as the case of the priest John Huss in the fifteenth century and the forced conversion to Catholicism of a great many of the people in the seventeenth.... Thus even history admonishes us that in this Council the principle of religious liberty and liberty of conscience must be proclaimed very clearly and without any restriction, in a spirit of penitence for the sins of the past.

Most of the bishops in missionary areas favoured the Declaration strongly. Many of them were uncomfortable about state recognition of Roman Catholicism. Bishop Lourdusamy of

[7] *America*, 15 June 1963. Interview by Walter Abbott S.J.

India spoke of this as difficult to understand today and as an 'obstacle to the spread of Catholicism in non-Catholic regions'.

The chief opponents of the Declaration naturally were to be found in Italy, Spain, Portugal, and Latin America with not a few interventions clearly springing from these historical circumstances. Cardinal Arriba y Castro said: 'The Council must be careful not to decree the ruin of Catholicism in countries where it represents the only religion.' Bishop Del Campo spelled it out clearly: 'With the present declaration a centuries-old religious patrimony is endangered.' One of the suspicions aroused by debate is that one's opponents speak not from principle, but from circumstance. Bishop Del Campo said: 'The sociological fact of religious pluralism and the existence of numerous Constitutions which recognize religious liberty are presented as valid arguments, as though sociological data could modify and correct the doctrinal principles of the Church and as though the Council were a juridico-civil organism and existing civil Constitutions could be considered as sources of Catholic doctrine.'

Outline of the Declaration on Religious Liberty

The Right of the Person and of Communities to Social and Civil Freedom in Matters Religious

Introduction:

(1) State of the Problem and the Catholic doctrine of the one true religion

I The General Principles of Religious Liberty
(2) The object and foundation of religious liberty
(3) Religious liberty and man's need of God
(4) The liberty of religious groups
(5) The religious liberty of the family
(6) The protection of religious liberty
(7) The limits of religious liberty
(8) Education for practicing liberty

II Religious Freedom in the Light of Revelation
(9) The doctrine of religious liberty has its roots in revelation
(10) The freedom of the act of faith
(11) Behavior of Christ and the Apostles

(12) The Church follows the steps of Christ and the Apostles
(13) The freedom of the Church
(14) The Task of the Church
(15) Conclusion

Analysis and Comment

1. The basic assertion of the whole declaration and the theme
that keeps recurring in the symphony of its development is that
religious liberty is an expression of the dignity of the human
person.

A sense of the dignity of the human person has been impressing
itself more and more deeply on the consciousness of contemporary
man, and the demand is increasingly made that men should act on
their own judgment, enjoying and making use of a responsible
freedom, not driven by coercion but motivated by a sense of duty.
The demand is likewise made that constitutional limits should be
set to the powers of government, in order that there may be no
encroachment on the religious freedom of the person and of associations.

One would expect that the document which has now given
the concept of religious liberty the meaning of freedom from
coercion would next proceed to elaborate on this theme. Indeed, this was the order of development in an earlier draft. The
final document, however, inserts a section on 'this one true
religion' in 'the Catholic and Apostolic Church' and 'leaves
untouched traditional Catholic doctrine on the moral duty of
men and societies toward the true religion and toward the one
Church of Christ'.

There is a serious question here about the value of this addition. The point is not so much the validity of this traditional
Roman Catholic teaching well known to everyone, but the
question of why it needs insertion here. The declaration is
about the social and civil religious liberty of individuals and
groups. Technically this theological doctrine is 'out of order'
in this connexion. It is an irrelevance since the problem is the
legal question of religious rights. It is a digression that interrupts
the harmony of the document. It certainly weakens the effectiveness of the document for the reader who is not a Roman

Catholic, whether he be a Christian, a Buddhist, an agnostic, or an atheist. Presumably one purpose of the document, as can be gathered from its fine general orientation elsewhere, is to address the outsider. A demand for religious liberty is being made on all states whether they are religious, non-religious, or anti-religious. One ought therefore to employ concepts and formulations that are understandable to all men and all states. This purpose is diminished by claims at this point about one particular religious body and also by the reassertion of just those dogmatic points that have been historically used by the conservatives to deny religious freedom. In situations of saying 'yes, but!' there is danger that the 'but' drowns out the 'yes'. It gives the unfortunate impression that a Roman Catholic is not free to discuss religious liberty as an issue in itself without talking about the one true Church.

It is necessary now to qualify this criticism. Ecumenical statements by the World Council of Churches on religious liberty are not predicated upon indifferentism to truth or on a relativism that puts all religions on the same level theologically. One does not ask the Roman Catholic Church to relativize its position as such but simply to deal with the issue at hand, namely, civil and social religious liberty, which can be discussed apart from the truth-claims of religious groups in pluralistic societies. The document does this when it speaks foundationally of religious liberty as an expression of the dignity of the human person. Perhaps the most charitable way for us to evaluate this insertion is that somehow it was needed for domestic consumption and that it was the means of getting through the Council the great good of the Declaration itself.

There is another important issue connected with this traditional insertion. It is not so 'traditional' after all. The Secretariat has used language that enlarges the scene ecumenically. Nowhere is the exclusive identity of the 'one true religion' with the Roman Catholic Church asserted. 'We believe that this one true religion subsists in the Catholic and Apostolic Church.' The verb 'subsists' leaves open the possibility that the 'one true religion' also subsists in non-Roman-Catholic Churches. In other words, the passage may be interpreted really as making truth-claims primarily for the Christian faith and the Church Universal rather than an exclusive identification of these with the Roman Catholic Church. The conservatives who insisted on this insertion may have been the instrument for eroding their own traditionalism by imparting a new orientation to old phrases.

(2) The second section has an admirably clear description of religious liberty.

This freedom means that all men are to be immune from coercion on the part of individuals or of social groups and of any human power in such wise that no one is to be forced to act in a manner contrary to his own beliefs, whether privately or publicly, whether alone or in association with others, within due limits.

The problem of 'due limits' will be discussed later.

It is asserted that, because religious liberty inheres in the nature of the human person and not in his subjective consciousness, even those who do not satisfy the requirements of seeking truth are not to be molested provided they do not harm the rights of others. This is an important addition. It helps to reassure those who might be worried by possible conclusions drawn from the section on the one true religion. Even the insincere person is not to be coerced; put in another way, governments are incompetent to judge any man's religious sincerity or insincerity. One wishes the document had explicitly stressed the right of disbelief, for surely the general insights adduced as a foundation for religious liberty apply also to the freedom not to believe. So do the specific Christian insights that will later be invoked in the Declaration. It goes without demonstration that a statement affirming the religious right to believe, and to believe even from insincere motives, if universalized by the specific inclusion of the right not to believe, would make for a stronger dialogue with atheists. Since many of the conservatives feared just this point, it is understandable that the document does not specifically affirm the right to hold no religion or to be anti-religious. The point made here, however, is not the expediential one of fostering dialogue, but the moral one that the dimension of universal application to all men is grounded in the very concept itself. The New Delhi

Assembly of the World Council of Churches recognized this point: 'Implicit in this right is the right freely to maintain one's belief or disbelief without external coercion or disability.'

(3) The third section states that God's law is the supreme norm for man and that man recognizes this law through his conscience which he is obliged to follow. Religious freedom includes more, however, than just internal liberty; because man is a social being he must have the right to give social expression to the leading of conscience. Because religious acts 'transcend the earthly and temporal order', civil power exceeds its limits if it offers directions or hindrances in this area. All of this is really a further development of the second section.

(4) There is a very full exposition of the liberty of religious groups. 'The freedom or immunity from coercion in matters religious, which is the endowment of persons as individuals, is also to be recognized as their right when they act in community', because of the social nature of man as well as the social nature of religion itself. The right of worship, association, and public teaching by the spoken and written word must be recognized.

Religious communities also have the right not to be hindered, either by legal measures or by administrative action on the part of government, in the selection, training, appointment, and transferral of their own ministers, in communicating with religious authorities and communities abroad, in erecting buildings for religious purposes and in the acquisition and use of suitable funds or properties.

Reading this, Anglicans may well ask whether the time has come for the provinces of York and Canterbury to request their government to allow them the religious freedom of free elections of their episcopate.

The section closes with a statement of the right of men to hold meetings and to 'establish educational, cultural, charitable, and social organizations.' All of this is, of course, an extremely important issue in Communist countries.

The problem of the censure of 'unworthy' or 'dishonorable' practices by religious bodies in this section will be considered later.

(5) This short paragraph states the religious right of the family unit, particularly the right of parents to determine the kind of religious training to be given their children and the right freely to choose their schools. It will be interesting to see whether there will be future modifications of the present demand that the non-Roman Catholic partner in a mixed marriage give away the right of raising his children in his faith. Present canonical legislation is defective here in due respect for the religious liberty of the non-Roman Catholic partner.

(6) The protection of religious liberty is the responsibility of all citizens, social groups, government, the Church, and other religious communities. Legal recognition is not enough; the practice of the state must also favour religious liberty.

Finally, government is to see to it that the equality of citizens before the law, which is itself an element of the common good, is never violated, whether openly or covertly, for religious reasons. Nor is there to be discrimination among citizens.

This careful description is admirable especially in its shifted and strengthened position from previous texts, for it now follows a section on forms of state recognition of a special religion. The emphasis on non-discrimination is especially vital because of the great dangers usually accompanying religious establishment. There was considerable debate about the propriety of these forms of Constantinianism that survive today and considerable defence of them by many conservatives. The decree takes a middle ground by casting the description in a hypothetical clause.

If, in view of peculiar circumstances obtaining among peoples, special civil recognition is given to one religious community in the constitutional order of society, it is at the same time imperative that the right of all citizens and religious communities to religious freedom should be recognized and made effective in practice.

An interesting argument on behalf of religious liberty is set forth which does not seem to have been made previously in statements of the World Council of Churches. It is that 'society itself may profit by the moral qualities of justice and peace which have their origin in man's faithfulness to God and to His holy will.'

(7) Any discussion of the limits to be placed on the exercise of religious liberty is fraught with difficulty. In ecumenical discussions under the auspices of the World Council of Churches it has often been observed that the representatives of religious minorities in states where some one religious body is overwhelmingly dominant are very reluctant to have the churches even discuss these limitations. They know only too well how readily majority interests in a reactionary situation can use seemingly reasonable statements of limitation as means for persecution or discrimination. Meticulous precision is obviously required in this area.

The decree speaks first of the moral law as a needed guide for both individuals and groups in having due regard for the rights of others and for the welfare of the community. This first section then deals with the responsible exercise of religious liberty, which cannot of course be legislated. The most difficult problem comes with legal limitations:

Furthermore, society has the right to defend itself against possible abuses committed on the pretext of freedom of religion. It is the special duty of government to provide this protection. However, government is not to act in an arbitrary fashion or in an unfair spirit of partisanship. Its action is to be controlled by juridical norms which are in conformity with the objective moral order. These norms arise out of the need for the effective safeguard of the rights of all citizens and for the peaceful settlement of conflicts of rights, also out of the need for an adequate care of genuine public peace, which comes about when men live together in good order and true justice, and finally out of the need for a proper guardianship of public morality.

It can be seen from this quotation and from three other phrases before in the document that 'public order' is the norm for limitation. It must be said at once that this is superior as a phrase to 'the public good or welfare' which grants too much to the supervisory agency of the state. But even 'public order' can become a hole in the dike. The phrase is particularly current in the Anglo-Saxon heritage in which it has generally been used in a reasonable manner. In this context it usually is expressed negatively and more precisely as the duty of the state in religious matters to prevent the actual breakdown of public order rather than to prevent some imagined future impairment. The trouble with 'public order' as a criterion is that it often bears a different context in the dictatorial state or even in some states of Latin culture in which the government paternalistically exceeds its competence in this area by manipulating its people ideologically. The addition of the adjective 'just' ('just demands of public order') in the final version introduced a very helpful restraining influence. This qualification makes the Declaration a more careful document that the July 1965 statement on religious liberty approved by the Executive Committee of the Churches' Commission on International Affairs and 'received' by the Executive Committee of the World Council of Churches. In this document there is no qualifying adjective like 'just' to modify the phrase 'solely in the interest of public order'.

In this connexion there is a very real problem in the English translation of the official Latin text. In general the English text has a lofty diction that is far superior to the rather colourless Latin of the original. The English text endorsed by the National Catholic Welfare Conference of the U.S.A. is widely believed to be, very appropriately, the work of Father John Courtney Murray. The technical problem is found at the beginning of the second paragraph under section four: 'Provided the just demands of public order are observed, religious communities rightly claim freedom . . .' The translator's 'observed' stands for 'not violated' (*non violentur*) in Latin. To paraphrase from the negative to the positive in the verb introduces quite different possibilities and ranges of interpretation. In the hands of an ultra-conservative the English text could be wrenched to give the police authority of a state much more power paternalistically in setting up norms itself and faulting religious groups for not measuring up to them than would be possible under the Latin text which casts the problem in the negative, i.e. 'non-violation' rather than 'observance'. It is to be hoped that the official English version will be changed to read 'provided the just demands of public order are not violated'.

There is an admonition earlier in section four that needs comment here. After developing the right of religious groups to public expression of their faith 'provided the just demands of public order are observed' there follows immediately what might be called a warning about unfair methods of evangelism or proselytism, although this word itself is not used.

However, in spreading religious faith and in introducing religious practices everyone ought at all times to refrain from any manner of action which might seem to carry a hint of coercion or of a kind of persuasion that would be dishonorable or unworthy especially when dealing with poor or uneducated people. Such a manner of action would have to be considered an abuse of one's right and a violation of the right of others.

This is excellent advice and needs to be said, but is there not a danger that a hard-core conservative can find a loophole here? Such a bishop or official of a confessional state might well declare evengelicals guilty in fact of such practice, because of a low level of education among their converts, and as disqualified to continue their activities. The picture of government officials deciding who are and who are not 'rice Christians' is disquieting. One cannot of course provide in advance against every conceivable contingency, but there would seem to be some ground for disquiet here. A suggestion will be made later in the essay directed toward meeting this problem. Archbishop Aramburu of Argentina had a clear perception of the limitations of 'public order' as a norm when he said: 'It could be remembered that Christ himself was condemned as a disturber of the public peace. Taking public order as the ultimate limit to the exercise of religious liberty, the elimination of racial discrimination could also be presented as something which disturbs peace.'

(8) In this short section there is a special appeal to educators to do all they can 'to form men who, on the one hand, will respect the moral order and will be obedient to lawful authority, and, on the other hand, will be lovers of true freedom'. While the Declaration is presumably directed to religious liberty as a civil right and while conservatives have denied that it had to do with 'liberty within the Church' this is a point

fraught with great potential hopefulness ecumenically for the future. There are overtones here of 'liberty' as a principle of an authentically responsible life. This evaluation may in time revolutionize the internal forum of the Roman Catholic Church. Just as 'collegiality' which in the Constitution on the Church is used to express the interrelationships of the episcopal and papal order may spread as a principle in the future to embrace more collegial relations between hierarchy, priests, and laity, so 'liberty' may have its field of influence increased. Greater freedom for biblical scholars in the *schema* on Revelation is perhaps an earnest of more to come when the 'indivisibility' of liberty is fully grasped. As it stands now without a specific application of 'liberty' within the Church, and with the emphasis on human dignity as a civil right within the state's sphere of influence, the question could be raised: What happens to human dignity when one becomes a believer? or, What happens to human dignity when one becomes a priest? Recent 'silencing' of priests in the United States for their activities in civil rights and the peace movements dramatize the problem.

(9) The next section brings the light of revelation to bear on religious liberty, which up until now has been described chiefly as grounded in the dignity of the human person. Now it is asserted that it is even more rooted in revelation itself.

There has been some criticism in the last few years from various quarters that the Roman Catholic Church was really only rehabilitating a rationalistic principle of religious liberty and that the scriptural texts employed did not refer to religious liberty as a civil right. This section considerably clarifies the confusion. By speaking first of religious liberty as grounded in the dignity of the human person it has been able to appeal to a broader audience than just those who accept the Christian revelation. It is altogether essential that the Church accept this responsibility as part of what it means to live in a pluralistic world. The Church's language must be in dialogue with the actual world. Many non-Christians understand the phrase 'dignity of the human person' so that there can be rational discourse. It is wrong to lock up the Church in a vocabulary totally dependent upon revelation for this isolates the Church from the world. Once this point is granted, then it is important for the Church to show that 'the dignity of the human person' can be more profoundly understood in the light of revelation and that it is this perspective 'even more' that leads the Church to be concerned for religious liberty. In this way theology is not isolated from life, but springs from it without diminishing in any way the theological obligation of the Church to speak from 'revelation'.

This section makes it clear (1) that revelation does not formally and explicitly affirm the right of the person not to be externally coerced in his faith, but (2) that the dignity of the human person has, however, its deepest roots in revelation and is in harmony with it.

Revelation 'gives evidence of the respect which Christ showed toward the freedom with which man is to fulfill his duty of belief in the word of God and it gives us lessons in the spirit which disciples of such a Master ought to adopt and continually follow.'

(10) This unit, concerned with the freedom of the act of faith, appropriately follows the rooting of religious liberty in revelation.

'The act of faith is of its very nature a free act. Man, redeemed by Christ the Saviour and through Christ Jesus called to be God's adopted son, cannot give his adherence to God revealing Himself unless, under the drawing of the Father, he offers to God the reasonable and free submission of faith.'

This description carefully excludes the humanist conception of freedom as just 'natural free will' or the Pelagian idea of faith as an independent, self-initiated human faculty by recognizing the divine initiative in which faith is seen as 'a gift of grace'. Yet at the same time it makes it clear that man in faith responds in freedom and in responsible obedience.

(11) Here we have a long list of some forty scriptural texts and footnotes illustrating the style of life of Christ and the Apostles to show their non-coerciveness in word and deed. Christ is described as 'gentle and lowly in heart', as patiently calling his disciples, as refusing to be a political Messiah, as

rather saying that he came 'to serve and to give his life a ransom for many.' Even Christ's miracles were not done to compel faith, but to elicit it freely. He counselled giving to Caesar the things that belong to Caesar, but to God the things that belong to God. Likewise the Apostles, 'taught by the word and example of Christ, followed the same path.'

There has been criticism of the use of scripture both by conservatives during the debate and by some evangelical Christians, but they appear to miss the mark because of the careful context in which the scriptural texts are set. It has been frankly stated in the Declaration that we do not have here a literal, explicit 'proof' of religious liberty in the modern sense. The appeal is not to single passages in the Bible nor to groups of them; it is rather Christ's whole method of approaching men that provides the clue. On the whole the Council's appeal to biblical revelation is supported by the penetrating and new classic study of 'Freedom in the New Testament and Religious Liberty' by Professor Amos Wilder. His conclusions follow:

(1) In this freedom the ultimate responsibility for choice and decision on the part of the believer is presupposed.

(2) This freedom is not solely inner and private freedom, but is understood by Paul as having a *historical-social* and indeed cosmic outreach and effect.

(3) The Christian is obliged to recognize the freedom of his fellow believers in this sense.

(4) The temporal power even of the pagan state is viewed as similarly obliged.[8]

(12) This section deals with the history of the Church with respect to religious liberty, trying to establish continuity with Christ and the Apostles. Earlier versions erred on the side of too much institutional self-justification in the light of the actual facts of persecution and of intolerance. The final version has reduced these claims considerably to the maintenance of 'the doctrine' of non-coercion in faith and by the recognition of failure in practice 'at times'.

'In the life of the People of God, as it has made its pilgrim way through the vicissitudes of human history, there has at

[8] Amos Wilder in *The Ecumenical Review*, July 1961, p. 416.

times appeared a way of acting that was hardly in accord with the spirit of the Gospel or even opposed to it. Nevertheless, the doctrine of the Church that no one is to be coerced into faith has always stood firm.'

One may be thankful for these changes, but at the same time regret that the document nowhere makes a clear confession of past sin nor a request for forgiveness. On this score the Declaration falls below the one on Ecumenism in which there is a recognition of sins against unity and need for mutual forgiveness. A great opportunity for healing with respect to other Christians and to non-Christians has been missed. If only the Declaration could have carried this note in the introduction instead of the 'doctrine of the one true religion' its impact would have been much more powerful. None of the historic Churches of Christendom can escape judgement for their sins against mankind on the subject of religious liberty. The Statement on Religious Liberty at the New Delhi Assembly of the World Council of Churches began to approach this situation.

'It is for the churches in their own life and witness, recognizing their own past failures in this regard, to play their indispensable role in promoting the realization of religious liberty for all men.'

(13) This section asserts the right of the Church to perform the mission divinely entrusted to her by Christ free from interference by the state.

'In human society and in the face of government the Church claims freedom for herself in her character as a spiritual authority, established by Christ the Lord, upon which there rests, by divine mandate, the duty of going out into the whole world and preaching the Gospel to every creature.'

(14) Here the duty of the Church is described:

'For the Church is, by the will of Christ, the teacher of the truth. It is her duty to give utterance to, and authoritatively to teach, that truth which is Christ Himself, and also to declare and confirm by her authority those principles of the moral order which have their origins in human nature itself.'

The method of dealing with unbelief is the way of love, never of force: '. . . the charity of Christ urges him (i.e., the disciple) to love and have prudence and patience in his dealings with those in error or in ignorance with regard to the faith.'

(15) The conclusion deserves quotation:

'The fact is that men of the present day want to be able freely to profess their religion in private and in public. Indeed, religious freedom has already been declared to be a civil right in most constitutions, and it is solemnly recognized in international documents. The further fact is that forms of government still exist under which, even though freedom of religious worship receives constitutional recognition, the powers of government are engaged in the effort to deter citizens from the profession of religion and to make life very difficult and dangerous for religious communities.'

'The Church hails the first with joy and denounces the second with sorrow and urges all men to consider how necessary religious liberty is, especially in the historical circumstances of today's world with its mixing of cultures and closer interrelationships of the human family.'

To sum up, the Declaration on Religious Liberty is one of the most substantial results of the Council. It represents a decisive break with the traditional principle of 'tolerance'. It is a victory for churchmen aware of the contemporary world with its religious pluralism and increased sense of personal responsibility for religious truth. It is no mere 'updating', but a new direction of movement with the dignity of the person central and the freedom of the Gospel increasingly operative. The Declaration makes credible the decrees on Ecumenism and on the Relation of the Church to the Non-Christian Religions. By doing this it practically guarantees a greater influence upon the non-Roman Catholic Churches of the Constitutions On the Church and On the Sacred Liturgy.

Not everything, however, is solved. It remains to be seen how the 249 opponents will act in the countries in which Roman Catholicism is overwhelmingly dominant and in those in which there are concordats with a confessional state. Will they ignore the Declaration, or will they twist its phrases in a minimalist direction? Will they as great advocates of obedience have the grace to change their minds and actions now that the Church has spoken? Will the Pope and perhaps, when it is implemented, the Senate of Bishops help them in these matters?

One of the pressing responsibilities now upon both the World Council of Churches and the Roman Catholic Church is to work towards a joint declaration on religious liberty. It is both an ecumenical opportunity of the highest order and a clear ecumenical imperative. The Secretariat for Religious Liberty of the World Council of Churches and the Secretariat for Promoting Christian Unity have in the course of the evolution of the text been in an informal dialogue. Let them now make the dialogue open and official. Only in this way can richer formulations of religious liberty be achieved, the problems of proselytism faced, and the difficulties in describing necessary limitations to religious liberty more fully explored. Bishop Rupp of the Principality of Monaco expressed the needed spirit and the direction of history in his frank critique at one point in the development of the Declaration: 'The *schema* is too negative and corresponds to an abstract concept of liberty, which bears the mark of the last century. It risks saying that again the Church is tardy in her ideas, her reforms and her evolution. . . . It would be very opportune to insert in our Declaration the seven propositions on religious liberty recently published by the World Council of Churches in Geneva.'

These seven points that sum up the ecumenical experience of the World Council of Churches would also profit much by further illumination from the Roman Catholic side in a dialogue on the official level open to the guiding of the Holy Spirit. They are included here both as a yardstick for comparison with the Declaration and as a challenge for further dialogue on the agenda of 'unfinished ecumenical cooperation.'

'1. While holding a distinctive Christian basis for religious liberty, the civil freedom which Christians claim for themselves must be guaranteed to all men everywhere, whatever their religion or belief.

'2. Religious liberty includes freedom to change one's religion or belief without consequent social, economic, and political disabilities. Implicit in this right is the right freely to maintain one's belief or disbelief without external coercion or disability.

'3. Religious liberty further includes freedom to manifest religion or belief. Worship, teaching, practice and observance are essential forms of religious manifestation, and any elaboration of the standard of religious liberty must expressly provide for them.

'4. To every person there should be assured the right to manifest his religion or belief, whether alone or in community, and in public or private.

'5. Religious liberty also includes freedom to maintain individual or collective bonds with religious communities or associations, the character of which transcends national boundaries. It also includes freedom to express opinions or convictions and to impart information and ideas through any media and regardless of frontiers.

'6. The standard of religious liberty should be international. The international standard should not be restrictively interpreted to make it conform to existing national constitutions and laws, but every effort should be made to cause national constitutions and laws to conform to the international standard.

'7. The exercise of religious freedom, as well as that of other civil rights, may be subject to such limitations as are determined by law solely in the interest of public order. Religious rights shall be available for all without discrimination on grounds of religion or belief.'[9]

[9] *The Ecumenical Review*, October 1965, pp. 385–6.

8 The Church in the Modern World

JOHN FINDLOW

*Representative of the Archbishop of Canterbury
at the Vatican and Director of
the Anglican Centre in Rome*

The Foreword

This Constitution with its address of friendly fellow appeal is in happy contrast to that thundering at the people which has been characteristic from the start of some Christian preachers and teachers, as it was of many Hebrew prophets whose utterances are recorded in the Old Testament. This thundering has been frequently supposed to be God's—mediated equally through mouth of prophet or preacher. A particularly dramatic example is when God commissioned the prophet Ezekiel saying that he sent him 'to the children of Israel, to nations that are rebellious, that have rebelled against me . . . I do send thee unto them: and thou shalt say unto them, Thus saith the Lord God. And they, whether they will hear, or whether they will forbear (for they are a rebellious house) yet shall know that there hath been a prophet among them.'(Ezek. 2. 3–5)

'Whether they will hear or whether they will forbear' might even so be added as the text introducing the Council's Pastoral Constitution on the Church in the Modern World; and it might be assumed, as it was by the God of Ezekiel, that the world will choose to forbear, like the rebellious nations of that remote time, rather than to hear the message coming, as is continuously claimed, from God.

Spiritually-minded men filled with a high sense of mission naturally turn their minds to their more numerous materially-minded fellow-men whose sense of mission in life is less high-falutin, more unformulated and more mundane. The traffic is usually one-way, for the mass always tends to forbear from hearing the message, though it could be contended that, at any rate until quite recently, parts of the message have seeped through into the so-called civilized system. The Christian spirit of love has but rarely and fitfully permeated either the Church or the world. It was not always uppermost in fact in the early Church, nor in the Eastern or Western European civilization of the Middle Ages, nor afterwards—a fact which, it could be argued, has since the French Revolution more than anything else increasingly given the lie to the Christian claim on modern man. Christianity, he tends to think, has been tried and failed (G. K. Chesterton notwithstanding). The saying first quoted by Tertullian 'See how these Christians love one another' has become as satirical and bitter as the proverb 'cold as charity'.

This is not of course to say that because of much mistrust among the masses a message should of set purpose not be broadcast. But it is to put the brake on ecclesiastical optimism and to react against the easy assumption still surprisingly made in many circles within Christendom that, the message once delivered, it is for the world to take it or leave it. It is all too significant that the weakest of the Council documents is the Decree on the Means of Social Communication promulgated on 4 December 1963 at the end of the Second Session. This decree looked to the setting up of a post-conciliar commission to do all its work without giving any sound guide-lines about how this was to be done. The key to unlock the means of communication from Church to world today seems to have been lost (and could hardly be said to have been found again in the pastoral constitution). One thing however is certain: if Pope John, the instigator of the Council, had no clear idea of the actual methods of communication, he had a very precious insight into the modern mentality. At the opening of the First Session on 11 October 1962 he was at pains to make clear that the Church should give *pastoral* teaching (hence the adjective attached to this constitution alone) and that this teaching should be *positive*: 'Today the Bride of Christ prefers to have recourse to the medicine of mercy rather than to brandish the weapons of wrath; she considers that, instead of condemning, she better responds to the needs of our time by placing more stress on the riches of her doctrine.' So it was that anathemas were dropped and the spirit of commination was ousted from the start.

The Recent Background in Brief

In recent times, through a series of Papal encyclicals (e.g. Leo XIII's *Rerum Novarum* 1891; Pius XI's *Quadragesimo Anno* 1931; John XXIII's *Mater et Magistra* 1961 and *Pacem in Terris* 1963; Pope Paul's *Ecclesiam Suam* 1964 and *Populorum Progressio* 1967), and now with this Pastoral Constitution of the Council, the Roman Catholic Church has shown herself alive to the burning social and moral issues of the age. The bishops of the Anglican Communion have attempted repeatedly, and not least at Lambeth Conferences, to speak to the world, in dealing with the life of the Christian community and its witness. The World Council of Churches has inherited the concern of most of its constituent bodies for the application of the Christian Gospel to the life and work of mankind. Can any of all these most commendable efforts be said to have broken through the thick wall dividing the sacristy from the street?

Rather is it true that the witness and work of individuals such as William Langland in *Piers Plowman*, remote in time though that be, through William Temple to Pope John XXIII (to name only three of the most outstanding in Western Christendom), have exercised immeasurably greater influence because they and their like have quite simply themselves gone out of the sacristy into the street. Such men have appealed at least to the imagination of mankind with their message where official or semi-official statements by a Church or group of Churches have dismally failed.

A real doubt about the Council's Pastoral Constitution on the Church in the Modern World is whether it will ever get across (and, if so, how) to the very people to whom it is primarily addressed. It is of course too long, too long-winded, and too wordy—most ecclesiastical pronouncements are—but also like many of these it is, for all its faults, really weighty. Such a document, bearing as it does the approval of 2,111 bishops out of 2,362 representing some half of Christendom, could not but carry weight. But, again (it is pertinent to ask) will the weight be brought to bear at the point where it is most required to counterbalance the portentous horrors hurriedly heaping up on the other side of the scale?

The History and Title of the Document

Before we turn to a summary of the subject, the history of the document should be briefly considered together with its title. Latterly during the Council it was referred to as *Schema* 13, coming as it did in that order out of the revised agenda advocated by Cardinal Suenens of Malines and Brussels in his noteworthy intervention of 4 December 1962. Towards the end of its first session the Council was clearly in rough seas. Only the Liturgy Constitution, of the many documents prepared, had been considered suitable in substance. Some 3,000 pages of unsatisfactory material were, it was only too well known, awaiting attention and the Council seemed likely to land on the rocks of disintegration rather than to be tending towards the righting of the bark of Peter in the midst of a naughty sea.

It was at this critical moment that, following the mind and known wishes of Pope John (expressed in a broadcast on 11 September 1962, one month before the opening of the Council) Cardinal Suenens plotted and explained the chart for future steering. The Church was to be the Council's preoccupation and theme, first looking inwardly (*ad intra*) at herself for *aggiornamento* and renewal and then, thus refreshed and brought up to date, looking outwards (*ad extra*) to all men to give them renewed faith, hope, and love from God the Source of their, as well as of the Church's, whole being. (This idea has perhaps been most succinctly expressed, from a strict Roman Catholic point of view, in the present Pope's Encyclical *Ecclesiam Suam*, 1964.) Concerning the Church's outward looking, the Cardinal referred to four specific points: the dignity of the human person, the responsibility of parents, social justice, peace and war. The Church, as the light of the nations, *lumen gentium* (another phrase beloved of Pope John, and the opening words of the Dogmatic Constitution *De Ecclesia*) should enter into dialogue with the world. On 5 December, the following day, the Archbishop of Milan, who was then Cardinal Montini, openly supported the new plan which, with great practical insight for the Council's future progress, the Belgian cardinal had outlined as the way out of the impasse and into the second session.

For the Church's outward looking little had so far been prepared and it was necessary to envisage and make ready a new *schema*. The replanning of the Council's work involved the formation in January 1963 of a new Commission of Coordination. This in its turn entrusted to a Joint Commission (comprising the already existing Commissions on theology and on the lay apostolate) the new *schema*, which had now to be written, on the presence of the Church in the Modern World. This was a difficult and lengthy task and it was not until the third session, some twenty months later, that the Council Fathers received the *schema De Ecclesia in Mundo Huius Temporis* accompanied by *adnexa*, a sort of appendix longer than the actual draft itself. Only in the fourth session, after much work on this *schema* in the third session and afterwards, did the next and now nearly final text appear. This was then debated, modified in consequence, and finally promulgated at the penultimate public session of the Council on 7 December 1965.

Partly owing to the inadequacy of Latin for such a theme, it was thought at one time that a text in French (in which much of the *schema* had actually been written) should be issued, but this was abandoned and the fully official text is in Latin. This in itself, in spite of translations appearing, might be a better reason than many for forbearing rather than hearing. It is no good after all addressing the world in a dead language, it being difficult enough to get anything across anyway in a living tongue. Whatever may be thought about Latin, Greek, Slavonic or Cranmerian English in the Liturgy, there can be nothing said for promulgating a message to the world of today in one only official language whose neologisms may be a delight to Latinists but which is wholly incomprehensible to the overwhelming majority of those to whom it is addressed. The translation used here, with some modifications, is that of the National Catholic Welfare Conference endorsed by the Bishops of the United States of America.

A possibly controversial word in the title, apart of course from differing interpretations of the *Church*, is the *World*. Hastings's *Dictionary of Christ and the Gospels* pointed out long ago that the first three evangelists only rarely use the word *world* (usually *kosmos* in Greek), and then 'in no dark or ominous colouring'. In the earlier part of St. John's Gospel a similar use is made. But, with the growing distinction between Christ and his followers on the one hand and those who opposed him on the other, the *world* seems to assume some of the darkness involved in opposing the Light. (St. Peter's, St. Paul's, and St. James's references to the world are usually in a similar vein too.) The Comforter 'when he is come will convict the world . . .' (John 16. 8ff., R.V.); and Hastings's *Dictionary* regards the teaching of the First Epistle of St. John on the world as a commentary, in particular, on our Lord's frequent utterances on these 'convictions'. Quoting Westcott, it states that in that passage the world appears as separate from God 'yet not without hope'. The Constitution, like all the Council documents, stresses the positive side and avoids anathemas. Following modern ideas and usage, and particularly in the spirit of Pope John, as has been shown already, the Constitution conceives of the world in this context as 'the whole of humanity'.

The Summary of the Document

Therefore, the Council focuses its attention on the world of men, the whole human family along with the sum of those realities in the midst of which it lives; that world which is the theatre of man's history, and the heir of his energies, his tragedies and his triumphs; that world which the Christian sees as created and sustained by its Maker's love, fallen indeed into bondage of sin, yet emancipated now by Christ, Who was crucified and rose again to break the stranglehold of personified Evil, so that the world might be fashioned anew according to God's design and reach its fulfilment.

That is the third paragraph of the preface which begins with an ecumenical sentence: 'The joys and the hopes, the griefs and the anxieties of the men of this age, especially those who are poor or in any way afflicted, these are the joys and hopes, the griefs and anxieties of the followers of Christ.' (It is not enough realized by those outside clerical and even some lay circles in the Roman Catholic Church, especially where Roman

Catholics are in the minority, how revolutionary this open approach of that Church to other Christians and to the world really is. This may be inconceivable to most modern men. To take a recent example, it would have been equally inconceivable to most Roman Catholics, until but a short time ago, that the doors of the Venerable English College, the ancient seminary for English Roman Catholic ordinands, in Rome should be opened to the Archbishop of Canterbury, where Dr. Ramsey actually stayed in March 1966 during his visit to the Pope. The generous gesture of the Roman Catholic Archbishop of Westminster, Cardinal Heenan, on this occasion marked a real break-through, not only to the Church of England but to all the Churches of the Anglican Communion and beyond. The external impact of such Christian solidarity on the world is probably less than the internal impact within Christendom itself.)

The *Preface* (just over one quarto page) of the Pastoral Constitution ends with the significant words, 'And Christ entered this world to give witness to the truth, to rescue and not to sit in judgement, to serve and not to be served'. The short preface leads into a longer *Introduction—Statement about the Situation of Man in the Modern World* (5 pages). Part I (28 pages) follows, treating of *The Church and Man's Calling* (*Vocatio*). The longer Part II (40 pages) is concerned with *Some Problems of Special Urgency*, a practical application of some of the principles outlined in the first part. *The Conclusion* covers less than 2 pages. The whole Constitution, including notes, is 88 quarto pages in length.

The Introductory Statement

In the *Introductory Statement on the Situation of Men in the Modern World* it is stated that the Church has always interpreted in the light of the Gospel the signs of the times to the men of each generation. Today the human race is involved in a new stage of history whose cultural and social transformation impinges also on the religious life of man. Growth involves crisis and this particular change brings serious difficulties in its train. Never before has mankind been so wealthy, so rich in resources and economic power; yet the old scourges of hunger, poverty and illiteracy still remain. Freedom meets slavery in new forms. World unity is stressed yet nationalism is still rampant. Peace is threatened by potentially totally destructive war. Words no longer have the same universal meaning in spite of increase in the exchange of ideas. There is much idealism abroad without sufficient spiritual progress. (This first section is appropriately headed *De Spe et Angore, Concerning Hope and Anguish*. The heading might almost be the *Agony and the Ecstasy*—a theme so old and yet so new.) The new technology is causing a profound revolution in the world-wide cultural sphere. Advances in biology, psychology, and historical studies increase the influence of mankind on the life of social groups. The human race is giving steadily increasing thought to forecasting and regulating its own population growth. Universal human progress is now noted where until recently the various groups of men had a kind of private history of their own. Traditional local communities are moving into the industrial type of society and city living is increasingly becoming the norm, whilst mass means of communication bring these changes home to all. Migration is widespread, involving a new attitude towards personal liberty. Young people especially, sensing these rapid changes and their own consequent insecurity, tend to become rebellious, which produces new problems for parents and teachers.

Finally, these new conditions have their impact on religion. On the one hand a more critical ability to distinguish religion from a magical view of the world and from the superstitions which still circulate purifies it and exacts day by day a more personal and explicit adherence to faith. As a result many persons are achieving a more vivid sense of God. On the other hand, growing numbers of people are abandoning religion in practice. Unlike former days, the denial of God or of religion, or the abandonment of them, are no longer unusual and individual occurrences. For today it is not rare for such things to be presented as requirements of scientific progress or of a certain new humanism. In numerous places these views are voiced not only in the teachings of philosophers, but on every side they influence literature, the arts, the interpretation of the humanities and of history and civil laws themselves. As a consequence many people are shaken.

As a result of this profound shaking, differences between persons, races, nations, ideologies, and within families are multiplied. Before the modern world lies the path to freedom or to slavery, to progress or retreat, to brotherhood or hatred. The present imbalances are linked with a more fundamental imbalance in the heart of man himself. The agelong questionings concerning the meaning of pain, evil, death, and about the after life persist. The Church remains confident in Christ who, through His Spirit, offers man the light and strength to live up to his destiny. Christ alone is the changeless reality and in His light, which is the light of God Himself, the Council wants to speak to all men in order to shed light on the mystery of man and to co-operate in finding the solution to the outstanding problems of our time.

Part I, *The Church and Man's Calling*. This consists of a short introduction and four chapters:

Chapter I   The Dignity of the Human Person,
Chapter II   The Community of Mankind,
Chapter III Man's Activity throughout the World,
Chapter IV   The Role of the Church in the Modern World.

The short introduction begins with a phrase here used for the first time in this Constitution—a significant paraphrase of the word *Church*—*The People of God*, which harks back to the Old Testament and looks forward with current trends in ecclesiology. *The People of God* is the title of the second chapter of the Dogmatic Constitution on the Church with which the Pastoral Constitution is thus linked at this point. That chapter ends with these words full of relevance to the present theme. 'It is the purpose of the Church's prayer and work that the fullness of the whole world should pass over to join the People of God, the Lord's Body and the Temple of the Holy Spirit, and that all honour and glory be paid in Christ, the Head of all to the Creator and Father of all.' Thus 'it will be increasingly clear that the People of God and the human race in whose midst it lives render service to each other', as our introduction states.

That man is the centre and crown of all things on earth is

recognized by nearly all, believers and unbelievers alike. So begins Chapter I on the *Dignity of the Human Person*. Man,
made in the image of God, exalts or debases himself. He is a
social rather than a solitary being. God's creation, though very
good, was corrupted through the Evil One when at the outset
man abused his liberty. Consequently man is split within himself; struggle between good and evil, light and darkness, is
common to all human life individual and collective. The agony
and the ecstasy are explicable only through the work of Christ
who renews man inwardly and casts out the 'prince of this
world'. Made of body and soul, man is one. He is a microcosm
but also reaches beyond the world to God. Thus, when he sees
within himself a soul, this is a true vision and not a fantasy. He
shares in the light of the divine mind and thereby attains great
heights. But wisdom, often found amongst poorer peoples, is
necessary more than ever today to apply his attainments to
human ends. An objective law is discerned in his conscience
which is the most secret core and sanctuary of a man; this
law is fulfilled by love of God and neighbour. Freedom rightly
used is a prerequisite of right action and can only be fulfilled
with the help of God's grace. The mystery of life is death and
the torment of suffering on earth is accompanied by fear of perpetual extinction. Abhorrence and repudiation of this fear is a
right intuition of man's heart. The mystery of death indeed
beggars the imagination, but the Church, taught by God's
revelation, firmly teaches that man's end is eternally blissful.
Bodily death will be finally vanquished through Christ's victory in the resurrection. Union with those whom he loves but
who are departed this life is given to man through faith in
Christ.

The root reason for human dignity lies in man's call to
communion with God. Many today have never recognized this
or have explicitly rejected it, and thus atheism is among the
most serious problems of this age. There are many kinds of
'atheism' ranging from what is called scientific agnosticism
to a gross misunderstanding of the God of the gospel who is rejected. Manifestations of atheism today can be due to deficiencies in the faith and witness of believers. Not to be

overlooked among the forms of modern atheism is that which anticipates the liberation of man through his economic and social emancipation—hence comes militant atheism, especially in the education of youth in those places where the proponents of this doctrine have gained governmental power. Sorrowfully but firmly the Church repudiates, in her loyal devotion to God and men, these poisonous doctrines which contradict reason and the common experience of humanity, dethroning man from his native excellence. Yet still she strives to detect in the atheistic mind the hidden causes for the denial of God which involves the most grievous wounding of man's dignity, as current events often prove. Every man is to himself an unsolved puzzle to which only God provides the solution. The remedy for atheism, attested by many past and present martyrs, is the presence and, in a sense, visibility of God the Father and His incarnate Son in the individual and corporate faith and love of believers. All alike, believers and unbelievers, ought to work to make the world a better place, but this is rendered impossible where there is State discrimination between them prejudicial to the fundamental rights of the human person. The Church courteously invites atheists to examine the gospel of Christ with an open mind for the restlessness of man can only be quieted in God, according to St. Augustine. The first Adam is fulfilled in Christ, the last Adam, who, 'the image of the invisible God', by His incarnation, life, passion, death and resurrection unites man with God. The mystery of Easter is offered, in a manner known only to God, by His Holy Spirit to all men so that 'as sons in the Son, we can cry out in the Spirit: Abba, Father!'

In the second chapter, the *Community of Mankind* involving brotherly dialogue among men is stated to be based on relationship between persons which is greatly promoted by the Christian revelation. Love of God and love of neighbour are inseparable and the divine unity implies the unity of men in truth and love. The human person is paramount in society; both are interdependent and both are contaminated by pride and selfishness. Social groups are, or should be, equally interdependent and all are responsible to the entire human family.

Every man has a right to certain basic necessities, physical, economic, political, and religious, which are due to his dignity. Good neighbourliness should extend to every person without exception. Evils opposed to life itself, including murder, abortion, euthanasia, suicide, arbitrary imprisonment and torture, slavery, prostitution, and disgraceful working conditions poison human society, harm the inflictor more than the afflicted and supremely dishonour the Creator. General toleration is to be commended, though this does not exclude a proper repudiation of error. All social and cultural discrimination is contrary to God's intent and here women have equal marital, vocational, educational, and cultural rights with men. True morality and true citizenship are always social. Christ himself shared in the human fellowship, and the Church, His Body, is called to do this too.

Man's Activity throughout the World (Chapter III) has recently been greatly increased through science and technology; it is tending towards a single world community and has produced many benefits formerly sought from heavenly powers. Man's achievements through the centuries have been colossal and this accords with God's will for him and the earth and all it contains, so long as this human activity accords also with the genuine good of the whole human race, society and the individual. Faith and science are not mutually opposed and a rightful independence is due to science. 'Indeed whoever labours to penetrate the secrets of reality with a humble and steady mind, even though he is unaware of the fact, is nevertheless being led by the hand of God, who holds all things in existence, and gives them their identity. . . . When God is forgotten, however, the creature becomes unintelligible.' All human progress involves indeed a great temptation and, in our own day, is threatened by self-destruction. All true human activity continually needs to be purified and perfected by the power of Christ's cross and resurrection. His love is relevant to the whole of man's life. The meal of brotherly solidarity, a foretaste of the heavenly banquet, is that sacrament of faith where natural elements refined by man are gloriously changed into Christ's Body and Blood—a pledge of hope and the strength for life's journey. Thus on earth God's Kingdom is already present in mystery but when the Lord comes it will be consummated.

Chapter IV on the *Role of the Church in the Modern World* follows upon what has been said in the foregoing chapters and presupposes everything declared by the Council on the mystery of the Church. The Church is pre-eternal, present, and to come; she is mystically within human history making it more human. Also, the (Roman) Catholic Church appreciates what other Christian Churches and Communities have done towards this end as well as the help coming from individuals and human society as a whole. Thus the Church, by virtue of the gospel committed to her, proclaims the right of man and infuses, but not by any external dominion, faith and charity into modern society. She is committed to no one earthly system but by her universality and with great respect supports and promotes the unity of mankind. There must be no false opposition set up between the sacred and the secular. Here the layman's free role is of paramount importance and undue clericalism should be avoided, though bishops and priests must realize their responsibilities to the full. Inevitably there is a discrepancy between theory and practice in the Church's life and witness, as there is in the life of humanity; but even so Church and world are complementary, to one another's mutual profit. This even extends as far as the Church's profiting by antagonism and persecution. The ultimate end is the Kingdom of God on earth as it is in heaven, for Christ is at once the beginning and the end of all things and all men.

Part II, *Some Problems of Special Urgency*. This consists of a short introduction and five chapters:

Chapter I   Promoting the Dignity of Marriage and the Family,

Chapter II   The Proper Development of Culture (introduction and three sections),

Chapter III Economic and Social Life (introduction and two sections),

Chapter IV The Life of the Political Community,

Chapter I

(This chapter, even more than those sections of the constitution where atheism and war and peace are discussed, was naturally the centre of chief public interest while it was being debated in council. Of all the questions discussed, birth control loomed largest in the public eye and also marked most clearly the dividing line between conservatives like Cardinal Ruffini of Palermo [opposing 'the pill which has so impudently been called Catholic'] and the progressives like Cardinal Suenens [calling for more scientific research into sexual life in marriage and the psychological aspects of self-control] and the Melchite Patriarch Maximos's vicar in Egypt, Archbishop Zoghby [going so far as to advocate relaxation in the Church's laws on the dissolution of the marriage bond].

Cardinal Heenan of Westminster took a moderate line and was in favour of dropping the whole chapter. He thought that it gave hardly any valuable guidance to married couples in their intimate problems. 'The fact is', he said, 'that, although moral principles remain fixed and certain, we still await guidance from doctors, physiologists and other experts. It was the wish of the Pope that there should be no public discussion of this question [birth control], and it was wisely taken from our agenda in the last [i.e. the third] session.' The Council came to an end without any directives about this having been issued by the Pope which most commentators, aided by certain indiscretions, interpreted as a sign that the appointed commission had so far failed to agree on the advice which should be proferred.)

At the beginning of the chapter it is emphasized that the well-being of the individual and of human and Christian society is connected with marriage and the family. There are many distortions and disfigurements of this institution including 'illicit practices against human generation'. World problems resulting from population growth are also mentioned. God himself is the author of matrimony, which is ordained for the procreation and education of children and finds in them its ultimate crown. Marriage is sacramental and for life; in it the actions of mutual love are noble and worthy when they are expressed in a manner which is truly human. Seasonable instruction of young people in the dignity, duty, and works of married love is advocated especially in the heart of their own families. Marriage and conjugal love being by their nature ordained for the begetting and education of children (though the other purposes of marriage should not be made of less account), it is for the parents, after due consideration, to decide about having and bringing up children, and that not arbitrarily but conscientiously in accordance with the divine law, and submissively towards the Church's teaching office which authentically interprets the law in the light of the gospel. Marriage is certainly not instituted solely for procreation.

Modern conditions make it hard to arrange married life harmoniously. At times it is necessary to limit the size of the family, which involves strain in maintaining the full exercise of love. From this may ensue the danger of infidelity and difficulty in conception. Some dishonourable solutions suggested involve the taking of life. God the Lord of life has conferred on men the surpassing ministry of safeguarding life in a manner worthy of man. Therefore from the moment of its conception life must be guarded with the greatest care. Relying on principles stemming from this, sons of the Church may not undertake methods of birth control which are found blameworthy by the Church in its unfolding of the divine law. (There is a note attached here referring amongst other papal pronouncements to Pius XI's Encyclical *Casti Connubii* and ending with this explanation: 'Certain questions requiring further and more careful investigation have, by order of the Supreme Pontiff, been handed over to a Commission for the study of population, of the family and of birth, in order that when it has completed this duty, the Supreme Pontiff may pronounce judgment. Such being the present teaching of the *Magisterium* [*sic stante doctrina Magisterii*], the holy Synod does not intend immediately to propose concrete solutions.')

Note: the Votum on Matrimony

Because of its relevance to Chapter I of the Constitution, this separate document may conveniently be dealt with here.

The Preparatory Commission (of which the President was Cardinal Masella) on *The Discipline of the Sacraments* held 66 plenary meetings (371 hours) between 11 November 1960 and 17 March 1962, that on 27 February 1961 being presided over by Pope John. The Commission presented nine schemes for the consideration of the Central Preparatory Commission including the following six on marriage:

1. On the form of the marriage service
2. On consent in matrimony
3. On impediments to matrimony
4. On matrimonial causes
5. On mixed marriages
6. On preparation for marriage.

The other three dealt with the sacraments of penance, confirmation, and holy order.

Between 3 December 1962 and 28 October 1964 the Commission on the Discipline of the Sacraments met many times and the sub-commissions even more. Two schemes on marriage were in preparation and under discussion:

(i) the scheme of the Decree on the Sacrament,
(ii) the scheme of the *Votum* on the Sacrament.

'Of the numerous schemes,' (originally prepared on the seven sacraments) Fr. Antoine Wenger remarks on p. 219 of *Vatican II Troisième Session* (Editions Centurion Paris 1965), 'there was to remain only one project of a *votum* on the sacrament of matrimony—a *votum* (*voeu*) because it was a question of elaborating new legislation on the sacrament of marriage which would be forwarded in the form of a *votum* to the commission set up by Pope Paul VI for the reform of the Code of Canon Law. As it was a question of practical measures more than doctrine and as the Council was not concerned with reform of the Code, it could only formulate a *votum* for the consideration of this Commission. If the Fathers had better considered this aspect of the text, certain of them would have been less surprised by the proposal made at the opening of the last session on Friday 20 November 1964 by Cardinal Döpfner that the *votum* should be proferred not to the Commission for the reform of the Code of Canon Law but to the Pope, in order that he should make a decree on the subject *motu proprio* without too much delay in application.'

In fact, on 20 November 1964 the Scheme of the *Votum* on the Sacrament of Matrimony with emended text (introduction, *relatio*, the actual *Schema de Matrimonii Sacramento*, notes on the form of celebration of matrimony) was discussed and presented for approval to the Council Fathers who were asked to vote according to the following formula:

Does it please the Fathers that the *votum* on matrimony which has already been discussed should be sent to the Holy Father, with the emendments (note: oral as well as written) presented in *Aula* in order that he may pronounce on the argument examined by the Fathers?

There were 2,024 votes: 1,592 for, 427 against, with 2 *juxta modum* and 3 abstentions.

In particular, the still vexed question of mixed marriages, which figured large in the many discussions preceding this and especially in the first project sent to the Council Fathers at the beginning of the summer of 1964, has become almost a subject in itself and cannot be dealt with directly here.

Chapter II

Chapter II on *The Proper Development of Culture* defines *culture* as the cultivation by man of the goods and values of nature including the historical and social aspects of this. It is possible now to speak of a new age of human history characterized by scientific and technical progress, standardization, urbanization, more leisure and more international commercial exchange. A new humanism is being born which arouses new hopes and new anxieties. How is the dynamism and expansion of a new culture to be fostered without the loss of vital continuity with tradition? How can a synthesis be made of the various branches of study in the service of wisdom? How can the refinements of culture be made available for all? Finally, how can the autonomy of the new culture be established without producing a merely material and possibly anti-religious humanism?

All good manual work and all sound learning should, by serving and enlightening humanity, lead to deeper understanding of the Wisdom of God revealing himself in the world as 'the light which enlightens every man'. Scientific methods by themselves cannot penetrate to the intimate notion (*rationes*) of things; though they tend to lead man to think that he is self-sufficient, this should not blind us to their positive value. The Church is not essentially bound to any one way of life or culture but rather renews all life and culture and is herself enriched by them. Culture cannot develop without a just liberty; wherefore, recalling the teaching of the First Vatican Council about 'two distinct orders of knowledge' (faith and reason), the Council affirms the legitimate autonomy of human culture and especially of the sciences. It is thus not within the function of the public authority to use culture for its own political or economic ends.

Culture should be made free and open for all and efforts undertaken, especially through education in the family, towards that synthesis of the various disciplines of knowledge and the arts which it is so difficult to achieve today. Theologians and other scholars should co-operate in this and for them, be they clerical or lay, lawful freedom of inquiry, of thought and of expression at once humble and courageous must be recognized. It is also important to recognize the positive role which literature and the arts have played and still play in the life of the Church.

Chapter III

Dealing with *Economic and Social Life*, Chapter III consists of an introduction and two sections, the first on economic development and the second on certain principles governing social and economic life as a whole of which man is the source, the centre and the purpose. In spite of improved methods of production and exchange of goods, extravagance and wretchedness still exist side by side in too many places. The very peace of the world can be threatened by this. The

Church through the centuries, and particularly in recent times, has, in the light of the gospel, worked out the principles of justice and equity for individual, social, and international life. It is important that economic development should be directed towards the good of persons and not to serve the purposes of only a few men or powerful groups or nations. Economic inequalities are to be combated not least in the case of agricultural workers. Likewise discrimination against migrant workers, the sick, and the aged is to be avoided and their status guaranteed in accordance with their right to a livelihood and their worth as persons. Work, to which every man has a right, has been sanctified by Christ Himself, and its remuneration must be just and be consistent with the needs of the whole man and of his dependents. Since free and independent persons created in the image of God are the basis of all economic enterprises, due active sharing of all in the administration and profits of these enterprises and the institutions controlling them is to be encouraged. The right to strike even in present-day circumstances must be upheld together with the duty of dialogue between the parties conducive to reconciliation of differences. The right to private property must be balanced by the Christian necessity of contributing to the communal good, especially in relief of the poor and hungry, who in extreme necessity have the right to procure what they need for themselves out of the riches of others. Family and social services are to be developed but individual responsibility should not thereby be diminished, leading to passivity towards society and its claims. Investments, both individual and corporate, should be made with an eye on present needs and the needs of the future. Private property and ownership of some goods is necessary for the autonomy of the person and is thus one of the conditions for civil liberties; it should not however be abused as it still is, not least on some large rural estates where the workers' conditions are unworthy of a human being. Those who seek first the Kingdom of God have the greater incentive to helping their brethren.

Chapter IV

Chapter IV on *The Life of the Political Community* first considers the increase of civic and religious freedom, still denied however under some political systems. It is men who under God create political community and public authority, which are expressed in various systems of government according to the free will of the citizens. Public authority must therefore be exercised within the limits of the moral order and towards the common good. Where oppression results from excess of public authority, the citizens should not protest in those matters requisite for the common good; but they may defend their own and the common rights against this abuse, keeping in due regard those limits drawn by the natural law and the gospels. All should bear in mind the right and duty of using the free vote to further the common good. In our day increase and development of social organization is inevitable; it is however inhuman for public authority to fall back on dictatorial systems or totalitarian methods which violate the rights of the person or social groups. Patriotism should be tempered by attention to the good of the whole human family. Church and State are each autonomous and independent. The Church is not identified in any way with the political community nor bound to any political system but both serve the same men individually and corporately. The Church requires true freedom for this at all times and in all places.

Chapter V

This final chapter concerns *The Fostering of Peace and the Promotion of a Community of Nations.* The introduction states that the human family is facing a supreme crisis in its advance towards maturity, confronted as it is by the ravages of war and the necessity of peace. Peace is not merely the absence of war; it is the fruit of love which goes beyond what justice can provide. Christians have therefore the greater responsibility.

The first section deals with the avoidance of war, which owing to scientific development is more savage and far-reaching now than ever before. Terrorism and guerilla action in the complex international situation add to this savagery. The

Council therefore wishes above all things else to recall the permanent binding force of universal natural law and its all-embracing principles, dictated by man's conscience itself. Actions, of which the most infamous is genocide, conflicting with these principles are criminal, and blind obedience cannot excuse those who commit them. Agreements made to reduce the horror of war, including such matters as the treatment of the wounded and of prisoners, should be honoured. Conscientious objection is, it seems, rightly made legal provided that those who thus do not bear arms serve the community in some other way. A distinction must be made between offensive and defensive war. Those who engage in military service should consider themselves as agents of the security and freedom of the nations.

Total war, now a possibility should all the available armaments held by the great nations once be unleashed, would involve the infliction of destruction far exceeding the limits of legitimate defence. In the notes at this point appears the following quotation from John XXIII's Encyclical *Pacem in Terris* (1963): 'Thus, in this age, which boasts of its atomic power, it no longer makes sense to maintain that war is a fit instrument with which to repair the violation of justice.' This declaration is then made in the text: 'Any act of war aimed indiscriminately at the destruction of entire cities or extensive areas along with their population is a crime against God and man himself. It merits unequivocal and unhesitating condemnation.' The hazard of modern war is increased by the fact that the possession of modern scientific weapons makes just this possible. Scientific weapons are also, indeed, held as a deterrent, and this is regarded by many as the most effective guarantee of peace at present. Nevertheless, the balance of power resulting from the arms race is not a safe way to preserve peace; and the peace consequent upon it is neither sure nor authentic. Divine providence urgently demands of us that we free ourselves from the age-old slavery of war. The alternative evil is indescribable. It is therefore clearly incumbent upon all to spare no effort in working for the time when all war can be completely outlawed by international consent, which involves the establishment of some universal public authority acknowledged by all. Disarmament, not unilateral, should be truly begun with genuine practicable safeguards. What has been done already to eliminate the danger of war should not be underrated and to this should be added not only further concerted action but a deep change of men's attitudes towards one another. We all need a change of heart. We should not be lulled into false hope, or the dreadful peace of death may be all that awaits mankind. The Church continues however firm in hope.

In Section 2 there are four norms stated for the setting up of that international community without which the various needs of man, especially his need of peace, will not be met:

(a) The developing nations must realize that, for the fulfilment of all their citizens, they must take the initiative in developing their own resources, economic, cultural, and traditional, and not only rely on foreign aid.

(b) The advanced nations should make the necessary spiritual and material readjustments to equip them for world-wide co-operation and not exact an unjust profit in business dealings with the weaker and poorer nations.

(c) The international community, in co-ordinating and promoting development, is to see that complete equity be observed in the allocation of resources made available for this purpose. The promotion and regulation of international business affairs should be undertaken by suitable organizations in order to compensate losses resulting from excessive inequality of power among the various nations and to help the developing nations to advance economically.

(d) Economic and social structures in many cases need re-examination, though untimely technical solutions should be guarded against lest some portion of the spiritual treasure entrusted by God to albeit unwitting humanity be lost.

Rapid population increases demand full and universal co-operation, especially by the richer nations, to meet the resultant human needs. The adoption of modern methods of farming and fairer land distribution are also urgent. Governments have rights and duties, within the proper limits, to see that the problems of population are dealt with—for example by social and family legislation and migration policies.

Many today, however, are in favour of radically curbing the increase in world population by every means possible and by any kind of intervention on the part of public authority. In view of this contention the Council urges everyone to guard against solutions, whether publicly or privately supported, or at times even imposed, which are contrary to the moral law. It is for the parents to decide on the number of children they will have, though, for this, more education in social, religious, and moral values is sometimes required. 'Men should discreetly be informed, furthermore, of scientific advances in exploring methods of family planning (*methodis quibus coniuges iuvari possint in ordinando numero prolis*) whose safeness has been well proven and whose harmony with the moral order has been ascertained.'

Extremes of wealth and poverty still existing in many places recall Christians to that spirit of poverty and charity which is the glory and witness of the Church of Christ. The duty of the People of God is to do all they can to alleviate the sufferings of the modern age and that not only out of their superfluity. Collection and distribution of aid may well often be arranged by Catholics and their other Christian brethren in co-operation, particularly in the service of the developing nations, and this should be done after due training.

Education in the principles and practice of international community is of prime importance in both religious and civil education. As the Church serves mankind, helping to build up peace everywhere on earth, and in view of the immensity of the greater part of the world's hardships, the Council recommends the setting up of some organization of the universal Church to stimulate the Catholic community to promote progress in needy areas and international social justice. (This has now been done by a *motu proprio* of 10 January 1967 setting up the Pontifical Commission for International Social Justice and Development under the presidency of Cardinal Roy, Archbishop of Quebec.)

The Conclusion, stressing lawful diversity within the Church, quotes the phrase '*Sit in necessariis unitas, in dubiis libertas, in omnibus caritas.*' It envisages the development and further application of the proposals set forth, in co-operation with Christians of other traditions, with all who acknowledge God and with

those who cultivate outstanding qualities of the human spirit without as yet acknowledging their Source. We include those who oppress the Church and harass her in manifold ways. Since God the Father is the origin and end of all men, we are all called to be brothers. Therefore if we have been summoned to the same destiny, human and divine, we can and we should work together without violence and deceit in order to build up the world in genuine peace. . . . Not everyone who cries 'Lord, Lord' will enter the kingdom of heaven but those who do the Father's will, by taking a strong grip on the work at hand.

The Final Comment

Those who from outside followed the formation of this Pastoral Constitution most closely in the many vicissitudes of its preparation must be full of praise for the persistence with which its protagonists plodded along and worked for this outgoing and forward-looking .conciliar document. The other sheep, which are not of the Roman fold and conscientiously cannot recognize all the present claims of its shepherd on earth, may yet joyfully join with him and his sheep in the gigantic common effort to direct the modern Church and the modern world to its origins in Christ, the one Shepherd of the whole flock. What we are all perhaps trying to do is *reculer pour mieux sauter.* This is very applicable both to shepherd and to sheep. But the jump has to be made and we have not yet made it.

It seems therefore that the matter of the Pastoral Constitution is presented too piecemeal, its manner is too pedestrian and its moral too pedantically pointed. Lest this seem a too trite criticism let it be briefly justified in conclusion.

It can hardly be said that the Pastoral Constitution is a worthy companion for its dogmatic counterpart on the Church. These two were meant to be the main pillars supporting the whole work of the Council. It is a task almost beyond hope of success for a Church so widely extended as the Roman to produce a satisfying action document on itself in the modern world. The matter is presented piecemeal because of this. There is too much theological assumption without enough sociological perception partly because most of the compilers and all the judges of the work were celibate clerics, and many of the compilers academics too. The impression produced, most prominently by the section on marriage and family life, is one of detached observation from outside, as indeed in these circumstances it had to be. There is a lack of co-ordination, not indeed theologically but ontologically, of the material available, a sense of groping in a realm unfamiliar, a lack of sense of responsibility on the part of the hierarchical Church for a state of affairs which is to some extent of its own making. The Christian Socialism in England of a century ago was born of two convictions: that the eighteenth-century Church and the Church of that day had failed and was failing the working man and that, in the words of its real founder, J. M. F. Ludlow, 'the new Socialism must be Christianized'. G. C. Binyon in *The Christian Socialist Movement in England* summing up the net result of the Christian Socialism of 1848–1854 (p. 84) notes that

largely through Ludlow's influence there has been in England a comparative absence of that complete alienation between organised Religion and the Socialist movement which is all too common in the rest of the world; and that, largely owing to Maurice, there has been in England, and particularly in the Anglican Church, a development, unparalleled in any other country or Church, of a theology consonant with the principles and ideals of Socialism, tending at once to infuse religion with a social purpose and fulfil social inspiration by religious faith.[1]

The late-coming of these tendencies to the Church of Rome is not a little of the reason for the matter of the constitution being so piecemeal, theology, so to say, not having digested sociology sufficiently. Not unfairly nor unkindly (but perhaps

[1] Quoted by S. C. Carpenter, *Church and People 1789–1889* (S.P.C.K., London, 1933), p. 325.

slightly *de haut en bas*) did an Anglican observer remark that a lot of the material in this constitution is for Anglicans rather *vieux jeu*.

The manner of presentation is often pedestrian, prosaic, and dull. There is unnecessary repetition, particularly in those parts which deal with atheism and peace. The length is inordinate and it is most unlikely that many of those to whom the Constitution is addressed will in fact ever read it. There is every appearance of sections having been hurriedly compiled and revised, as indeed particularly in the latter stages they were. The suggested modifications were so great in number, and the time before the end of the final session was so brief and overburdened, that this all-important constitution, in addition to not having been well enough thought out from the start, received somewhat short shrift in the last weeks of the Council's last session. Had the pressure, brought to bear too late by those who wanted overt references to Communism and condemnation of it, been successful, the text would have been somewhat enlivened. But it was the firm mind of the Fathers to adhere to Pope John's wish to affirm rather than to condemn. There were rumours that some Cardinals with intimate experience of Communism favoured the openly anti-Communist initiative but the issue of this 'last-ditch battle', as the London *Times* called it at the time, was already decided and could, given the general atmosphere prevailing in the Council at the period, not have been otherwise.

The general moral, that the Church must address the modern world and deal with contemporary issues positively and co-operatively even with those who are openly opposed to her, is too pedantically pointed. The intention is clear and good but the means adopted too doctrinaire for an age in which quotation from the Scriptures, with which the text is rife, is becoming increasingly meaningless. It is no longer sufficient to quote scriptural and other ecclesiastical texts in order to gain a hearing and to prove a point in the public forum. The whole new way of thought and life, acknowledged and outwardly accepted by the Constitution, requires a new approach and orientation which are lamentably lacking in it. It is a new thing prepared and presented largely in the old way. Until this new wine is put into new bottles, few of those for whom it is made can be expected to taste it, much less to drink deep and become convinced of its genuine worth for them now. What form these new communication bottles should take must be the concern and practical care of all Christian Churches and Communities co-operating closely. If the Pastoral Constitution achieves that, it will have done less than it set out to do but it will have begun a new chapter in the somewhat 'Cinderella' subject of Christian sociology. Whether the world will drink, be the bottles old or new, or whether it will forbear is doubtful indeed. The rather pessimistic doubt expressed by Ezekiel and his like would seem to be confirmed in most prophetic parts of the New Testament. But the Constitution is not prophetic. May it succeed in being what it set out to be—pastoral. There is no thunder to steal from a shepherd.

8a The Church and Non-Christian Religions

HOWARD E. ROOT

Professor of Theology in the
University of Southampton

This Declaration (which will always be known popularly as 'the declaration on the Jews') began life as Chapter IV ('On the Jews') in the 1963 text of *De Oecumenismo*. Its subsequent history, through the second, third, and fourth Sessions, was one of the most dramatic features in the Council's life and regularly made newspaper headlines. We shall not attempt to trace the long and complicated history of the text through its several versions. All the details can be found in Cardinal Bea's own book and in the books by Xavier Rynne.[1]

It is widely known that the original idea for the Council to make a statement on the Jews came from Pope John. He expressed this to Cardinal Bea and was deeply concerned with the progress of the text right up until his death. But we can also properly surmise that the subject was always very close to the heart of Cardinal Bea himself. Quite apart from the general merits of a statement repudiating any kind of anti-Semitism, the sufferings of the Jews under Hitler would touch very deeply

[1] Augustin Cardinal Bea, *The Church and the Jewish People* (London, 1966), which is indispensable, and Xavier Rynne, *The Second Session* (London, 1964), pp. 216 ff. Rynne most usefully includes here the text of Cardinal Bea's speech of 18 November 1963, introducing the Chapter on the Jews. *The Third Session* (London, 1965) continues the story (esp. pp. 31 ff.) and in an appendix prints the texts of two versions which were successively before the Fathers. *The Fourth Session* (London, 1966) concludes the tale (pp. 160 ff.) and gives the full text of the final version in an appendix. A very brief account can be found in Abbott, op. cit., pp. 656 ff. in an introduction to the Declaration by Fr. R. A. Graham, S. J. The translation given in Abbott is provided with lengthy and informative notes. Quotations here will be from this translation, which is itself based on one made by the Secretariat for Unity.

a man of the character and sensitivity of the German Augustin Cardinal Bea.

It would seem, then, that nothing could be simpler than for the Council to make a brief and clear statement on the Jews, proclaiming its horror of persecution, and removing once for all any possible doubt about the Roman Catholic position. It is a plain fact of history that the whole Christian Church—and not Rome only— has much to be ashamed of in its past actions and statements about the Jews. As Cardinal Bea himself pointed out, the obscene horror of Hitler's 'final solution' may itself owe something to Christian behaviour in the past. The Council, then, seemed to present a magnificent occasion for a kind of act of reparation, and repudiation of anything in past or present Christian attitudes which could lead to discrimination or persecution. A repugnance towards the persecution of the Jews is not a matter of controversy in the Roman Catholic (or any other) Church. There may, sadly, be individual Christians who harbour anti-Semitic prejudice, but there should be no difficulty in getting the Fathers of the Council to state the Church's feelings unequivocally.

Alas, so far from being simple, the drafting and approving of this document proved to be one of the Council's most difficult tasks. For this the Council was not to blame. The difficulties were forced on it by pressures from outside. The only thing which may have been a mistake was the initial placing of the statement as a chapter in the Decree on Ecumenism. (Although, it is said, Cardinal Bea felt there was no other way to get it put before the Council.) The moment the debate began it was clear that there would be much opposition to this placing. In all fairness, the criticism was pertinent. The Decree on Ecumenism was concerned with relations between Christian churches, or within the Christian family. Strictly speaking, a discussion of the Jews was out of place in this context. The relation of Christianity to Judaism raises real theological questions, but they are not the same as the question of ecumenism.

It should be recorded here that observers from other churches were themselves extremely critical. To their mind, the presence of this chapter in this Decree would weaken the image of Roman Catholic intentions which the Decree was trying to create. Inclusion of a discussion of the Jews would, they felt, have been viewed with great suspicion—as though Rome really didn't draw much distinction between other Christians, Jews, and adherents of any other religion. All, so to speak, would seem to be equidistant from the truth which Rome uniquely possesses. Ecumenism, understood in that way, would be nothing more than a kind of benevolent gesture of goodwill towards Jews, Anglicans, Moslems, Humanists, Orthodox, or what you will. Since many were in any case likely to be suspicious of Rome's real intentions it would have been most unfortunate to feed those suspicions by introducing the question of the Jews in this Decree. On this point the observers and many of the Fathers were of one mind.

But there was another kind of criticism. The Fathers from the Eastern (Uniate) churches were unanimous in their hostility towards a special treatment of the Jews. Most of them live in Arab lands. Any kind of statement about the Jews would be interpreted by their Moslem neighbours as official Roman Catholic support for the Zionist theories which led to the partition of Palestine. In other words, no matter what the Decree said, it would be interpreted politically in that part of the world. (It must also be said here that certain Israeli voices fed fuel to the flames by claiming that this declaration *would* imply Vatican approval of their aspirations.) It is difficult for those who do not know the Middle East to realize the depth and the despair in Arab feeling on this question. Unlike Christians, Moslems do not have a shameful history of persecution of the Jews. And yet (as Arabs see it) they have been sacrificed by Western Christian nations. Men have, in Palestine, been dispossessed of their homes and lands. Why? Not because they were guilty of the horrors of persecution but because the Christian West was conscience-driven to do something to help the Jews, and then did it not at their own expense but at the expense of the Arabs. Given this strong feeling, the whole Arab world has felt betrayed by Christian powers. If Rome were now to give even the slightest evidence of pro-Israeli feelings, Christian Arabs (of whom there are more than most people realize) would scarcely be able to face their Moslem neighbours. This was the predicament of the Eastern bishops at the Council. In their pastoral responsibility to their own people they had to warn of the very grave risks to the Christian Church which any kind of statement on the Jews would run. They also pointed out—with some reason—that if the Council were to make some conciliatory and charitable gesture to the Jews, it ought certainly to do the same for the Moslems.

And so the debate went. Some thought that the statement belonged in the Constitution on the Church. Others thought that it should be only a very brief paragraph or two on its own. Meanwhile the press was taking note of the controversy and leading many people to think (even if unintentionally) that the Council could not make up its mind on whether or not to condemn anti-Semitism. This widespread impression could not be further from the truth. No one, Eastern or Western, had any hesitation at all about the vileness of anti-Semitism. But the political realities (themselves created by Christian nations) made the situation extraordinarily delicate.

In the end a solution was found which produced a much better document than the 1963 chapter. It took two more Sessions of the Council before it was completed and approved, but the delay was in a good cause. By the end of 1965 much of the Eastern opposition had lessened, and, when the Declaration was promulgated, Arab reactions were relatively mild. All through the period, of course, various pressures were also being brought to bear by Jewish opinion, especially in the United States. The final text does not perhaps entirely satisfy Jewish opinion, but responsible Jewish spokesmen have expressed a very general satisfaction that the Council was able to do what it did.

The solution took the form of placing the statement on the Jews in an entirely new context, i.e. a declaration 'On the relation of the Church to non-Christian religions.' It is a brief document (only 1,117 words), divided into five sections. It is wholly admirable, doing precisely what it sets out to do. Obviously it was not possible to describe or discuss any particular religion in detail. But in each case just enough is said to show that the drafters knew whereof they spoke and were glad to point to positive features in other faiths which Christians should respect and esteem.

The first section stresses the unity of mankind and points to those ultimate questions which all men ask and which find embodiment in religious systems. The second section refers specifically to Hinduism and Buddhism, positively and appreciatively, and with a view to future dialogue. 'The Catholic Church rejects nothing which is true and holy in these religions. She looks with sincere respect upon those ways of conduct and of life, those rules and teachings which, though differing in many particulars from what she holds and sets forth, nevertheless often reflect a ray of that truth which enlightens all men.' The following section, of much the same temper, addresses itself to Islam and enumerates beliefs and traditions which Moslems and Christians have in common.

The fourth and longest section deals with the Jews. The points made are straightforward and clearly expressed. Christians and Jews are bound together by the unique bond of a common spiritual patrimony, and dialogue is to be fostered. Then, 'True, authorities of the Jews and those who followed their lead pressed for the death of Christ; still, what happened in this passion cannot be blamed upon all the Jews then living, without distinction, nor upon the Jews of today . . . the Jews should not be presented as repudiated or cursed by God, as if such views followed from the Holy Scriptures.' Further, 'the Church repudiates (*reprobat*) all persecution against any man . . . She deplores the hatred, persecutions and displays of anti-Semitism directed against the Jews at any time and from any source.' There is no ambiguity or equivocation here.

The fifth and final section simply enlarges this repudiation to universal scope. 'The Church rejects (*reprobat*), as foreign to the mind of Christ, any discrimination against men or harassment of them because of their race, colour, condition of life, or religion.'

As will be seen this Declaration really does two quite separate though related things. By incorporating the substance of the original chapter on the Jews it makes Rome's views on this question absolutely clear, and it also does not miss the opportunity to reprove any kind of discrimination or persecution on other grounds. But the first three sections contain the strongest possible kind of gesture towards the great religions of the world. That the prospect of dialogue is meant seriously was established by the setting up of a special Secretariat for the Non-Christian Religions under Cardinal Marella. A further gesture in this direction was Pope Paul's meeting with Hindu and other religious leaders in Bombay. Some will no doubt find this all astonishing, but I can recall in the debate no voice raised against this part of the Declaration on the grounds of any 'false irenicism'.

It is of course true that traditional Roman Catholic theology allows for much more flexibility in the approach to other religions than does, say, the reformed theology of a conservatively Lutheran or Calvinist stamp. This derives in part from a conviction about the importance and necessity of natural theology. The Catholic attitude is that Christian faith is not compromised by the search for things held in common with other religions. A Protestant theology which rejects natural theology (and any natural knowledge of God by man) is much more likely to see other religions not as proximations to the fullness revealed in Christ, but as so man-centred as to be anti-Christ. Dr. W. A. Visser 't Hooft is recorded as having found this part of the Declaration 'very, very weak'.[2] This is not surprising because Visser 't Hooft, former Secretary of the World Council of Churches, comes from that tradition in continental Protestantism which is represented, for example, in the work of his fellow-countryman, the late Hendrik Kraemer. In this tradition, any such positive word to other religions is not only 'false irenicism', but indeed a betrayal of the gospel. At this point, one feels, Canterbury is much nearer to Rome and Constantinople than to Geneva, and this, perhaps, because both feel closer to that common theological tradition which is at least as old as the Greek Apologists of the earliest Christian centuries.

We cannot conclude this brief account of the Declaration

[2] Quoted by Graham in Abbott, op. cit., pp. 658–9.

without adverting to a situation which seems to leap at us from the page. In discussing the Decree on Ecumenism we noticed the problem for Roman Catholic thought posed by other Christian churches, the difficulty in finding theological resources to resolve that problem. And now, almost paradoxically, we see the relative ease with which Roman Catholic thought can find resources to approach the problem of other religions. It is as though in some way it were easier to adjust to the existence of Buddhism and Islam than to that of Orthodoxy and Anglicanism. This is a point worth pondering for the future. Is it possible that as we take more seriously and have more contact with other religions, we may find unexpected hints to help us in the development of a theological language which will enable us to resolve the ecumenical problem?

Appendix I

THE COUNCIL DOCUMENTS

The sixteen documents promulged at the Council are here listed by (a) their titles as commonly given in English; translations vary somewhat, e.g. '. . . the Church in the Modern World' or '. . . the Church in the World of Today'; (b) their Latin titles, where these have become generally known; (c) their opening words which, as with earlier papal encyclicals, etc., are used by many writers to refer to them: thus '*Lumen Gentium*' is the same as *De Ecclesia*, the Dogmatic Constitution on the Church.

FOUR CONSTITUTIONS:

The Dogmatic Constitution on the Church. *De Ecclesia* ('*Lumen Gentium* . . .')
The Dogmatic Constitution on Divine Revelation. *De Divina Revelatione* ('*Dei Verbum* . . .')
The Pastoral Constitution on the Church in the Modern World. *De Ecclesia in Mundo Huius Temporis* ('*Gaudium et Spes* . . .')
The Constitution on the Liturgy. *De Sacra Liturgia* ('*Sacrosanctum Concilium* . . .')

NINE DECREES, ON:

The Instruments of Social Communication ('*Inter Mirifica* . . .')
Ecumenism. *De Oecumenismo* ('*Unitatis Redintegratio* . . .')
The Oriental Catholic Churches ('*Orientalium Ecclesiarum* . . .')
The Pastoral Office of Bishops ('*Christus Dominus* . . .')
The Life and Ministry of Priests ('*Presbyterorum Ordinis* . . .')
The Renewal of the Religious Life ('*Perfectae Caritatis* . . .')
Training for the Priesthood, also known as 'Priestly Formation') ('*Optatam totius Ecclesiae* . . .')
The Apostolate of the Laity ('*Apostolicam Actuositatem* . . .')
The Missionary Activity of the Church ('*Ad Gentes* . . .')

THREE DECLARATIONS, ON:

The Relations of the Church with the Non-Christian Religions ('*Nostra Aetate* . . .')
Christian Education ('*Gravissimum Educationis* . . .')
Religious Liberty ('*Dignitatis Humanae* . . .')

Appendix II

THE DIRECTORIUM ON ECUMENICAL MATTERS, PART I

This document, issued at Pentecost (14 May) 1967 by the Secretariat for Promoting Christian Unity, comprises an Introduction and Chapters I-IV (nos. 1–63). It could be subject to revision at a later date, and at the time of going to press is still incomplete, Part II and any further Parts being yet to come. As with Council documents, only the Latin is authoritative, but an English version is issued, for convenience, by the Secretariat, under the full title *Directory for the Application of the Decisions of the Second Ecumenical Council of the Vatican concerning Ecumenical Matters: Part I*.[1] The Introduction recalls the principles laid down by the Council, and Chapter I, 'The Setting Up of Ecumenical Commissions', urges that these be established in the Roman Catholic Church on a diocesan and territorial basis; Chapter II concerns 'The Validity of Baptism Conferred by Ministers of Churches and Ecclesial Communities Separated from Us'; it deals with the status (in Roman Catholic terms) of persons who have received baptism in the Orthodox Churches or in other Christian Communities, and merits careful study; especially noteworthy is the direction (no. 14) 'Indiscriminate conditional baptism of all who desire full communion with the Catholic Church cannot be approved...'. This firmly reverses a practice, prevalent before the Council, by which doubt was in effect cast on the validity of *all* non-Roman Catholic baptisms. Chapter III, 'Fostering Spiritual Ecumenism in the Catholic Church', is of mainly domestic relevance, though highly significant. The sections which bear most directly on Anglican-Roman relations occur in Chapter IV, 'Sharing of Spiritual Activity and Resources with our Separated Brethren', viz. nos. 25–37 and 59–63, as follows:

A. Introduction

25. Fraternal charity in the relations of daily life is not enough to foster the restoration of unity among all Christians. It is right and

---

[1] The curious double use of the word in 'Ecumenical' in rather differing senses is worth noting.

proper that there should also be allowed a certain 'communicatio in spiritualibus'—i.e. that Christians should be able to share that spiritual heritage they have in common, in a manner and to a degree permissible and appropriate in their present divided state. From those 'elements and endowments which together go to build up and give life to the Church herself, some, even very many, can exist outside the visible boundaries of the Catholic Church' (Decree on Ecumenism n. 3). These elements 'which come from Christ and lead to Him rightly belong to the one Church of Christ' (Ibid); they can contribute appropriately to our petitioning for the grace of unity; they can manifest and strengthen the bonds which still bind Catholics to their separated brethren.

26. But these spiritual endowments are found in different ways in the several Christian communities, and sharing in spiritual activity and resources cannot be independent of this diversity; its treatment must vary according to the conditions of the people, Churches and communities involved. For present conditions the following guiding principles are offered:

27. There should be regard for a certain give-and-take ('reciprocity') if sharing in spiritual activity and resources, even within defined limits, is to contribute, in a spirit of mutual goodwill and charity, to the growth of harmony among Christians. Dialogues and consultations on the subject between Catholic local or territorial authorities and those of other Communions are strongly recommended.

28. In some places and with some communities, sects and persons, the ecumenical movement and the wish for peace with the Catholic Church have not yet grown strong (cf. Decree on Ecumenism n. 19), and so this reciprocity and mutual understanding are more difficult; the local Ordinary or, if need be, the episcopal conference may indicate suitable measures for preventing the dangers of indifferentism and proselytism* among their faithful in these circumstances. It is to be hoped, however, that through the grace of the Holy Spirit and the prudent pastoral care of the bishops, ecumenical feeling and mutual regard will so increase both among Catholics and among their separated brethren that the need for these special measures will gradually vanish.

* The word 'proselytism' is here used to mean a manner of behaving, contrary to the spirit of the gospel, which makes use of dishonest methods to attract men to a community—e.g. by exploiting their ignorance or poverty. (Cf. Declaration on Religious Liberty n. 4.) [Footnote in the Directorium]

29. The term, sharing of spiritual activity and resources (*Communicatio in spiritualibus*) is used to cover all prayer offered in common, common use of sacred places and objects, as well as all sharing in liturgical worship (*communicatio in sacris*) in the strict sense.

30. There is '*communicatio in sacris*' when anyone takes part in the liturgical worship or in the sacraments of another Church or ecclesial community.

31. By 'liturgical worship' is meant worship carried out according to the books, prescriptions or customs of a Church or community, celebrated by a minister or delegate of such Church or community, in his capacity as minister of that community.

B. Prayer in Common

32. 'In certain special circumstances, such as prayer services "for unity" and during ecumenical gatherings, it is allowable, indeed desirable that Catholics should join in prayer with their separated brethren. Such prayers in common are certainly a very effective means of petitioning for the grace of unity, and they are a genuine expression of the ties which still bind Catholics to their separated brethren.' (Decree on Ecumenism n. 8.) The Decree is dealing with prayers in which members and even ministers of different communities take an 'active' part. Where Catholics are concerned, this kind of participation is committed to the guidance and encouragement of local ordinaries. The following points should be noted.

33. It is to be hoped that Catholics and their other brethren will join in prayer for any common concern in which they can and should cooperate—e.g. peace, social justice, mutual charity among men, the dignity of the family and so on. The same may be said of occasions when according to circumstances a nation or community wishes to make a common act of thanksgiving or petition to God, as on a national feast-day, at a time of public disaster or mourning, on a day set aside for remembrance of those who have died for their country. This kind of prayer is also recommended so far as is possible at times when Christians hold meetings for study or common action.

34. However, common prayer should particularly be concerned with the restoration of Christian unity. It can centre on e.g. the mystery of the Church and her unity, baptism as a sacramental

bond of unity however incomplete, the renewal of personal and social life as a necessary way to achieving unity and the other themes set out under n. 22.

35. The form of the Service.
   a) Representatives of the Churches or communities concerned should agree and cooperate in arranging such prayer—in deciding who should take part, what themes, hymns, scripture readings, prayers and the like should be used.
   b) In such a service there is room for any reading, prayer and hymn which manifests the faith or spiritual life shared by all Christians. There is a place for an exhortation, address or biblical meditation drawing on the common Christian inheritance which may lead to mutual good will and promote unity among Christians.
   c) It is desirable that the structure of services of this kind, whether confined to Catholics, or held in common with our separated brethren, should conform to the pattern of community prayer recommended by the liturgical revival. (Cf. Constitution on the Sacred Liturgy, v.gr. nn. 30, 34, 35.)[2]

36. The Place.
   a) A place should be chosen which is acceptable to all those taking part. Care should be taken that everything is properly prepared and conducive to devotion.
   b) Although a church building is the place in which a community is normally accustomed to celebrating its own liturgy, there is nothing which in itself prevents holding the common services mentioned in nn. 32–35, in the church of one or other of the communities concerned if there is need for this and the local Ordinary approves. In fact the situation may make this the suitable thing.[2]

37. Dress. There is nothing against the use of choir dress, where circumstances may indicate this and there is common agreement among the participants.

C. Sharing in Liturgical Worship

. . . . .

59. Catholics may be allowed to attend occasionally the liturgical services of other brethren if they have reasonable ground, e.g. arising out of a public office or function, blood relationship or friendship, desire to be better informed, an ecumenical gathering

[2] [Nos. 35(d) and 36(c) concern the Eastern Churches, as do nos. 39–51—Ed.]

etc. In these cases, with due regard to what has been said above—there is nothing against Catholics taking some part in the common responses, hymns and actions of the Community of which they are guests—so long as they are not at variance with Catholic faith. The same principles govern the manner in which our separated brethren may assist at services in Catholic churches. This participation, from which reception of the Eucharist is always excluded, should lead the participants to esteem the spiritual riches we have in common and at the same time make them more aware of the gravity of our separations.

60. When taking part in services which do not call for sacramental sharing, ministers of other Communions may, by mutual consent, take a place suitable to their dignity. So too Catholic ministers who are present at ceremonies celebrated by other Communions, may, with due regard for local customs, wear choir dress.

61. If the separated brethren have no place in which to carry out their religious rites properly and with dignity, the local Ordinary may allow them the use of a Catholic building, cemetery or church.

62. The authorities of Catholic schools and institutions should take care to offer to ministers of other Communions every facility for giving spiritual and sacramental ministration to their own communicants who attend Catholic institutions. These ministrations may be given in Catholic buildings, in accordance with the above, n. 61.

63. In hospitals and similar institutions conducted by Catholics, the authorities in charge should promptly advise ministers of other Communions of the presence of their communicants and afford them every facility for visiting the sick and giving them spiritual and sacramental ministrations.

Bibliography

A. LATIN TEXTS: COLLECTED

Sacrosanctum Concilium Vaticanum Secundum: Constitutiones, Decreta, et Declarationes (Vatican Press, Vatican City.)

B. ENGLISH TRANSLATIONS (WITH COMMENTARY): COLLECTED

The Documents of Vatican II ed. Walter M. Abbott, S.J. (paperback, Guild Press, New York: Geoffrey Chapman, London.)
Contains Eng. tr. of each document, with 'Introduction' and 'Response' by R.C. and non-R.C. writers.

The Documents of Vatican II (library edition, boards: Herder & Herder, New York: Geoffrey Chapman, London.) Contents same as above.

C. SEPARATE DOCUMENTS: TEXT AND/OR TRANSLATION AND COMMENTARY

1. *Constitutions*

(a) *De Ecclesia: the Constitution on the Church.* Commentary and Eng. trans. by Gregory Baum, O.S.A. Foreword by the Rt. Rev. Bishop B. C. Butler, O.S.B. (Darton, Longman & Todd, London: Paulist Press, Glen Rock, U.S.A.)
Vatican II: The Church Constitution. The full text of the Constitution and of the Motu Proprio on the Synod of Bishops, with commentaries by priests and lay people. Edited by Austin Flannery, O.P. (Scepter Books, Dublin and Chicago.)

(b) *The Dogmatic Constitution on Divine Revelation of the Second Vatican Council.* Commentary and translation by George H. Tavard. (Darton, Longman & Todd, London: Paulist Press, Glen Rock, U.S.A.)

(c) *Vatican II: The Liturgy Constitution.* Text, translation, and commentary. Edited by Austin Flannery, O.P. (Scepter Books, Dublin and Chicago.)
The Liturgy Revised: A Doctrinal Commentary on the Conciliar Constitution on the Liturgy. By Louis Bouyer. (Darton, Longman & Todd, London: University of Notre Dame Press, U.S.A.)

(See also fuller bibliography at end of Chapter 6)

2. *Decrees*

(a) *Vatican II on Ecumenism.* Text and commentaries. Edited by
Michael Adams. (Scepter Books, Dublin and Chicago.)

The Vatican Council and Christian Unity: A commentary on
the Decree on Ecumenism of the Second Vatican Council,
with a translation of the text. By Bernard Leeming, S.J.
(Darton, Longman & Todd, London.)

(b) *Vatican II: The Catholic Eastern Churches.* An introduction
and commentary by Patrick O'Connell, S.J., with the text
of the decree. (Scepter Books, Dublin and Chicago.)

3. *Declarations*

(a) *The Declaration on Religious Freedom of the Second Vatican
Council.* Commentary and translation by Enda McDonagh.
(Darton, Longman & Todd, London.)

(b) *The Church and the Jewish People:* A Commentary on the
Second Vatican Council's Declaration on the Relation of
the Church to Non-Christian Religions, by Augustin
Cardinal Bea. (Geoffrey Chapman, London.)

4. *General*

The Council Documents are published in translation in two
series of low-priced booklets: most of them in England by the
Catholic Truth Society, London (Nos. Do. 349, 351, and
356–366), and all of them in U.S.A. by the National
Catholic Welfare Conference Publications Office, Washington, D.C. (Nos. EC—1 to 16.)

D. SOME GENERAL WORKS (a small selection)

Rynne, Xavier, *Letters from Vatican City* (Faber & Faber,
London; Farrar, Straus and Giroux, Inc., New York, 1963).
—— *The Second Session* (same publishers, 1964).
—— *The Third Session* (same publishers, 1965).
—— *The Fourth Session* (same publishers, 1966).

Grant, Frederick C., *Rome and Reunion* (Oxford University
Press, New York and London, 1965).

Moorman, John (Bishop of Ripon), *Vatican Observed.* An
Anglican Impression of Vatican II. (Darton, Longman &
Todd, London, 1967.)

O'Brien, John A. (ed.), *Steps to Christian Unity* (Doubleday
& Co. Inc., New York, 1964).

Romeu, Luis V. (ed.), *Ecumenical Experiences* (Burns & Oates, London, 1965) (translation of *Diálogos de la Cristiandad*, Editiones Sígueme, 1964).

Pawley, Bernard C., *Looking at the Vatican Council* (S.C.M. Press, London): U.S. edition, *An Anglican View of the Vatican Council* (Moorhouse-Barlow Co., New York, 1962).

—— *Anglican-Roman Relations and the Second Vatican Council* (Church Information Office, London, 1964).

Caird, George B., *Our Dialogue with Rome* (Oxford University Press, London and New York, 1967). [A Congregational Observer's comments.]

Horton, Douglas, *Vatican Diary* (United Church Press, Philadelphia, 1966).

Brown, Robert McAfee, *Observer in Rome* (first session) (Methuen, London, 1964).

Lindbeck, G. A. (ed.) *Dialogue on the Way* (Augsburg Publishing House, Minneapolis, 1965).

Index

Abbott, Walter M., S.J., 59n., 122n., 124n., 138n., 147, 189n.

Abraham, 70

'absolute' consecration, 92–93

Ad Gentes (Missionary Activity of the Church, Decree on the), 72n.

Ad Petri Cathedram (Encyclical), 4

aggiornamento, 99, 109, 114, 146 ('up-dating'), 154, 203

agnostics, 192

Alcuin, 151

Alfrink, Cardinal, 31, 187

allegorism, 52

Ambrose, St., 58

America, United States of, *see* United States

America (review), 189n.

angels, 38

Anglican Communion, the, 1ff., 11, 25, 26, 27, 36, 47, 49, 97, 101, 107, 108, 133, 146, 159 & n., 208, 212; in debates and Decree on Ecumenism, 121–2, 137, 147–8; 235; liturgy in, 164, 166–7, 170; and non-Christian religions, 238 (*see also* Prayer, Book of Common)

Anglican-Methodist Conversations, 91–92

Anglican Orders, question of, 11f., 121, 140

Anglican viewpoint, etc., on: R. C. Church, 7, 25–26, 51, 140, 144–145; developments connected with Council, 8, 20, 22, 23–24, 51–52, 77, 131, 132, 144–6; Holy Scripture, 38, 40–41, 48, 50, 51, 127–8, 144; divine revelation, 44; church order, 57n., 91–92, 136–7, 143 (*see also* Prayer Book, Ordinal), training for ministry, 97–99, 100; position of

non-R.C. churches, 121, 139; Liturgy Constitution, 149, 158 & n., 159–60, 164–70; liturgical art, 170; appointment of bishops, 194

anti-clericalism, 23

Antioch, Patriarchate of, 31

Apocrypha, the, 37, 38

Apostles, the, 37, 45, 46, 71, 73, 75–76, 85, 127, 128, 190–1, 200–1

Apostolicae curae (Bull), 12, 140

Apostolicam Actuositatem, *see* Laity, Decree on the Apostolate of the

Arab countries, 117, 235

Aramburu, Abp., 198

Argentina, 198

Arriba y Castro, Cardinal, 186–7 190

art and furnishings, sacred, 150, 169

Articles, the Thirty-nine, 10, 24, 26, 37, 38

Assisi, liturgical conference at (1956), 157

Assumption of the B.V.M., 80

atheism, 9, 181, 192, 193, 215–16, 219, 231

Augustine, St., 44, 49, 58, 216; *De doctrina Christiana*, 47

Bacci, Cardinal, 99

baptism, 7, 69, 72, 101–2, 124, 128–129, 131, 140, 142, 144, 159, 163, 169, 241

Baptists, 4

Baum, Gregory, O.S.B., 89n.

Bea, Augustin Cardinal, 27, 31, 34, 106, 156–7, 176, 182, 183, 184, 233–4; *The Study of the Synoptic Gospels*, 48; *The Church and the Jewish People*, 233

Belgium, 2, 31